SECOND EDITION

RESTful Java with JAX-RS 2.0

Bill Burke

Beijing · Boston · Farnham · Sebastopol · Tokyo

RESTful Java with JAX-RS 2.0, Second Edition

by Bill Burke

Published by O'Reilly Media, Inc., 1005 Gravenstein Highway North, Sebastopol, CA 95472.

O'Reilly books may be purchased for educational, business, or sales promotional use. Online editions are also available for most titles (*http://safaribooksonline.com*). For more information, contact our corporate/institutional sales department: 800-998-9938 or *corporate@oreilly.com*.

Editor: Meghan Blanchette
Production Editor: Melanie Yarbrough
Copyeditor: Charles Roumeliotis
Proofreader: Rachel Monaghan
Indexer: Ellen Troutman-Zaig
Cover Designer: Karen Montgomery
Interior Designer: David Futato
Illustrator: Rebecca Demarest

November 2013:   Second Edition

Revision History for the Second Edition:

2013-11-11:   First release

2015-08-14:   Second release

See *http://oreilly.com/catalog/errata.csp?isbn=9781449361341* for release details.

ISBN: 978-1-449-36134-1

[LSI]

Table of Contents

Part II.   JAX-RS Workbook

Foreword

REST is an architectural style that defines a set of constraints that, when applied to the architecture of a distributed system, induce desirable properties like loose coupling and horizontal scalability. RESTful web services are the result of applying these constraints to services that utilize web standards such as URIs, HTTP, XML, and JSON. Such services become part of the fabric of the Web and can take advantage of years of web engineering to satisfy their clients' needs.

The Java API for RESTful web services (JAX-RS) is a new API that aims to make development of RESTful web services in Java simple and intuitive. The initial impetus for the API came from the observation that existing Java Web APIs were generally either:

- Very low level, leaving the developer to do a lot of repetitive and error-prone work such as URI parsing and content negotiation, or
- Rather high level and proscriptive, making it easy to build services that conform to a particular pattern but lacking the necessary flexibility to tackle more general problems.

A Java Specification Request (JSR 311) was filed with the Java Community Process (JCP) in January 2007 and approved unanimously in February. The expert group began work in April 2007 with the charter to design an API that was flexible and easy to use, and that encouraged developers to follow the REST style. The resulting API, finalized in October 2008, has already seen a remarkable level of adoption, and we were fortunate to have multiple implementations of the API under way throughout the development of JAX-RS. The combination of implementation experience and feedback from users of those implementations was invaluable and allowed us to refine the specification, clarify edge cases, and reduce API friction.

JAX-RS is one of the latest generations of Java APIs that make use of Java annotations to reduce the need for standard base classes, implementing required interfaces, and out-of-band configuration files. Annotations are used to route client requests to matching Java class methods and declaratively map request data to the parameters of those methods. Annotations are also used to provide static metadata to create responses. JAX-RS also provides more traditional classes and interfaces for dynamic access to request data and for customizing responses.

Bill Burke led the development of one of the JAX-RS implementations mentioned earlier (RESTEasy) and was an active and attentive member of the expert group. His contributions to expert group discussions are too numerous to list, but a few of the areas where his input was instrumental include rules for annotation inheritance, use of regular expressions for matching request URIs, annotation-driven support for cookies and form data, and support for streamed output.

This book, *RESTful Java with JAX-RS 2.0*, provides an in-depth tutorial on JAX-RS and shows how to get the most from this new API while adhering to the REST architectural style. I hope you enjoy the book and working with JAX-RS.

—Marc Hadley
JAX-RS 1.0 Specification Lead

Preface

Author's Note

The bulk of my career has been spent working with and implementing distributed middleware. In the mid-'90s I worked for the parent company of Open Environment Corporation working on DCE tools. Later on, I worked for Iona, developing its next-generation CORBA ORB. Currently, I work for the JBoss division of Red Hat, which is entrenched in Java middleware, specifically Java EE. So, you could say that I have a pretty rich perspective when it comes to middleware.

I must tell you that I was originally very skeptical of REST as a way of writing SOA applications. It seemed way too simple and shortsighted, so I sort of blew it off for a while. One day, though, back in mid-2007, I ran into my old Iona boss and mentor, Steve Vinoski, while grabbing a sandwich at D'Angelo in Westford, Massachusetts, near Red Hat's offices. We ended up sitting down, having lunch, and talking for hours. The first shocker for me was that Steve had left Iona to go work for a start-up. The second was when he said, "Bill, I've abandoned CORBA and WS-* for REST." For those of you who don't know Steve, he contributed heavily to the CORBA specification, wrote a book on the subject (which is basically the CORBA bible), and is a giant in the distributed computing field, writing regularly for C++ Report and IEEE. How could the guy I looked up to and who was responsible for my foundation in distributed computing abandon CORBA, WS-*, and the distributed framework landscape he was instrumental in creating? I felt a little betrayed and very unnerved. (OK, maybe I'm exaggerating a little…)

We ended up arguing for a few hours about which was better—WS-*/CORBA or REST. This conversation spilled into many other lengthy email messages, with me trying to promote WS-* and him defending REST. The funniest thing to me was that as I researched REST more and more I found that my arguments with Steve were just another endless replay of debates that had been raging across the blogosphere for years. They are still raging to this day.

It took months for me to change my mind and embrace REST. You would figure that my distributed computing background was an asset, but it was not. DCE, CORBA, WS-*, and Java EE were all baggage. All were an invisible barrier for me to accept REST as a viable (and better) alternative for writing SOA applications. I think that's what I liked most about REST. It required me to rethink and reformulate the foundation of my distributed computing knowledge. Hopefully your journey isn't as difficult as mine and you will be a little less stubborn and more open-minded than I was.

Who Should Read This Book

This book teaches you how to design and develop distributed web services in Java using RESTful architectural principles on top of the HTTP protocol. It is mostly a comprehensive reference guide on the JAX-RS specification, which is a JCP standardized annotation framework for writing RESTful web services in Java.

While this book does go into many of the fundamentals of REST, it does not cover them all and focuses more on implementation rather than theory. You can satisfy your craving for more RESTful theory by obtaining *RESTful Web Services* by Leonard Richardson and Sam Ruby (O'Reilly). If you are familiar with writing Java EE applications, you will be very comfortable reading this book. If you are not, you will be at a disadvantage, but some experience with web application development, HTTP, and XML is a huge plus. Before reading this book, you should also be fairly fluent in the Java language and specifically know how to use and apply Java annotations. If you are unfamiliar with the Java language, I recommend *Learning Java* by Patrick Niemeyer and Jonathan Knudsen (O'Reilly).

How This Book Is Organized

This book is organized into two parts: the technical manuscript, followed by the JAX-RS workbook. The technical manuscript explains what REST and JAX-RS are, how they work, and when to use them. The JAX-RS workbook provides step-by-step instructions for installing, configuring, and running the JAX-RS examples from the manuscript with the JBoss RESTEasy framework, an implementation of JAX-RS.

Part I, REST and the JAX-RS Standard

Part I starts off with a brief introduction to REST and HTTP. It then guides you through the basics of the JAX-RS specification, and then in later chapters shows how you can apply JAX-RS to build RESTful web services:

Chapter 1, Introduction to REST
    This chapter gives you a brief introduction to REST and HTTP.

Chapter 2, Designing RESTful Services

This chapter walks you through the design of a distributed RESTful interface for an ecommerce order entry system. For the second edition, this chapter has been revised to include a simple client using the new JAX-RS 2.0 Client API.

Chapter 3, Your First JAX-RS Service

This chapter walks you through the development of a RESTful web service written in Java as a JAX-RS service.

Chapter 4, HTTP Method and URI Matching

This chapter defines how HTTP requests are dispatched in JAX-RS and how you can use the `@Path` annotation and subresources. For the second edition, I talk about some of the ambiguities of the request matching algorithm.

Chapter 5, JAX-RS Injection

This chapter walks you through various annotations that allow you to extract information from an HTTP request (URI parameters, headers, query parameters, form data, cookies, matrix parameters, encoding, and defining default values). For the second edition, this chapter has been revised to include the new `@BeanParam` and `ParamConverter` features introduced in JAX-RS 2.0.

Chapter 6, JAX-RS Content Handlers

This chapter explains how to marshal HTTP message bodies to and from Java objects using built-in handlers or writing your own custom marshallers.

Chapter 7, Server Responses and Exception Handling

This chapter walks through the JAX-RS `Response` object and how you use it to return complex responses to your client (`ResponseBuilder`). It also explains how exception and error handling work in JAX-RS. This chapter has been revised a little bit to talk about the new exception hierarchy that was added in JAX-RS 2.0.

Chapter 8, JAX-RS Client API

This chapter is new to the second edition and describes in detail the new Client API added to JAX-RS 2.0.

Chapter 9, HTTP Content Negotiation

This chapter explains how HTTP content negotiation works, its relationship to JAX-RS, and how you can leverage this within RESTful architectures.

Chapter 10, HATEOAS

This chapter dives into Hypermedia As The Engine Of Application State (HATEOAS) and how it relates to JAX-RS (`UriInfo` and `UriBuilder`). This chapter has been revised for the second edition to include additions to the `UriBuilder` API and the new classes for building links.

Chapter 11, Scaling JAX-RS Applications
> This chapter explains how you can increase the performance of your services by leveraging HTTP caching protocols. It also shows you how to manage concurrency conflicts in high-volume sites.

Chapter 12, Filters and Interceptors
> This chapter is new to the second edition. It talks about the new filter and interceptor APIs added to JAX-RS 2.0 and how you can use them to write extensions to JAX-RS.

Chapter 13, Asynchronous JAX-RS
> This is a new chapter for the second edition. It walks you through the new server- and client-side asynchronous interfaces available in JAX-RS 2.0.

Chapter 14, Deployment and Integration
> This chapter explains how you can deploy and integrate your JAX-RS services within Java Enterprise Edition, servlet containers, EJB, Spring, and JPA. It has been revised in the second edition.

Chapter 15, Securing JAX-RS
> This chapter walks you through the most popular mechanisms to perform authentication on the Web. It then shows you how to implement secure applications with JAX-RS. It has been revised in the second edition to walk you through configuring client-side SSL and also now includes an introduction to OAuth 2.0. I also talk about JSON Web Signatures and encryption.

Chapter 16, Alternative Java Clients
> This chapter talks about alternative Java clients you can use to communicate with RESTful services (`java.net.URL`, Apache HTTP Client, and RESTEasy Proxy).

Part II, JAX-RS Workbook

The JAX-RS workbook shows you how to execute examples from chapters in the book that include at least one significant example. You'll want to read the introduction to the workbook to set up RESTEasy and configure it for the examples. After that, just go to the workbook chapter that matches the chapter you're reading. For example, if you are reading Chapter 3 on writing your first JAX-RS service, use Chapter 18 of the workbook to develop and run the examples with RESTEasy.

Conventions Used in This Book

The following typographical conventions are used in this book:

Italic
> Indicates new terms, URLs, email addresses, filenames, and file extensions.

`Constant width`

> Used for program listings, as well as within paragraphs to refer to program elements such as variable or function names, databases, data types, environment variables, statements, and keywords.

`Constant width bold`

> Shows commands or other text that should be typed literally by the user.

`Constant width italic`

> Shows text that should be replaced with user-supplied values or by values determined by context.

 This icon signifies a tip, suggestion, or general note.

 This icon indicates a warning or caution.

Using Code Examples

Supplemental material (code examples, exercises, etc.) is available for download at *https://github.com/oreillymedia/restful_java_jax-rs_2_0*.

This book is here to help you get your job done. In general, if example code is offered with this book, you may use it in your programs and documentation. You do not need to contact us for permission unless you're reproducing a significant portion of the code. For example, writing a program that uses several chunks of code from this book does not require permission. Selling or distributing a CD-ROM of examples from O'Reilly books does require permission. Answering a question by citing this book and quoting example code does not require permission. Incorporating a significant amount of example code from this book into your product's documentation does require permission.

We appreciate, but do not require, attribution. An attribution usually includes the title, author, publisher, and ISBN. For example: "*RESTful Java with JAX-RS 2.0*, Second Edition by Bill Burke. Copyright 2014 Bill Burke, 978-1-449-36134-1."

If you feel your use of code examples falls outside fair use or the permission given here, feel free to contact us at *permissions@oreilly.com*.

Safari® Books Online

 *Safari Books Online* is an on-demand digital library that delivers expert content in both book and video form from the world's leading authors in technology and business.

Technology professionals, software developers, web designers, and business and creative professionals use Safari Books Online as their primary resource for research, problem solving, learning, and certification training.

Safari Books Online offers a range of plans and pricing for enterprise, government, education, and individuals.

Members have access to thousands of books, training videos, and prepublication manuscripts in one fully searchable database from publishers like O'Reilly Media, Prentice Hall Professional, Addison-Wesley Professional, Microsoft Press, Sams, Que, Peachpit Press, Focal Press, Cisco Press, John Wiley & Sons, Syngress, Morgan Kaufmann, IBM Redbooks, Packt, Adobe Press, FT Press, Apress, Manning, New Riders, McGraw-Hill, Jones & Bartlett, Course Technology, and hundreds more. For more information about Safari Books Online, please visit us online.

How to Contact Us

Please address comments and questions concerning this book to the publisher:

O'Reilly Media, Inc.
1005 Gravenstein Highway North
Sebastopol, CA 95472
800-998-9938 (in the United States or Canada)
707-829-0515 (international or local)
707-829-0104 (fax)

We have a web page for this book, where we list errata, examples, and any additional information. You can access this page at *http://oreil.ly/restful_java_jax-rs_2_0*.

To comment or ask technical questions about this book, send email to *bookquestions@oreilly.com*.

For more information about our books, courses, conferences, and news, see our website at *http://www.oreilly.com*.

Find us on Facebook: *http://facebook.com/oreilly*

Follow us on Twitter: *http://twitter.com/oreillymedia*

Watch us on YouTube: *http://www.youtube.com/oreillymedia*

Acknowledgments

First, I'd like to thank Steve Vinoski for introducing me to REST. Without our conversations and arguments, I would never have written this book. Next, I'd like to thank Marek Potociar and Santiago Pericas-Geertsen, the JAX-RS 2.0 spec leads. They ran an excellent expert group and put up with a lot of crap from me. I'd like to thank Sergey Beryozkin for contributing the Apache CXF section. It is cool when competitors can be on good terms with each other. Fernando Nasser, Jeff Mesnil, and Michael Musgrove were instrumental in reviewing this book and provided a lot of great feedback. Subbu Allaraju helped tremendously in making sure my understanding and explanation of RESTful theory was correct. By the way, I strongly suggest you check out his blog (*http://www.subbu.org*). Heiko Braun helped on the first few chapters as far as reviewing goes. I'd also like to thank the contributors to the RESTEasy project, specifically Ron Sigal, Wei Nan Li, Solomon Duskis, Justin Edelson, Ryan McDonough, Attila Kiraly, and Michael Brackx. Without them, RESTEasy wouldn't be where it is. Finally, I'd like to thank Meghan Blanchette and the O'Reilly team for helping make this book a reality.

REST and the JAX-RS Standard

CHAPTER 1

Introduction to REST

For those of us with computers, the World Wide Web is an intricate part of our lives. We use it to read the newspaper in the morning, pay our bills, perform stock trades, and buy goods and services, all through the browser, all over the network. "Googling" has become a part of our daily vocabulary as we use search engines to do research for school, find what time a movie is playing, or just search for information on old friends. Door-to-door encyclopedia salesmen have gone the way of the dinosaur as Wikipedia has become the summarized source of human knowledge. People even socialize over the network using sites like Facebook and Google+. Professional social networks are sprouting up in all industries as doctors, lawyers, and all sorts of professionals use them to collaborate. The Web is an intricate part of our daily jobs as programmers. We search for and download open source libraries to help us develop applications and frameworks for our companies. We build web-enabled applications so that anybody on the Internet or intranet can use a browser to interact with our systems.

Really, most of us take the Web for granted. Have you, as a programmer, sat down and tried to understand why the Web has been so successful? How has it grown from a simple network of researchers and academics to an interconnected worldwide community? What properties of the Web make it so viral?

One man, Roy Fielding, did ask these questions in his doctoral thesis, "Architectural Styles and the Design of Network-based Software Architectures."[1] In it, he identifies specific architectural principles that answer the following questions:

- Why is the Web so prevalent and ubiquitous?
- What makes the Web scale?

---

1. Architectural Styles and the Design of Network-based Software Architectures (*http://www.ics.uci.edu/~field ing/pubs/dissertation/top.htm*)

- How can I apply the architecture of the Web to my own applications?

The set of these architectural principles is called REpresentational State Transfer (REST) and is defined as:

Addressable resources
> The key abstraction of information and data in REST is a resource, and each resource must be addressable via a URI (Uniform Resource Identifier).

A uniform, constrained interface
> Use a small set of well-defined methods to manipulate your resources.

Representation-oriented
> You interact with services using representations of that service. A resource referenced by one URI can have different formats. Different platforms need different formats. For example, browsers need HTML, JavaScript needs JSON (JavaScript Object Notation), and a Java application may need XML.

Communicate statelessly
> Stateless applications are easier to scale.

Hypermedia As The Engine Of Application State (HATEOAS)
> Let your data formats drive state transitions in your applications.

For a PhD thesis, Fielding's paper is actually very readable and, thankfully, not very long. It, along with Leonard Richardson and Sam Ruby's book *RESTful Web APIs* (O'Reilly), is an excellent reference for understanding REST. I will give a much briefer introduction to REST and the Internet protocol it uses (HTTP) within this chapter.

REST and the Rebirth of HTTP

REST isn't protocol-specific, but when people talk about REST, they usually mean REST over HTTP. Learning about REST was as much of a rediscovery and reappreciation of the HTTP protocol for me as learning a new style of distributed application development. Browser-based web applications see only a tiny fraction of the features of HTTP. Non-RESTful technologies like SOAP and WS-* use HTTP strictly as a transport protocol and thus use a very small subset of its capabilities. Many would say that SOAP and WS-* use HTTP solely to tunnel through firewalls. HTTP is actually a very rich application protocol that provides a multitude of interesting and useful capabilities for application developers. You will need a good understanding of HTTP in order to write RESTful web services.

HTTP is a synchronous request/response-based application network protocol used for distributed, collaborative, document-based systems. It is the primary protocol used on the Web, in particular by browsers such as Firefox, MS Internet Explorer, Safari, and Netscape. The protocol is very simple: the client sends a request message made up of the HTTP method being invoked, the location of the resource you are interested in invoking, a variable set of headers, and an optional message body that can basically be anything you want, including HTML, plain text, XML, JSON, and even binary data. Here's an example:

```
GET /resteasy HTTP/1.1
Host: jboss.org
User-Agent: Mozilla/5.0
Accept: text/html,application/xhtml+xml,application/xml;q=0.9,*/*;q=0.8
Accept-Language:      en-us,en;q=0.5
Accept-Encoding:      gzip,deflate
```

Your browser would send this request if you wanted to look at *http://jboss.org/resteasy*. GET is the method we are invoking on the server. /resteasy is the object we are interested in. HTTP/1.1 is the version of the protocol. Host, User-Agent, Accept, Accept-Language, and Accept-Encoding are all message headers. There is no request body, as we are querying information from the server.

The response message from the server is very similar. It contains the version of HTTP we are using, a response code, a short message that explains the response code, a variable set of optional headers, and an optional message body. Here's the message the server might respond with using the previous GET query:

```
HTTP/1.1 200 OK
X-Powered-By: Servlet 2.4; JBoss-4.2.2.GA
Content-Type: text/html

<head>
<title>JBoss RESTEasy Project</title>
</head>
<body>
<h1>JBoss RESTEasy</h1>
<p>JBoss RESTEasy is an open source implementation of the JAX-RS specification...
```

The response code of this message is 200, and the status message is "OK." This code means that the request was processed successfully and that the client is receiving the information it requested. HTTP has a large set of response codes. They can be informational codes like 200, "OK," or error codes like 500, "Internal Server Error." Visit the w3c's website (*http://bit.ly/19djuCx*) for a more complete and verbose listing of these codes.

This response message also has a message body that is a chunk of HTML. We know it is HTML by the Content-Type header.

RESTful Architectural Principles

Roy Fielding's PhD thesis describing REST was really an explanation of why the human-readable Web had become so pervasive in the past 18 years. As time went on, though, programmers started to realize that they could use the concepts of REST to build distributed services and model service-oriented architectures (SOAs).

The idea of SOA is that application developers design their systems as a set of reusable, decoupled, distributed services. Since these services are published on the network, conceptually, it should be easier to compose larger and more complex systems. SOA has been around for a long time. Developers have used technologies like DCE, CORBA, and Java RMI to build them in the past. Nowadays, though, when you think of SOA, you think of SOAP-based web services.

While REST has many similarities to the more traditional ways of writing SOA applications, it is very different in many important ways. You would think that a background in distributed computing would be an asset to understanding this new way of creating web services, but unfortunately this is not always the case. The reason is that some of the concepts of REST are hard to swallow, especially if you have written successful SOAP or CORBA applications. If your career has a foundation in one of these older technologies, there's a bit of emotional baggage you will have to overcome. For me, it took a few months of reading, researching, and intense arguing with REST evangelists (aka RESTafarians). For you, it may be easier. Others will never pick REST over something like SOAP and WS-*.

Let's examine each of the architectural principles of REST in detail and why they are important when you are writing a web service.

Addressability

Addressability is the idea that every object and resource in your system is reachable through a unique identifier. This seems like a no-brainer, but if you think about it, standardized object identity isn't available in many environments. If you have tried to implement a portable J2EE application, you probably know what I mean. In J2EE, distributed and even local references to services are not standardized, which makes portability really difficult. This isn't such a big deal for one application, but with the new popularity of SOA, we're heading to a world where disparate applications must integrate and interact. Not having something as simple as standardized service addressability adds a whole complex dimension to integration efforts.

In the REST world, addressability is managed through the use of URIs. When you make a request for information in your browser, you are typing in a URI. Each HTTP request must contain the URI of the object you are requesting information from or posting information to. The format of a URI is standardized as follows:

```
scheme://host:port/path?queryString#fragment
```

The scheme is the protocol you are using to communicate with. For RESTful web services, it is usually http or https. The host is a DNS name or IP address. It is followed by an optional port, which is numeric. The host and port represent the location of your resource on the network. Following host and port is a path expression. This path expression is a set of text segments delimited by the "/" character. Think of the path expression as a directory list of a file on your machine. Following the path expression is an optional query string. The "?" character separates the path from the query string. The query string is a list of parameters represented as name/value pairs. Each pair is delimited with the "&" character. Here's an example query string within a URI:

```
http://example.com/customers?lastName=Burke&zipcode=02115
```

A specific parameter name can be repeated in the query string. In this case, there are multiple values for the same parameter.

The last part of the URI is the fragment. It is delimited by a "#" character. The fragment is usually used to point to a certain place in the document you are querying.

Not all characters are allowed within a URI string. Some characters must be encoded using the following rules. The characters a–z, A–Z, 0–9, ., -, *, and _ remain the same. The space character is converted to +. The other characters are first converted into a sequence of bytes using a specific encoding scheme. Next, a two-digit hexadecimal number prefixed by % represents each byte.

Using a unique URI to identify each of your services makes each of your resources linkable. Service references can be embedded in documents or even email messages. For instance, consider the situation where somebody calls your company's help desk with a problem related to your SOA application. A link could represent the exact problem the user is having. Customer support can email the link to a developer who can fix the problem. The developer can reproduce the problem by clicking on the link. Furthermore, the data that services publish can also be composed into larger data streams fairly easily:

```
<order id="111">
   <customer>http://customers.myintranet.com/customers/32133</customer>
   <order-entries>
     <order-entry>
        <quantity>5</quantity>
        <product>http://products.myintranet.com/products/111</product>
 ...
```

In this example, an XML document describes an ecommerce order entry. We can reference data provided by different divisions in a company. From this reference, we can not only obtain information about the linked customer and products that were bought, but we also have the identifier of the service this data comes from. We know exactly where we can further interact and manipulate this data if we so desired.

The Uniform, Constrained Interface

The REST principle of a constrained interface is perhaps the hardest pill for an experienced CORBA or SOAP developer to swallow. The idea behind it is that you stick to the finite set of operations of the application protocol you're distributing your services upon. This means that you don't have an "action" parameter in your URI and use only the methods of HTTP for your web services. HTTP has a small, fixed set of operational methods. Each method has a specific purpose and meaning. Let's review them:

GET

GET is a read-only operation. It is used to query the server for specific information. It is both an *idempotent* and *safe* operation. Idempotent means that no matter how many times you apply the operation, the result is always the same. The act of reading an HTML document shouldn't change the document. Safe means that invoking a GET does not change the state of the server at all. This means that, other than request load, the operation will not affect the server.

PUT

PUT requests that the server store the message body sent with the request under the location provided in the HTTP message. It is usually modeled as an insert or update. It is also idempotent. When using PUT, the client knows the identity of the resource it is creating or updating. It is idempotent because sending the same PUT message more than once has no effect on the underlying service. An analogy is an MS Word document that you are editing. No matter how many times you click the Save button, the file that stores your document will logically be the same document.

DELETE

DELETE is used to remove resources. It is idempotent as well.

POST

POST is the only nonidempotent and unsafe operation of HTTP. Each POST method is allowed to modify the service in a unique way. You may or may not send information with the request. You may or may not receive information from the response.

HEAD

HEAD is exactly like GET except that instead of returning a response body, it returns only a response code and any headers associated with the request.

OPTIONS

OPTIONS is used to request information about the communication options of the resource you are interested in. It allows the client to determine the capabilities of a server and a resource without triggering any resource action or retrieval.

There are other HTTP methods (like TRACE and CONNECT), but they are unimportant when you are designing and implementing RESTful web services.

You may be scratching your head and thinking, "How is it possible to write a distributed service with only four to six methods?" Well…SQL only has four operations: SELECT, INSERT, UPDATE, and DELETE. JMS and other message-oriented middleware

(MOM) really only have two logical operations: *send* and *receive*. How powerful are these tools? For both SQL and JMS, the complexity of the interaction is confined purely to the data model. The addressability and operations are well defined and finite, and the hard stuff is delegated to the data model (in the case of SQL) or the message body (in the case of JMS).

Why Is the Uniform Interface Important?

Constraining the interface for your web services has many more advantages than disadvantages. Let's look at a few:

Familiarity

If you have a URI that points to a service, you know exactly which methods are available on that resource. You don't need an IDL-like file describing which methods are available. You don't need stubs. All you need is an HTTP client library. If you have a document that is composed of links to data provided by many different services, you already know which method to call to pull in data from those links.

Interoperability

HTTP is a very ubiquitous protocol. Most programming languages have an HTTP client library available to them. So, if your web service is exposed over HTTP, there is a very high probability that people who want to use your service will be able to do so without any additional requirements beyond being able to exchange the data formats the service is expecting. With CORBA or SOAP, you have to install vendor-specific client libraries as well as loads and loads of IDL- or WSDL-generated stub code. How many of you have had a problem getting CORBA or WS-* vendors to interoperate? It has traditionally been very problematic. The WS-* set of specifications has also been a moving target over the years. So with WS-* and CORBA, you not only have to worry about vendor interoperability, but you also have to make sure that your client and server are using the same specification version of the protocol. With REST over HTTP, you don't have to worry about either of these things and can just focus on understanding the data format of the service. I like to think that you are focusing on what is really important: *application interoperability*, rather than *vendor interoperability*.

Scalability

Because REST constrains you to a well-defined set of methods, you have predictable behavior that can have incredible performance benefits. GET is the strongest example. When surfing the Internet, have you noticed that the second time you browse to a specific page it comes up faster? This is because your browser caches already visited pages and images. HTTP has a fairly rich and configurable protocol for defining caching semantics. Because GET is a read method that is both idempotent and safe, browsers and HTTP proxies can cache responses to servers, and this can save a huge amount of network traffic and hits to your website. Add HTTP caching semantics to your web services, and you have an incredibly rich way of defining caching policies for your services. We will discuss HTTP caching in detail within Chapter 11.

It doesn't end with caching, though. Consider both PUT and DELETE. Because they are idempotent, neither the client nor the server has to worry about handling duplicate message delivery. This saves a lot of bookkeeping and complex code.

Representation-Oriented

The third architectural principle of REST is that your services should be representation-oriented. Each service is addressable through a specific URI and representations are exchanged between the client and service. With a GET operation, you are receiving a representation of the current state of that resource. A PUT or POST passes a representation of the resource to the server so that the underlying resource's state can change.

In a RESTful system, the complexity of the client-server interaction is within the representations being passed back and forth. These representations could be XML, JSON, YAML, or really any format you can come up with.

With HTTP, the representation is the message body of your request or response. An HTTP message body may be in any format the server and client want to exchange. HTTP uses the Content-Type header to tell the client or server what data format it is receiving. The Content-Type header value string is in the Multipurpose Internet Mail Extension (MIME) format. The MIME format is very simple:

```
type/subtype;name=value;name=value...
```

type is the main format family and subtype is a category. Optionally, the MIME type can have a set of name/value pair properties delimited by the ";" character. Some examples are:

```
text/plain
text/html
application/xml
text/html; charset=iso-8859-1
```

One of the more interesting features of HTTP that leverages MIME types is the capability of the client and server to negotiate the message formats being exchanged between them. While not used very much by your browser, HTTP content negotiation is a very powerful tool when you're writing web services. With the Accept header, a client can list its preferred response formats. Ajax clients can ask for JSON, Java for XML, Ruby for YAML. Another thing this is very useful for is versioning of services. The same service can be available through the same URI with the same methods (GET, POST, etc.), and all that changes is the MIME type. For example, the MIME type could be application/vnd+xml for an old service, while newer services could exchange application/vnd+xml;version=1.1 MIME types. You can read more about these concepts in Chapter 9.

All in all, because REST and HTTP have a layered approach to addressability, method choice, and data format, you have a much more decoupled protocol that allows your service to interact with a wide variety of clients in a consistent way.

Communicate Statelessly

The fourth RESTful principle I will discuss is the idea of statelessness. When I talk about statelessness, though, I don't mean that your applications can't have state. In REST, stateless means that there is no client session data stored on the server. The server only records and manages the state of the resources it exposes. If there needs to be session-specific data, it should be held and maintained by the client and transferred to the server with each request as needed. A service layer that does not have to maintain client sessions is a lot easier to scale, as it has to do a lot fewer expensive replications in a clustered environment. It's a lot easier to scale up because all you have to do is add machines.

A world without server-maintained session data isn't so hard to imagine if you look back 12–15 years ago. Back then, many distributed applications had a fat GUI client written in Visual Basic, Power Builder, or Visual C++ talking RPCs to a middle tier that sat in front of a database. The server was stateless and just processed data. The fat client held all session state. The problem with this architecture was an IT operations one. It was very hard for operations to upgrade, patch, and maintain client GUIs in large environments. Web applications solved this problem because the applications could be delivered from a central server and rendered by the browser. We started maintaining client sessions on the server because of the limitations of the browser. Around 2008, in step with the growing popularity of Ajax, Flex, and Java FX, the browsers became sophisticated enough to maintain their own session state like their fat-client counterparts in the mid-'90s used to do. We can now go back to that stateless scalable middle tier that we enjoyed in the past. It's funny how things go full circle sometimes.

HATEOAS

The final principle of REST is the idea of using Hypermedia As The Engine Of Application State (HATEOAS). Hypermedia is a document-centric approach with added support for embedding links to other services and information within that document format. I did indirectly talk about HATEOAS in "Addressability" on page 6 when I discussed the idea of using hyperlinks within the data format received from a service.

One of the uses of hypermedia and hyperlinks is composing complex sets of information from disparate sources. The information could be within a company intranet or dispersed across the Internet. Hyperlinks allow us to reference and aggregate additional data without bloating our responses. The ecommerce order in "Addressability" on page 6 is an example of this:

```
<order id="111">
    <customer>http://customers.myintranet.com/customers/32133</customer>
```

```
<order-entries>
  <order-entry>
     <quantity>5</quantity>
     <product>http://products.myintranet.com/products/111</product>
  ...
```

In that example, links embedded within the document allowed us to bring in additional information as needed. Aggregation isn't the full concept of HATEOAS, though. The more interesting part of HATEOAS is the "engine."

The engine of application state

If you're on *Amazon.com* buying a book, you follow a series of links and fill out one or two forms before your credit card is charged. You transition through the ordering process by examining and interacting with the responses returned by each link you follow and each form you submit. The server guides you through the order process by embedding where you should go next within the HTML data it provides your browser.

This is very different from the way traditional distributed applications work. Older applications usually have a list of precanned services they know exist, and they interact with a central directory server to locate these services on the network. HATEOAS is a bit different because with each request returned from a server it tells you what new interactions you can do next, as well as where to go to transition the state of your applications.

For example, let's say we wanted to get a list of products available on a web store. We do an HTTP GET on *http://example.com/webstore/products* and receive back:

```
<products>
  <product id="123">
     <name>headphones</name>
     <price>$16.99</price>
  </product>
  <product id="124">
     <name>USB Cable</name>
     <price>$5.99</price>
  </product>
  ...
</products>
```

This could be problematic if we had thousands of products to send back to our client. We might overload it, or the client might wait forever for the response to finish downloading. We could instead list only the first five products and provide a link to get the next set:

```
<products>
  <link rel="next" href="http://example.com/store/products?startIndex=5"/>
  <product id="123">
     <name>headphones</name>
     <price>$16.99</price>
```

```
        </product>
    ...
    </products>
```

When first querying for a list of products, clients don't have to know they're getting back a list of only five products. The data format can tell them that they didn't get a full set and that to get the next set, they need to follow a specific link. Following the next link could get them back a new document with additional links:

```
<products>
    <link rel="previous" href="http://example.com/store/products?startIndex=0"/>
    <link rel="next" href="http://example.com/webstore/products?startIndex=10"/>
    <product id="128">
        <name>stuff</name>
        <price>$16.99</price>
    </product>
...
</products>
```

In this case, there is the additional state transition of previous so that clients can browse an earlier part of the product list. The next and previous links seem a bit trivial, but imagine if we had other transition types like payment, inventory, or sales.

This sort of approach gives the server a lot of flexibility, as it can change where and how state transitions happen on the fly. It could provide new and interesting opportunities to surf to. In Chapter 10, we'll dive into HATEOAS again.

Wrapping Up

REST identifies the key architectural principles of why the Web is so prevalent and scalable. The next step in the evolution of the Web is to apply these principles to the Semantic Web and the world of web services. REST offers a simple, interoperable, and flexible way of writing web services that can be very different than the RPC mechanisms like CORBA and WS-* that so many of us have had training in. In the next chapter we will apply the concepts of REST by defining a distributed RESTful interface for an existing business object model.

CHAPTER 2

Designing RESTful Services

In Chapter 1, I gave you a brief overview of REST and how it relates to HTTP. Although it is good to obtain a solid foundation in theory, nothing can take the place of seeing theory put into practice. So, let's define a RESTful interface for a simple order entry system of a hypothetical ecommerce web store. Remote distributed clients will use this web service to purchase goods, modify existing orders in the system, and view information about customers and products.

In this chapter, we will start off by examining the simple underlying object model of our service. After walking through the model, we will add a distributed interface to our system using HTTP and the architectural guidelines of REST. To satisfy the addressability requirements of REST, we will first have to define a set of URIs that represent the entry points into our system. Since RESTful systems are representation-oriented, we will next define the data format that we will use to exchange information between our services and clients. Finally, we will decide which HTTP methods are allowed by each exposed URI and what those methods do. We will make sure to conform to the uniform, constrained interface of HTTP when doing this step.

The Object Model

The object model of our order entry system is very simple. Each order in the system represents a single transaction or purchase and is associated with a particular customer. Orders are made up of one or more line items. Line items represent the type and number of each product purchased.

Based on this description of our system, we can deduce that the objects in our model are Order, Customer, LineItem, and Product. Each data object in our model has a unique identifier, which is the integer id property. Figure 2-1 shows a UML diagram of our object model.

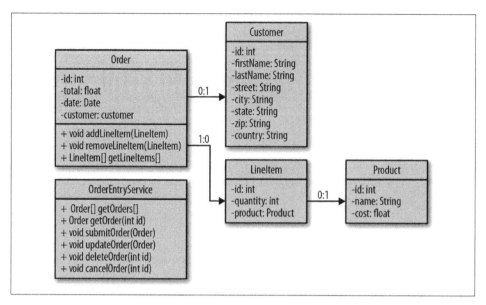

Figure 2-1. Order entry system object model

We will want to browse all orders as well as each individual order in our system. We will also want to submit new orders and update existing ones. Finally, we will want to have the ability to cancel and delete existing orders. The `OrderEntryService` object represents the operations we want to perform on our `Order`, `Customer`, `LineItem`, and `Product` objects.

Model the URIs

The first thing we are going to do to create our distributed interface is define and name each of the distributed endpoints in our system. In a RESTful system, endpoints are usually referred to as *resources* and are identified using a URI. URIs satisfy the addressability requirements of a RESTful service.

In our object model, we will be interacting with `Orders`, `Customers`, and `Products`. These will be our main, top-level resources. We want to be able to obtain lists of each of these top-level items and to interact with individual items. `LineItems` are aggregated within `Order` objects so they will not be a top-level resource. We could expose them as a subresource under one particular `Order`, but for now, let's assume they are hidden by the data format. Given this, here is a list of URIs that will be exposed in our system:

```
/orders
/orders/{id}
/products
/products/{id}
```

```
/customers
/customers/{id}
```

 You'll notice that the nouns in our object model have been represented as URIs. URIs shouldn't be used as mini-RPC mechanisms and should not identify operations. Instead, you should use a combination of HTTP methods and the data format to model unique operations in your distributed RESTful system.

Defining the Data Format

One of the most important things we have to do when defining a RESTful interface is determine how our resources will be represented over the wire to our clients. XML is perhaps one of the most popular formats on the Web and can be processed by most modern languages, so let's choose that. JSON is also a popular format, as it is more condensed and JavaScript can interpret it directly (great for Ajax applications), but let's stick to XML for now.

Generally, you would define an XML schema for each representation you want to send across the wire. An XML schema defines the grammar of a data format. It defines the rules about how a document can be put together. I do find, though, that when explaining things within an article (or a book), providing examples rather than schema makes things much easier to read and understand.

Read and Update Format

The XML format of our representations will look a tiny bit different when we read or update resources from the server as compared to when we create resources on the server. Let's look at our read and update format first.

Common link element

Each format for Order, Customer, and Product will have a common XML element called link:

```
<link rel="self" href="http://example.com/..."/>
```

The link[1] element tells any client that obtains an XML document describing one of the objects in our ecommerce system where on the network the client can interact with that particular resource. The rel attribute tells the client what relationship the link has with the resource the URI points to (contained within the href attribute). The self value

---

1. I actually borrowed the link element from the Atom format. Atom is a syndication format that is used to aggregate and publish blogs and news feeds. You can find out more about Atom at *http://www.w3.org/2005/ Atom*.

just means it is pointing to itself. While not that interesting on its own, link becomes very useful when we aggregate or compose information into one larger XML document.

The details

So, with the common elements described, let's start diving into the details by first looking at our Customer representation format:

```
<customer id="117">
    <link rel="self" href="http://example.com/customers/117"/>
    <first-name>Bill</first-name>
    <last-name>Burke</last-name>
    <street>555 Beacon St.<street>
    <city>Boston</city>
    <state>MA</state>
    <zip>02115</zip>
</customer>
```

Pretty straightforward. We just take the object model of Customer from Figure 2-1 and expand its attributes as XML elements. Product looks much the same in terms of simplicity:

```
<product id="543">
    <link rel="self" href="http://example.com/products/543"/>
    <name>iPhone</name>
    <cost>$199.99</cost>
</product>
```

In a real system, we would, of course, have a lot more attributes for Customer and Product, but let's keep our example simple so that it's easier to illustrate these RESTful concepts:

```
<order id="233">
    <link rel="self" href="http://example.com/orders/233"/>
    <total>$199.02</total>
    <date>December 22, 2008 06:56</date>
    <customer id="117">
        <link rel="self" href="http://example.com/customers/117"/>
        <first-name>Bill</first-name>
        <last-name>Burke</last-name>
        <street>555 Beacon St.<street>
        <city>Boston</city>
        <state>MA</state>
        <zip>02115</zip>
    </customer>
    <line-items>
        <line-item id="144">
            <product id="543">
                <link rel="self" href="http://example.com/products/543"/>
                <name>iPhone</name>
                <cost>$199.99</cost>
            </product>
```

```
            <quantity>1</quantity>
        </line-item>
    </line-items>
</order>
```

The Order data format has the top-level elements of total and date that specify the total cost of the order and the date the Order was made. Order is a great example of data composition, as it includes Customer and Product information. This is where the link element becomes particularly useful. If the client is interested in interacting with a Customer or Product that makes up the Order, it has the URI needed to interact with one of these resources.

Create Format

When we are creating new Orders, Customers, or Products, it doesn't make a lot of sense to include an id attribute and link element with our XML document. The server will generate IDs when it inserts our new object into a database. We also don't know the URI of a new object because the server also generates this. So, the XML for creating a new Product would look something like this:

```
<product>
    <name>iPhone</name>
    <cost>$199.99</cost>
</product>
```

Orders and Customers would follow the same pattern and leave out the id attribute and link element.

Assigning HTTP Methods

The final thing we have to do is decide which HTTP methods will be exposed for each of our resources and what these methods will do. It is crucial that we do not assign functionality to an HTTP method that supersedes the specification-defined boundaries of that method. For example, an HTTP GET on a particular resource should be read-only. It should not change the state of the resource it is invoking on. Intermediate services like a proxy-cache, a CDN (Akamai), or your browser rely on you to follow the semantics of HTTP strictly so that they can perform built-in tasks like caching effectively. If you do not follow the definition of each HTTP method strictly, clients and administration tools cannot make assumptions about your services, and your system becomes more complex.

Let's walk through each method of our object model to determine which URIs and HTTP methods are used to represent them.

Browsing All Orders, Customers, or Products

The Order, Customer, and Product objects in our object model are all very similar in how they are accessed and manipulated. One thing our remote clients will want to do is to browse all the Orders, Customers, or Products in the system. These URIs represent these objects as a group:

```
/orders
/products
/customers
```

To get a list of Orders, Products, or Customers, the remote client will call an HTTP GET on the URI of the object group it is interested in. An example request would look like the following:

```
GET /products HTTP/1.1
```

Our service will respond with a data format that represents all Orders, Products, or Customers within our system. Here's what a response would look like:

```
HTTP/1.1 200 OK
Content-Type: application/xml

<products>
   <product id="111">
      <link rel="self" href="http://example.com/products/111"/>
      <name>iPhone</name>
      <cost>$199.99</cost>
   </product>
   <product id="222">
      <link rel="self" href="http://example.com/products/222"/>
      <name>Macbook</name>
      <cost>$1599.99</cost>
   </product>
...
</products>
```

One problem with this bulk operation is that we may have thousands of Orders, Customers, or Products in our system and we may overload our client and hurt our response times. To mitigate this problem, we will allow the client to specify query parameters on the URI to limit the size of the dataset returned:

```
GET /orders?startIndex=0&size=5 HTTP/1.1
GET /products?startIndex=0&size=5 HTTP/1.1
GET /customers?startIndex=0&size=5 HTTP/1.1
```

Here we have defined two query parameters: startIndex and size. The startIndex parameter represents where in our large list of Orders, Products, or Customers we want to start sending objects from. It is a numeric index into the object group being queried. The size parameter specifies how many of those objects in the list we want to return.

These parameters will be optional. The client does not have to specify them in its URI when crafting its request to the server.

Obtaining Individual Orders, Customers, or Products

I mentioned in the previous section that we would use a URI pattern to obtain individual Orders, Customers, or Products:

```
/orders/{id}
/products/{id}
/customers/{id}
```

We will use the HTTP GET method to retrieve individual objects in our system. Each GET invocation will return a data format that represents the object being obtained:

```
GET /orders/233 HTTP/1.1
```

For this request, the client is interested in getting a representation of the Order with an order id of 233. GET requests for Products and Customers would work the same. The HTTP response message would look something like this:

```
HTTP/1.1 200 OK
Content-Type: application/xml

<order id="233">...</order>
```

The response code is 200, "OK," indicating that the request was successful. The Content-Type header specifies the format of our message body as XML, and finally we have the actual representation of the Order.

Creating an Order, Customer, or Product

There are two possible ways in which a client could create an Order, Customer, or Product within our order entry system: by using either the HTTP PUT or POST method. Let's look at both ways.

Creating with PUT

The HTTP definition of PUT states that it can be used to create or update a resource on the server. To create an Order, Customer, or Product with PUT, the client simply sends a representation of the new object it is creating to the exact URI location that represents the object:

```
PUT /orders/233 HTTP/1.1
PUT /customers/112 HTTP/1.1
PUT /products/664 HTTP/1.1
```

PUT is required by the specification to send a response code of 201, "Created," if a new resource was created on the server as a result of the request.

The HTTP specification also states that PUT is idempotent. Our PUT is idempotent, because no matter how many times we tell the server to "create" our Order, the same bits are stored at the /orders/233 location. Sometimes a PUT request will fail and the client won't know if the request was delivered and processed at the server. Idempotency guarantees that it's OK for the client to retransmit the PUT operation and not worry about any adverse side effects.

The disadvantage of using PUT to create resources is that the client has to provide the unique ID that represents the object it is creating. While it is usually possible for the client to generate this unique ID, most application designers prefer that their servers (usually through their databases) create this ID. In our hypothetical order entry system, we want our server to control the generation of resource IDs. So what do we do? We can switch to using POST instead of PUT.

Creating with POST

Creating an Order, Customer, or Product using the POST method is a little more complex than using PUT. To create an Order, Customer, or Product with POST, the client sends a representation of the new object it is creating to the parent URI of its representation, leaving out the numeric target ID. For example:

```
POST /orders HTTP/1.1
Content-Type: application/xml

<order>
   <total>$199.02</total>
   <date>December 22, 2008 06:56</date>
...
</order>
```

The service receives the POST message, processes the XML, and creates a new order in the database using a database-generated unique ID. While this approach works perfectly fine, we've left our client in a quandary. What if the client wants to edit, update, or cancel the order it just posted? What is the ID of the new order? What URI can we use to interact with the new resource? To resolve this issue, we will add a bit of information to the HTTP response message. The client would receive a message something like this:

```
HTTP/1.1 201 Created
Content-Type: application/xml
Location: http://example.com/orders/233

<order id="233">
   <link rel="self" href="http://example.com/orders/233"/>
   <total>$199.02</total>
   <date>December 22, 2008 06:56</date>
...
</order>
```

HTTP requires that if POST creates a new resource, it respond with a code of 201, "Created" (just like PUT). The Location header in the response message provides a URI to the client so it knows where to further interact with the Order that was created (i.e., if the client wanted to update the Order). It is optional whether the server sends the representation of the newly created Order with the response. Here, we send back an XML representation of the Order that was just created with the ID attribute set to the one generated by our database as well as a link element.

I didn't pull the Location header out of thin air. The beauty of this approach is that it is defined within the HTTP specification. That's an important part of REST—to follow the predefined behavior within the specification of the protocol you are using. Because of this, most systems are self-documenting, as the distributed interactions are already mostly defined by the HTTP specification.

Updating an Order, Customer, or Product

We will model updating an Order, Customer, or Product using the HTTP PUT method. The client PUTs a new representation of the object it is updating to the exact URI location that represents the object. For example, let's say we wanted to change the price of a product from $199.99 to $149.99. Here's what the request would look like:

```
PUT /products/111 HTTP/1.1
Content-Type: application/xml

<product id="111">
    <name>iPhone</name>
    <cost>$149.99</cost>
</product>
```

As I stated earlier in this chapter, PUT is great because it is idempotent. No matter how many times we transmit this PUT request, the underlying Product will still have the same final state.

When a resource is updated with PUT, the HTTP specification requires that you send a response code of 200, "OK," and a response message body or a response code of 204, "No Content," without any response body. In our system, we will send a status of 204 and no response message.

We could use POST to update an individual Order, but then the client would have to assume the update was nonidempotent and we would have to take duplicate message processing into account.

Removing an Order, Customer, or Product

We will model deleting an `Order`, `Customer`, or `Product` using the HTTP DELETE method. The client simply invokes the DELETE method on the exact URI that represents the object we want to remove. Removing an object will wipe its existence from the system.

When a resource is removed with DELETE, the HTTP specification requires that you send a response code of 200, "OK," and a response message body or a response code of 204, "No Content," without any response body. In our application, we will send a status of 204 and no response message.

Cancelling an Order

So far, the operations of our object model have fit quite nicely into corresponding HTTP methods. We're using GET for reading, PUT for updating, POST for creating, and DELETE for removing. We do have an operation in our object model that doesn't fit so nicely. In our system, `Orders` can be cancelled as well as removed. While removing an object wipes it clean from our databases, cancelling only changes the state of the `Order` and retains it within the system. How should we model such an operation?

Overloading the meaning of DELETE

Cancelling an `Order` is very similar to removing it. Since we are already modeling remove with the HTTP DELETE method, one thing we could do is add an extra query parameter to the request:

```
DELETE /orders/233?cancel=true
```

Here, the `cancel` query parameter would tell our service that we don't really want to remove the `Order`, but cancel it. In other words, we are overloading the meaning of DELETE.

While I'm not going to tell you not to do this, I will tell you that you shouldn't do it. It is not good RESTful design. In this case, you are changing the meaning of the uniform interface. Using a query parameter in this way is actually creating a mini-RPC mechanism. HTTP specifically states that DELETE is used to delete a resource from the server, not cancel it.

States versus operations

When modeling a RESTful interface for the operations of your object model, you should ask yourself a simple question: is the operation a state of the resource? If you answer yes to this question, the operation should be modeled within the data format.

Cancelling an `Order` is a perfect example of this. The key with cancelling is that it is a specific state of an `Order`. When a client follows a particular URI that links to a specific

Order, the client will want to know whether the Order was cancelled or not. Information about the cancellation needs to be in the data format of the Order. So let's add a cancelled element to our Order data format:

```
<order id="233">
  <link rel="self" href="http://example.com/orders/233"/>
  <total>$199.02</total>
  <date>December 22, 2008 06:56</date>
  <cancelled>false</cancelled>
...
</order>
```

Since the state of being cancelled is modeled in the data format, we can now use our already defined mechanism of updating an Order to model the cancel operation. For example, we could PUT this message to our service:

```
PUT /orders/233 HTTP/1.1
Content-Type: application/xml

<order id="233">
  <total>$199.02</total>
  <date>December 22, 2008 06:56</date>
  <cancelled>true</cancelled>
...
</order>
```

In this example, we PUT a new representation of our order with the cancelled element set to true. By doing this, we've changed the state of our order from viable to cancelled.

This pattern of modeling an operation as the state of the resource doesn't always fit, though. What if we expanded on our cancel example by saying that we wanted a way to clean up all cancelled orders? In other words, we want to purge all cancelled orders from our database. We can't really model purging the same way we did cancel. While purge does change the state of our application, it is not in and of itself a state of the application.

To solve this problem, we model this operation as a subresource of /orders and we trigger a purging by doing a POST on that resource. For example:

```
POST /orders/purge HTTP/1.1
```

An interesting side effect of this is that because purge is now a URI, we can evolve its interface over time. For example, maybe GET /orders/purge returns a document that states the last time a purge was executed and which orders were deleted. What if we wanted to add some criteria for purging as well? Form parameters could be passed stating that we only want to purge orders older than a certain date. In doing this, we're giving ourselves a lot of flexibility as well as honoring the uniform interface contract of REST.

Wrapping Up

So, we've taken an existing object diagram and modeled it as a RESTful distributed service. We used URIs to represent the endpoints in our system. These endpoints are called resources. For each resource, we defined which HTTP methods each resource will allow and how those individual HTTP methods behave. Finally, we defined the data format that our clients and services will use to exchange information. The next step is to actually implement these services in Java. This will be the main topic for the rest of this book.

CHAPTER 3

Your First JAX-RS Service

The first two chapters of this book focused on the theory of REST and designing the RESTful interface for a simple ecommerce order entry system. Now it's time to implement a part of our system in the Java language.

Writing RESTful services in Java has been possible for years with the servlet API. If you have written a web application in Java, you are probably already very familiar with servlets. Servlets bring you very close to the HTTP protocol and require a lot of boilerplate code to move information to and from an HTTP request. In 2008, a new specification called JAX-RS was defined to simplify RESTful service implementation.

JAX-RS is a framework that focuses on applying Java annotations to plain Java objects. It has annotations to bind specific URI patterns and HTTP operations to individual methods of your Java class. It has parameter injection annotations so that you can easily pull in information from the HTTP request. It has message body readers and writers that allow you to decouple data format marshalling and unmarshalling from your Java data objects. It has exception mappers that can map an application-thrown exception to an HTTP response code and message. Finally, it has some nice facilities for HTTP content negotiation.

This chapter gives a brief introduction to writing a JAX-RS service. You'll find that getting it up and running is fairly simple.

Developing a JAX-RS RESTful Service

Let's start by implementing one of the resources of the order entry system we defined in Chapter 2. Specifically, we'll define a JAX-RS service that allows us to read, create, and update Customers. To do this, we will need to implement two Java classes. One class will be used to represent actual Customers. The other will be our JAX-RS service.

Customer: The Data Class

First, we will need a Java class to represent customers in our system. We will name this class Customer. Customer is a simple Java class that defines eight properties: id, firstName, lastName, street, city, state, zip, and country. *Properties* are attributes that can be accessed via the class's fields or through public set and get methods. A Java class that follows this pattern is also called a *Java bean*:

```java
package com.restfully.shop.domain;

public class Customer {
    private int id;
    private String firstName;
    private String lastName;
    private String street;
    private String city;
    private String state;
    private String zip;
    private String country;

    public int getId() { return id; }
    public void setId(int id) { this.id = id; }

    public String getFirstName() { return firstName; }
    public void setFirstName(String firstName) {
                this.firstName = firstName; }

    public String getLastName() { return lastName; }
    public void setLastName(String lastName) {
                this.lastName = lastName; }

    public String getStreet() { return street; }
    public void setStreet(String street) { this.street = street; }

    public String getCity() { return city; }
    public void setCity(String city) { this.city = city;  }

    public String getState() { return state; }
    public void setState(String state) { this.state = state; }

    public String getZip() { return zip; }
    public void setZip(String zip) { this.zip = zip; }

    public String getCountry() { return country; }
    public void setCountry(String country) { this.country = country; }
}
```

In an Enterprise Java application, the Customer class would usually be a Java Persistence API (JPA) Entity bean and would be used to interact with a relational database. It could also be annotated with JAXB annotations that allow you to map a Java class directly to XML. To keep our example simple, Customer will be just a plain Java object and stored in memory. In Chapter 6, I'll show how you can use JAXB with JAX-RS to make translating between your customer's data format (XML) and your Customer objects easier. Chapter 14 will show you how JAX-RS works in the context of a Java EE (Enterprise Edition) application and things like JPA.

CustomerResource: Our JAX-RS Service

Now that we have defined a domain object that will represent our customers at runtime, we need to implement our JAX-RS service so that remote clients can interact with our customer database. A JAX-RS service is a Java class that uses JAX-RS annotations to bind and map specific incoming HTTP requests to Java methods that can service these requests. While JAX-RS can integrate with popular component models like Enterprise JavaBeans (EJB), Web Beans, JBoss Seam, and Spring, it does define its own lightweight model.

In vanilla JAX-RS, services can either be singletons or per-request objects. A *singleton* means that one and only one Java object services HTTP requests. *Per-request* means that a Java object is created to process each incoming request and is thrown away at the end of that request. Per-request also implies statelessness, as no service state is held between requests.

For our example, we will write a CustomerResource class to implement our JAX-RS service and assume it will be a singleton. In this example, we need CustomerResource to be a singleton because it is going to hold state. It is going to keep a map of Custom er objects in memory that our remote clients can access. In a real system, CustomerRe source would probably interact with a database to retrieve and store customers and wouldn't need to hold state between requests. In this database scenario, we could make CustomerResource per-request and thus stateless. Let's start by looking at the first few lines of our class to see how to start writing a JAX-RS service:

```java
package com.restfully.shop.services;

import ...;

@Path("/customers")
public class CustomerResource {

    private Map<Integer, Customer> customerDB =
                        new ConcurrentHashMap<Integer, Customer>();
    private AtomicInteger idCounter = new AtomicInteger();
```

As you can see, CustomerResource is a plain Java class and doesn't implement any particular JAX-RS interface. The @javax.ws.rs.Path annotation placed on the Customer Resource class designates the class as a JAX-RS service. Java classes that you want to be recognized as JAX-RS services must have this annotation. Also notice that the @Path annotation has the value of /customers. This value represents the relative root URI of our customer service. If the absolute base URI of our server is *http://shop.restfully.com*, methods exposed by our `CustomerResource` class would be available under *http://shop.restfully.com/customers*.

In our class, we define a simple map in the `customerDB` field that will store created `Customer` objects in memory. We use a `java.util.concurrent.ConcurrentHashMap` for `customerDB` because `CustomerResource` is a singleton and will have concurrent requests accessing the map. Using a `java.util.HashMap` would trigger concurrent access exceptions in a multithreaded environment. Using a `java.util.Hashtable` creates a synchronization bottleneck. `ConcurrentHashMap` is our best bet. The `idCounter` field will be used to generate IDs for newly created `Customer` objects. For concurrency reasons, we use a `java.util.concurrent.atomic.AtomicInteger`, as we want to always have a unique number generated. Of course, these two lines of code have nothing to do with JAX-RS and are solely artifacts required by our simple example.

Creating customers

Let's now take a look at how to create customers in our `CustomerResource` class:

```java
@POST
@Consumes("application/xml")
public Response createCustomer(InputStream is) {
    Customer customer = readCustomer(is);
    customer.setId(idCounter.incrementAndGet());
    customerDB.put(customer.getId(), customer);
    System.out.println("Created customer " + customer.getId());
    return Response.created(URI.create("/customers/"
                                + customer.getId())).build();
}
```

We will implement customer creation using the same model as that used in Chapter 2. An HTTP POST request sends an XML document representing the customer we want to create. The `createCustomer()` method receives the request, parses the document, creates a `Customer` object from the document, and adds it to our `customerDB` map. The `createCustomer()` method returns a response code of 201, "Created," along with a `Location` header pointing to the absolute URI of the customer we just created. So how does the `createCustomer()` method do all this? Let's examine further.

To bind HTTP POST requests to the `createCustomer()` method, we annotate it with the `@javax.ws.rs.POST` annotation. The `@Path` annotation we put on the `CustomerResource` class, combined with this `@POST` annotation, binds all POST requests going to the relative URI /customers to the Java method `createCustomer()`.

The `@javax.ws.rs.Consumes` annotation applied to `createCustomer()` specifies which media type the method is expecting in the message body of the HTTP input request. If the client POSTs a media type other than XML, an error code is sent back to the client.

The `createCustomer()` method takes one `java.io.InputStream` parameter. In JAX-RS, any non-JAX-RS-annotated parameter is considered to be a representation of the HTTP input request's message body. In this case, we want access to the method body in its most basic form, an `InputStream`.

 Only one Java method parameter can represent the HTTP message body. This means any other parameters must be annotated with one of the JAX-RS annotations discussed in Chapter 5.

The implementation of the method reads and transforms the POSTed XML into a `Customer` object and stores it in the `customerDB` map. The method returns a complex response to the client using the `javax.ws.rs.core.Response` class. The static `Response.created()` method creates a `Response` object that contains an HTTP status code of 201, "Created." It also adds a `Location` header to the HTTP response with the value of something like *http://shop.restfully.com/customers/333*, depending on the base URI of the server and the generated ID of the `Customer` object (333 in this example).

Retrieving customers

```
@GET
@Path("{id}")
@Produces("application/xml")
public StreamingOutput getCustomer(@PathParam("id") int id) {
    final Customer customer = customerDB.get(id);
    if (customer == null) {
        throw new WebApplicationException(Response.Status.NOT_FOUND);
    }
    return new StreamingOutput() {
        public void write(OutputStream outputStream)
                    throws IOException, WebApplicationException {
            outputCustomer(outputStream, customer);
        }
    };
}
```

We annotate the `getCustomer()` method with the `@javax.ws.rs.GET` annotation to bind HTTP GET operations to this Java method.

We also annotate `getCustomer()` with the `@javax.ws.rs.Produces` annotation. This annotation tells JAX-RS which HTTP `Content-Type` the GET response will be. In this case, it is `application/xml`.

In the implementation of the method, we use the `id` parameter to query for a `Customer` object in the `customerDB` map. If this customer does not exist, we throw the `javax.ws.rs.WebApplicationException`. This exception will set the HTTP response code to 404, "Not Found," meaning that the customer resource does not exist. We'll discuss more about exception handling in Chapter 7, so I won't go into more detail about the WebApplicationException here.

We will write the response manually to the client through a java.io.OutputStream. In JAX-RS, when you want to do streaming manually, you must implement and return an instance of the javax.ws.rs.core.StreamingOutput interface from your JAX-RS method. StreamingOutput is a callback interface with one callback method, write():

```
package javax.ws.rs.core;

public interface StreamingOutput {
   public void write(OutputStream os) throws IOException,
                                       WebApplicationException;
}
```

In the last line of our getCustomer() method, we implement and return an inner class implementation of StreamingOutput. Within the write() method of this inner class, we delegate back to a utility method called outputCustomer() that exists in our Cus tomerResource class. When the JAX-RS provider is ready to send an HTTP response body back over the network to the client, it will call back to the write() method we implemented to output the XML representation of our Customer object.

In general, you will not use the StreamingOutput interface to output responses. In Chapter 6, you will see that JAX-RS has a bunch of nice content handlers that can automatically convert Java objects straight into the data format you are sending across the wire. I didn't want to introduce too many new concepts in the first introductory chapter, so the example only does simple streaming.

Updating a customer

The last RESTful operation we have to implement is updating customers. In Chapter 2, we used PUT /customers/{id}, while passing along an updated XML representation of the customer. This is implemented in the updateCustomer() method of our CustomerResource class:

```
@PUT
@Path("{id}")
@Consumes("application/xml")
public void updateCustomer(@PathParam("id") int id,
                           InputStream is) {
   Customer update = readCustomer(is);
   Customer current = customerDB.get(id);
   if (current == null)
     throw new WebApplicationException(Response.Status.NOT_FOUND);

   current.setFirstName(update.getFirstName());
   current.setLastName(update.getLastName());
```

```
            current.setStreet(update.getStreet());
            current.setState(update.getState());
            current.setZip(update.getZip());
            current.setCountry(update.getCountry());
    }
```

We annotate the updateCustomer() method with @javax.ws.rs.PUT to bind HTTP PUT requests to this method. Like our getCustomer() method, updateCustomer() is annotated with an additional @Path annotation so that we can match /customers/{id} URIs.

The updateCustomer() method takes two parameters. The first is an id parameter that represents the Customer object we are updating. Like getCustomer(), we use the @Path Param annotation to extract the ID from the incoming request URI. The second parameter is an InputStream that will allow us to read in the XML document that was sent with the PUT request. Like createCustomer(), a parameter that is not annotated with a JAX-RS annotation is considered a representation of the body of the incoming message.

In the first part of the method implementation, we read in the XML document and create a Customer object out of it. The method then tries to find an existing Customer object in the customerDB map. If it doesn't exist, we throw a WebApplicationExcep tion that will send a 404, "Not Found," response code back to the client. If the Custom er object does exist, we update our existing Customer object with new updated values.

Utility methods

The final thing we have to implement is the utility methods that were used in create Customer(), getCustomer(), and updateCustomer() to transform Customer objects to and from XML. The outputCustomer() method takes a Customer object and writes it as XML to the response's OutputStream:

```
    protected void outputCustomer(OutputStream os, Customer cust)
                                                throws IOException {
        PrintStream writer = new PrintStream(os);
        writer.println("<customer id=\"" + cust.getId() + "\">");
        writer.println("   <first-name>" + cust.getFirstName()
                        + "</first-name>");
        writer.println("   <last-name>" + cust.getLastName()
                        + "</last-name>");
        writer.println("   <street>" + cust.getStreet() + "</street>");
        writer.println("   <city>" + cust.getCity() + "</city>");
        writer.println("   <state>" + cust.getState() + "</state>");
        writer.println("   <zip>" + cust.getZip() + "</zip>");
        writer.println("   <country>" + cust.getCountry() + "</country>");
        writer.println("</customer>");
    }
```

As you can see, this is a pretty straightforward method. Through string manipulations, it does a brute-force conversion of the `Customer` object to XML text.

The next method is `readCustomer()`. The method is responsible for reading XML text from an `InputStream` and creating a `Customer` object:

```
protected Customer readCustomer(InputStream is) {
   try {
      DocumentBuilder builder =
         DocumentBuilderFactory.newInstance().newDocumentBuilder();
      Document doc = builder.parse(is);
      Element root = doc.getDocumentElement();
```

Unlike `outputCustomer()`, we don't manually parse the `InputStream`. The JDK has a built-in XML parser, so we do not need to write it ourselves or download a third-party library to do it. The `readCustomer()` method starts off by parsing the `InputStream` and creating a Java object model that represents the XML document. The rest of the `read Customer()` method moves data from the XML model into a newly created `Customer` object:

```
Customer cust = new Customer();
if (root.getAttribute("id") != null
       && !root.getAttribute("id").trim().equals("")) {
   cust.setId(Integer.valueOf(root.getAttribute("id")));
}
NodeList nodes = root.getChildNodes();
for (int i = 0; i < nodes.getLength(); i++) {
   Element element = (Element) nodes.item(i);
   if (element.getTagName().equals("first-name")) {
      cust.setFirstName(element.getTextContent());
   }
   else if (element.getTagName().equals("last-name")) {
      cust.setLastName(element.getTextContent());
   }
   else if (element.getTagName().equals("street")) {
      cust.setStreet(element.getTextContent());
   }
   else if (element.getTagName().equals("city")) {
      cust.setCity(element.getTextContent());
   }
   else if (element.getTagName().equals("state")) {
      cust.setState(element.getTextContent());
   }
   else if (element.getTagName().equals("zip")) {
      cust.setZip(element.getTextContent());
   }
   else if (element.getTagName().equals("country")) {
      cust.setCountry(element.getTextContent());
   }
}
return cust;
```

```
        }
        catch (Exception e) {
            throw new WebApplicationException(e,
                        Response.Status.BAD_REQUEST);
        }
    }
}
```

I'll admit, this example was a bit contrived. In a real system, we would not manually output XML or write all this boilerplate code to read in an XML document and convert it to a business object, but I don't want to distract you from learning JAX-RS basics by introducing another API. In Chapter 6, I will show how you can use JAXB to map your Customer object to XML and have JAX-RS automatically transform your HTTP message body to and from XML.

JAX-RS and Java Interfaces

In our example so far, we've applied JAX-RS annotations directly on the Java class that implements our service. In JAX-RS, you are also allowed to define a Java interface that contains all your JAX-RS annotation metadata instead of applying all your annotations to your implementation class.

Interfaces are a great way to scope out how you want to model your services. With an interface, you can write something that defines what your RESTful API will look like along with what Java methods they will map to before you write a single line of business logic. Also, many developers like to use this approach so that their business logic isn't "polluted" with so many annotations. They think the code is more readable if it has fewer annotations. Finally, sometimes you do have the case where the same business logic must be exposed not only RESTfully, but also through SOAP and JAX-WS. In this case, your business logic would look more like an explosion of annotations than actual code. Interfaces are a great way to isolate all this metadata into one logical and readable construct.

Let's transform our customer resource example into something that is interface based:

```
package com.restfully.shop.services;

import ...;

@Path("/customers")
public interface CustomerResource {

    @POST
    @Consumes("application/xml")
    public Response createCustomer(InputStream is);

    @GET
    @Path("{id}")
    @Produces("application/xml")
```

```
    public StreamingOutput getCustomer(@PathParam("id") int id);

    @PUT
    @Path("{id}")
    @Consumes("application/xml")
    public void updateCustomer(@PathParam("id") int id, InputStream is);
}
```

Here, our `CustomerResource` is defined as an interface and all the JAX-RS annotations are applied to methods within that interface. We can then define a class that implements this interface:

```
package com.restfully.shop.services;

import ...;

public class CustomerResourceService implements CustomerResource {

    public Response createCustomer(InputStream is) {
        ... the implementation ...
    }

    public StreamingOutput getCustomer(int id)
        ... the implementation ...
    }

    public void updateCustomer(int id, InputStream is) {
        ... the implementation ...
    }
}
```

As you can see, no JAX-RS annotations are needed within the implementing class. All our metadata is confined to the `CustomerResource` interface.

If you need to, you can override the metadata defined in your interfaces by reapplying annotations within your implementation class. For example, maybe we want to enforce a specific character set for POST XML:

```
public class CustomerResourceService implements CustomerResource {

    @POST
    @Consumes("application/xml;charset=utf-8")
    public Response createCustomer(InputStream is) {
        ... the implementation ...
    }
```

In this example, we are overriding the metadata defined in an interface for one specific method. When overriding metadata for a method, you must respecify all the annotation metadata for that method even if you are changing only one small thing.

Overall, I do not recommend that you do this sort of thing. The whole point of using an interface to apply your JAX-RS metadata is to isolate the information and define it in one place. If your annotations are scattered about between your implementation class and interface, your code becomes a lot harder to read and understand.

Inheritance

The JAX-RS specification also allows you to define class and interface hierarchies if you so desire. For example, let's say we wanted to make our outputCustomer() and read Customer() methods abstract so that different implementations could transform XML how they wanted:

```
package com.restfully.shop.services;

import ...;

public abstract class AbstractCustomerResource {

    @POST
    @Consumes("application/xml")
    public Response createCustomer(InputStream is) {
        ... complete implementation ...
    }

    @GET
    @Path("{id}")
    @Produces("application/xml")
    public StreamingOutput getCustomer(@PathParam("id") int id) {
        ... complete implementation
    }
    @PUT
    @Path("{id}")
    @Consumes("application/xml")
    public void updateCustomer(@PathParam("id") int id,
                               InputStream is) {
        ... complete implementation ...
    }

    abstract protected void outputCustomer(OutputStream os,
                                   Customer cust) throws IOException;

    abstract protected Customer readCustomer(InputStream is);

}
```

You could then extend this abstract class and define the outputCustomer() and read Customer() methods:

```
package com.restfully.shop.services;

import ...;

@Path("/customers")
```

```
public class CustomerResource extends AbstractCustomerResource {

    protected void outputCustomer(OutputStream os, Customer cust)
                                            throws IOException {
        ... the implementation ...
    }

    protected Customer readCustomer(InputStream is) {
        ... the implementation ...
    }
```

The only caveat with this approach is that the concrete subclass must annotate itself with the @Path annotation to identify it as a service class to the JAX-RS provider.

Deploying Our Service

It is easiest to deploy JAX-RS within a Java EE–certified application server (e.g., JBoss) or standalone Servlet 3 container (e.g., Tomcat). Before we can do that, we need to write one simple class that extends `javax.ws.rs.core.Application`. This class tells our application server which JAX-RS components we want to register.

```
package javax.ws.rs.core;

import java.util.Collections;
import java.util.Set;

public abstract class Application {
    private static final Set<Object> emptySet = Collections.emptySet();

    public abstract Set<Class<?>> getClasses();


    public Set<Object> getSingletons() {
        return emptySet;
    }

}
```

The `getClasses()` method returns a list of JAX-RS service classes (and providers, but I'll get to that in Chapter 6). Any JAX-RS service class returned by this method will follow the per-request model mentioned earlier. When the JAX-RS vendor implementation determines that an HTTP request needs to be delivered to a method of one of these classes, an instance of it will be created for the duration of the request and thrown away. You are delegating the creation of these objects to the JAX-RS runtime.

The `getSingletons()` method returns a list of JAX-RS service objects (and providers, too—again, see Chapter 6). You, as the application programmer, are responsible for creating and initializing these objects.

These two methods tell the JAX-RS vendor which services you want deployed. Here's an example:

```
package com.restfully.shop.services;

import javax.ws.rs.ApplicationPath;
import javax.ws.rs.core.Application;
import java.util.HashSet;
import java.util.Set;

@ApplicationPath("/services")
public class ShoppingApplication extends Application {

    private Set<Object> singletons = new HashSet<Object>();
    private Set<Class<?>> empty = new HashSet<Class<?>>();

    public ShoppingApplication() {
        singletons.add(new CustomerResource());
    }

    @Override
    public Set<Class<?>> getClasses() {
        return empty;
    }

    @Override
    public Set<Object> getSingletons() {
        return singletons;
    }
}
```

The `@ApplicationPath` defines the relative base URL path for all our JAX-RS services in the deployment. So, in this example, all of our JAX-RS RESTful services will be prefixed with the `/services` path when we execute on them. For our customer service database example, we do not have any per-request services, so our `ShoppingApplication.getClasses()` method returns an empty set. Our `ShoppingApplication.getSingletons()` method returns the `Set` we initialized in the constructor. This `Set` contains an instance of `CustomerResource`.

In Java EE and standalone servlet deployments, JAX-RS classes must be deployed within the application server's servlet container as a Web ARchive (WAR). Think of a servlet container as your application server's web server. A WAR is a JAR file that, in addition to Java class files, also contains other Java libraries along with dynamic (like JSPs) and static content (like HTML files or images) that you want to publish on your website. We need to place our Java classes within this archive so that our application server can deploy them. Here's what the structure of a WAR file looks like:

```
<any static content>
WEB-INF/
        web.xml
```

```
classes/
        com/restfully/shop/domain/
                              Customer.class
        com/restfully/shop/services/
                              CustomerResource.class
                              ShoppingApplication.class
```

Our application server's servlet container publishes everything outside the *WEB-INF/* directory of the archive. This is where you would put static HTML files and images that you want to expose to the outside world. The *WEB-INF/* directory has two subdirectories. Within the *classes/* directory, you can put any Java classes you want. They must be in a Java package structure. This is where we place all of the classes we wrote and compiled in this chapter. The *lib/* directory can contain any third-party JARs we used with our application. Depending on whether your application server has built-in support for JAX-RS or not, you may have to place the JARs for your JAX-RS vendor implementation within this directory. For our customer example, we are not using any third-party libraries, so this *lib/* directory may be empty.

We are almost finished. All we have left to do is to create a *WEB-INF/web.xml* file within our archive.

```
<?xml version="1.0" encoding="UTF-8"?>
<web-app xmlns="http://java.sun.com/xml/ns/javaee"
        xmlns:xsi="http://www.w3.org/2001/XMLSchema-instance"
        xsi:schemaLocation="http://java.sun.com/xml/ns/javaee
                        http://java.sun.com/xml/ns/javaee/web-app_3_0.xsd"
        version="3.0">
</web-app>
```

Because this example deploys within a Java EE application server or standalone Servlet 3.x container, all we need is an empty *web.xml* file. The server will detect that an `Application` class is within your WAR and automatically deploy it. Your application is now ready to use!

Writing a Client

If you need to interact with a remote RESTful service like we just created, you can use the JAX-RS 2.0 Client API. The `Client` interface is responsible for managing client HTTP connections. I discuss the Client API in more detail in Chapter 8, but let's look at how we might create a customer by invoking the remote services defined earlier in this chapter.

```
import javax.ws.rs.client.ClientBuilder;
import javax.ws.rs.client.Client;
import javax.ws.rs.client.Entity;
import javax.ws.rs.core.Response;

public class MyClient {
    public static void main(String[] args) throws Exception {
```

```java
Client client = ClientBuilder.newClient();
try {
    System.out.println("*** Create a new Customer ***");

    String xml = "<customer>"
            + "<first-name>Bill</first-name>"
            + "<last-name>Burke</last-name>"
            + "<street>256 Clarendon Street</street>"
            + "<city>Boston</city>"
            + "<state>MA</state>"
            + "<zip>02115</zip>"
            + "<country>USA</country>"
            + "</customer>";

    Response response = client.target(
            "http://localhost:8080/services/customers")
            .request().post(Entity.xml(xml));
    if (response.getStatus() != 201) throw new RuntimeException(
            "Failed to create");
    String location = response.getLocation().toString();
    System.out.println("Location: " + location);
    response.close();

    System.out.println("*** GET Created Customer **");
    String customer = client.target(location).request().get(String.class);
    System.out.println(customer);

    String updateCustomer = "<customer>"
            + "<first-name>William</first-name>"
            + "<last-name>Burke</last-name>"
            + "<street>256 Clarendon Street</street>"
            + "<city>Boston</city>"
            + "<state>MA</state>"
            + "<zip>02115</zip>"
            + "<country>USA</country>"
            + "</customer>";
    response = client.target(location)
                    .request()
                    .put(Entity.xml(updateCustomer));
    if (response.getStatus() != 204)
        throw new RuntimeException("Failed to update");
    response.close();
    System.out.println("**** After Update ***");
    customer = client.target(location).request().get(String.class);
    System.out.println(customer);
} finally {
    client.close();
}
}
}
```

The Client API is a fluent API in that it tries to look like a domain-specific language (DSL). The Client API has a lot of method chaining, so writing client code can be as simple and compact as possible. In the preceding example, we first build and execute a POST request to create a customer. We then extract the URI of the created customer from a Response object to execute a GET request on the URI. After this, we update the customer with a new XML representation by invoking a PUT request. The example only uses Strings, but we'll see in Chapter 6 that JAX-RS also has content handlers you can use to marshal your Java objects automatically to and from XML and other message formats.

Wrapping Up

In this chapter, we discussed how to implement a simple customer database as a JAX-RS service. You can test-drive this code by flipping to Chapter 18. It will walk you through installing JBoss RESTEasy, implementing JAX-RS, and running the examples in this chapter within a servlet container.

CHAPTER 4

HTTP Method and URI Matching

Now that we have a foundation in JAX-RS, it's time to start looking into the details. In Chapter 3, you saw how we used the @GET, @PUT, @POST, and @DELETE annotations to bind Java methods to a specific HTTP operation. You also saw how we used the @Path annotation to bind a URI pattern to a Java method. While applying these annotations seems pretty straightforward, there are some interesting attributes that we're going to examine within this chapter.

Binding HTTP Methods

JAX-RS defines five annotations that map to specific HTTP operations:

- @javax.ws.rs.GET
- @javax.ws.rs.PUT
- @javax.ws.rs.POST
- @javax.ws.rs.DELETE
- @javax.ws.rs.HEAD

In Chapter 3, we used these annotations to bind HTTP GET requests to a specific Java method. For example:

```
@Path("/customers")
public class CustomerService {

    @GET
    @Produces("application/xml")
    public String getAllCustomers() {
    }
}
```

Here we have a simple method, getAllCustomers(). The @GET annotation instructs the JAX-RS runtime that this Java method will process HTTP GET requests to the URI /customers. You would use one of the other five annotations described earlier to bind to different HTTP operations. One thing to note, though, is that you may only apply one HTTP method annotation per Java method. A deployment error occurs if you apply more than one.

Beyond simple binding, there are some interesting things to note about the implementation of these types of annotations. Let's take a look at @GET, for instance:

```
package javax.ws.rs;

import ...;

@Target({ElementType.METHOD})
@Retention(RetentionPolicy.RUNTIME)
@HttpMethod(HttpMethod.GET)
public @interface GET {
}
```

@GET, by itself, does not mean anything special to the JAX-RS provider. In other words, JAX-RS is not hardcoded to look for this annotation when deciding whether or not to dispatch an HTTP GET request. What makes the @GET annotation meaningful to a JAX-RS provider is the meta-annotation @javax.ws.rs.HttpMethod. Meta-annotations are simply annotations that annotate other annotations. When the JAX-RS provider examines a Java method, it looks for any method annotations that use the meta-annotation @HttpMethod. The value of this meta-annotation is the actual HTTP operation that you want your Java method to bind to.

HTTP Method Extensions

What are the implications of this? This means that you can create new annotations that bind to HTTP methods other than GET, POST, DELETE, HEAD, and PUT. While HTTP is a ubiquitous, stable protocol, it is still constantly evolving. For example, consider the WebDAV standard.[1] The WebDAV protocol makes the Web an interactive readable and writable medium. It allows users to create, change, and move documents on web servers. It does this by adding a bunch of new methods to HTTP like MOVE, COPY, MKCOL, LOCK, and UNLOCK.

Although JAX-RS does not define any WebDAV-specific annotations, we could create them ourselves using the @HttpMethod annotation:

```
package org.rest.webdav;
```

---

1. For more information on WebDAV, see *http://www.webdav.org*.

```
import ...;

@Target({ElementType.METHOD})
@Retention(RetentionPolicy.RUNTIME)
@HttpMethod("LOCK")
public @interface LOCK {
}
```

Here, we have defined a new @org.rest.LOCK annotation using @HttpMethod to specify the HTTP operation it binds to. We can then use it on JAX-RS resource methods:

```
@Path("/customers")
public class CustomerResource {

    @Path("{id}")
    @LOCK
    public void lockIt(@PathParam("id") String id) {
        ...
    }
}
```

Now WebDAV clients can invoke LOCK operations on our web server and they will be dispatched to the lockIt() method.

> Do not use @HttpMethod to define your own application-specific HTTP methods. @HttpMethod exists to hook into new methods defined by standards bodies like the W3C. The purpose of the uniform interface is to define a set of well-known behaviors across companies and organizations on the Web. Defining your own methods breaks this architectural principle.

@Path

There's more to the @javax.ws.rs.Path annotation than what we saw in our simple example in Chapter 3. @Path can have complex matching expressions so that you can be more specific about what requests get bound to which incoming URIs. @Path can also be used on a Java method as sort of an object factory for subresources of your application. We'll examine both in this section.

Binding URIs

The @javax.ws.rs.Path annotation in JAX-RS is used to define a URI matching pattern for incoming HTTP requests. It can be placed upon a class or on one or more Java methods. For a Java class to be eligible to receive any HTTP requests, the class must be annotated with at least the @Path("/") expression. These types of classes are called JAX-RS *root resources*.

The value of the @Path annotation is an expression that denotes a relative URI to the context root of your JAX-RS application. For example, if you are deploying into a WAR archive of a servlet container, that WAR will have a base URI that browsers and remote clients use to access it. @Path expressions are relative to this URI.

To receive a request, a Java method must have at least an HTTP method annotation like @javax.ws.rs.GET applied to it. This method is not required to have an @Path annotation on it, though. For example:

```
@Path("/orders")
public class OrderResource {
  @GET
  public String getAllOrders() {
     ...
  }
}
```

An HTTP request of GET /orders would dispatch to the getAllOrders() method.

You can also apply @Path to your Java method. If you do this, the URI matching pattern is a concatenation of the class's @Path expression and that of the method's. For example:

```
@Path("/orders")
public class OrderResource {

    @GET
    @Path("unpaid")
    public String getUnpaidOrders() {
       ...
    }
}
```

So, the URI pattern for getUnpaidOrders() would be the relative URI /orders/unpaid.

@Path Expressions

The value of the @Path annotation is usually a simple string, but you can also define more complex expressions to satisfy your URI matching needs.

Template parameters

In Chapter 3, we wrote a customer access service that allowed us to query for a specific customer using a wildcard URI pattern:

```
@Path("/customers")
public class CustomerResource {

    @GET
    @Path("{id}")
    public String getCustomer(@PathParam("id") int id) {
       ...
```

```
        }
    }
```

These template parameters can be embedded anywhere within an @Path declaration. For example:

```
@Path("/")
public class CustomerResource {

    @GET
    @Path("customers/{firstname}-{lastname}")
    public String getCustomer(@PathParam("firstname") String first,
                              @PathParam("lastname") String last) {

        ...
    }
}
```

In our example, the URI is constructed with a customer's first name, followed by a hyphen, ending with the customer's last name. So, the request GET /customers/333 would no longer match to getCustomer(), but a GET/customers/bill-burke request would.

Regular expressions

@Path expressions are not limited to simple wildcard matching expressions. For example, our getCustomer() method takes an integer parameter. We can change our @Path value to match only digits:

```
@Path("/customers")
public class CustomerResource {

    @GET
    @Path("{id : \\d+}")
    public String getCustomer(@PathParam("id") int id) {
        ...
    }
}
```

Regular expressions are not limited in matching one segment of a URI. For example:

```
@Path("/customers")
public class CustomerResource {

    @GET
    @Path("{id : .+}")
    public String getCustomer(@PathParam("id") String id) {
        ...
    }

    @GET
    @Path("{id : .+}/address")
    public String getAddress(@PathParam("id") String id) {
```

```
        ...
    }

}
```

We've changed getCustomer()'s @Path expression to {id : .+}. The .+ is a regular expression that will match any stream of characters after /customers. So, the GET /customers/bill/burke request would be routed to getCustomer().

The getAddress() method has a more specific expression. It will map any stream of characters after /customers that ends with /address. So, the GET /customers/bill/burke/address request would be routed to the getAddress() method.

Precedence rules

You may have noticed that, together, the @Path expressions for getCustomer() and getAddress() are ambiguous. A GET /customers/bill/burke/address request could match either getCustomer() or getAddress(), depending on which expression was matched first by the JAX-RS provider. The JAX-RS specification has defined strict sorting and precedence rules for matching URI expressions and is based on a *most specific match wins* algorithm. The JAX-RS provider gathers up the set of deployed URI expressions and sorts them based on the following logic:

1. The primary key of the sort is the number of literal characters in the full URI matching pattern. The sort is in descending order. In our ambiguous example, getCustomer()'s pattern has 11 literal characters: /customers/. The getAddress() method's pattern has 18 literal characters: /customers/ plus address. Therefore, the JAX-RS provider will try to match getAddress()'s pattern before getCustomer().

2. The secondary key of the sort is the number of template expressions embedded within the pattern—that is, {id} or {id : .+}. This sort is in descending order.

3. The tertiary key of the sort is the number of nondefault template expressions. A default template expression is one that does not define a regular expression—that is, {id}.

Let's look at a list of sorted URI matching expressions and explain why one would match over another:

```
1 /customers/{id}/{name}/address
2 /customers/{id : .+}/address
3 /customers/{id}/address
4 /customers/{id : .+}
```

Expressions 1–3 come first because they all have more literal characters than expression 4. Although expressions 1–3 all have the same number of literal characters, expression 1 comes first because sorting rule #2 is triggered. It has more template expressions than either pattern 2 or 3. Expressions 2 and 3 have the same number of literal characters and same number of template expressions. Expression 2 is sorted ahead of 3 because it triggers sorting rule #3; it has a template pattern that is a regular expression.

These sorting rules are not perfect. It is still possible to have ambiguities, but the rules cover 90% of use cases. If your application has URI matching ambiguities, your application design is probably too complicated and you need to revisit and refactor your URI scheme.

Encoding

The URI specification only allows certain characters within a URI string. It also reserves certain characters for its own specific use. In other words, you cannot use these characters as part of your URI segments. This is the set of allowable and reserved characters:

- The US-ASCII alphabetic characters a–z and A–Z are allowable.
- The decimal digit characters 0–9 are allowable.
- All these other characters are allowable: _-!.~'()*.
- These characters are allowed but are reserved for URI syntax: ,;:$&+=?/\[]@.

All other characters must be encoded using the "%" character followed by a two-digit hexadecimal number. This hexadecimal number corresponds to the equivalent hexadecimal character in the ASCII table. So, the string bill&burke would be encoded as bill%26burke.

When creating @Path expressions, you may encode its string, but you do not have to. If a character in your @Path pattern is an illegal character, the JAX-RS provider will automatically encode the pattern before trying to match and dispatch incoming HTTP requests. If you do have an encoding within your @Path expression, the JAX-RS provider will leave it alone and treat it as an encoding when doing its request dispatching. For example:

```
@Path("/customers"
public class CustomerResource {

    @GET
    @Path("roy&fielding")
    public String getOurBestCustomer() {
        ...
    }
}
```

The @Path expression for getOurBestCustomer() would match incoming requests like GET /customers/roy%26fielding.

Matrix Parameters

One part of the URI specification that we have not touched on yet is *matrix parameters*. Matrix parameters are name-value pairs embedded within the path of a URI string. For example:

```
http://example.cars.com/mercedes/e55;color=black/2006
```

They come after a URI segment and are delimited by the ";" character. The matrix parameter in this example comes after the URI segment e55. Its name is color and its value is black. Matrix parameters are different than query parameters, as they represent attributes of certain segments of the URI and are used for identification purposes. Think of them as adjectives. Query parameters, on the other hand, always come at the end of the URI and always pertain to the full resource you are referencing.

Matrix parameters are ignored when matching incoming requests to JAX-RS resource methods. It is actually illegal to specify matrix parameters within an @Path expression. For example:

```
@Path("/mercedes")
public class MercedesService {

    @GET
    @Path("/e55/{year}")
    @Produces("image/jpeg")
    public Jpeg getE55Picture(@PathParam("year") String year) {
       ...
    }
```

If we queried our JAX-RS service with GET /mercedes/e55;color=black/2006, the getE55Picture() method would match the incoming request and would be invoked. Matrix parameters are not considered part of the matching process because they are usually variable attributes of the request. We'll see in Chapter 5 how to access matrix parameter information within our JAX-RS resource methods.

Subresource Locators

So far, I've shown you the JAX-RS capability to statically bind URI patterns expressed through the @Path annotation to a specific Java method. JAX-RS also allows you to dynamically dispatch requests yourself through subresource locators. Subresource locators are Java methods annotated with @Path, but with no HTTP method annotation, like @GET, applied to them. This type of method returns an object that is, itself, a JAX-RS annotated service that knows how to dispatch the remainder of the request. This is best described using an example.

Let's continue by expanding our customer database JAX-RS service. This example will be a bit contrived, so please bear with me. Let's say our customer database is partitioned into different databases based on geographic regions. We want to add this information to our URI scheme, but we want to decouple finding a database server from querying and formatting customer information. We will now add the database partition information to the URI pattern /customers/{database}-db/{customerId}. We can define a `CustomerDatabaseResource` class and have it delegate to our original `CustomerRe source` class. Here's the example:

```
@Path("/customers")
public class CustomerDatabaseResource {

    @Path("{database}-db")
    public CustomerResource getDatabase(@PathParam("database") String db) {
        // find the instance based on the db parameter
        CustomerResource resource = locateCustomerResource(db);
        return resource;
    }

    protected CustomerResource locateCustomerResource(String db) {
        ...
    }
}
```

The `CustomerDatabaseResource` class is our root resource. It does not service any HTTP requests directly. It processes the database identifier part of the URI and locates the identified customer database. Once it does this, it allocates a `CustomerResource` instance, passing in a reference to the database. The JAX-RS provider uses this `Custom erResource` instance to service the remainder of the request:

```
public class CustomerResource {
    private Map<Integer, Customer> customerDB =
                        new ConcurrentHashMap<Integer, Customer>();
    private AtomicInteger idCounter = new AtomicInteger();

    public CustomerResource(Map<Integer, Customer> customerDB)
    {
        this.customerDB = customerDB;
    }

    @POST
    @Consumes("application/xml")
    public Response createCustomer(InputStream is) {
        ...
    }

    @GET
    @Path("{id}")
    @Produces("application/xml")
    public StreamingOutput getCustomer(@PathParam("id") int id) {
        ...
    }
```

```
@PUT
@Path("{id}")
@Consumes("application/xml")
public void updateCustomer(@PathParam("id") int id, InputStream is) {
    ...
  }
}
```

So, if a client sends GET /customers/northamerica-db/333, the JAX-RS provider will first match the expression on the method CustomerDatabaseResource.getData base(). It will then match and process the remaining part of the request with the method CustomerResource.getCustomer().

Besides the added constructor, another difference in the CustomerResource class from previous examples is that it is no longer annotated with @Path. It is no longer a root resource in our system; it is a subresource and must not be registered with the JAX-RS runtime within an Application class.

Full Dynamic Dispatching

While our previous example does illustrate the concept of subresource locators, it does not show their full dynamic nature. The CustomerDatabaseResource.getDatabase() method can return any instance of any class. At runtime, the JAX-RS provider will introspect this instance's class for resource methods that can handle the request.

Let's say that in our example, we have two customer databases with different kinds of identifiers. One database uses a numeric key, as we talked about before. The other uses first and last name as a composite key. We would need to have two different classes to extract the appropriate information from the URI. Let's change our example:

```
@Path("/customers")
public class CustomerDatabaseResource {

    protected CustomerResource europe = new CustomerResource();
    protected FirstLastCustomerResource northamerica =
                            new FirstLastCustomerResource();

    @Path("{database}-db")
    public Object getDatabase(@PathParam("database") String db) {
       if (db.equals("europe")) {
           return europe;
       }
       else if (db.equals("northamerica")) {
           return northamerica;
       }
       else return null;
    }
}
```

Instead of our `getDatabase()` method returning a `CustomerResource`, it will return any `java.lang.Object`. JAX-RS will introspect the instance returned to figure out how to dispatch the request. For this example, if our database is europe, we will use our original `CustomerResource` class to service the remainder of the request. If our database is northamerica, we will use a new subresource class `FirstLastCustomerResource`:

```
public class FirstLastCustomerResource {
   private Map<String, Customer> customerDB =
                         new ConcurrentHashMap<String, Customer>();

   @GET
   @Path("{first}-{last}")
   @Produces("application/xml")
   public StreamingOutput getCustomer(@PathParam("first") String firstName,
                                @PathParam("last") String lastName) {

   ...
   }

   @PUT
   @Path("{first}-{last}")
   @Consumes("application/xml")
   public void updateCustomer(@PathParam("first") String firstName,
                         @PathParam("last") String lastName,
                         InputStream is) {

   ...
   }
}
```

Customer lookup requests routed to europe would match the /customers/{database}-db/{id} URI pattern defined in `CustomerResource`. Requests routed to northamerica would match the /customers/{database}-db/{first}-{last} URI pattern defined in `FirstLastCustomerResource`. This type of pattern gives you a lot of freedom to dispatch your own requests.

Gotchas in Request Matching

There are some fine print details about the URI request matching algorithm that I must go over, as there may be cases where you'd expect a request to match and it doesn't. First of all, the specification requires that potential JAX-RS class matches are filtered first based on the root @Path annotation. Consider the following two classes:

```
@Path("/a")
public class Resource1 {
   @GET
   @Path("/b")
   public Response get() {}
}

@Path("/{any : .*}")
```

```
public class Resource2 {

    @GET
    public Response get() {}

    @OPTIONS
    public Response options() {}
}
```

If we have an HTTP request GET /a/b, the matching algorithm will first find the best class that matches before finishing the full dispatch. In this case, class Resource1 is chosen because its @Path("/a") annotation best matches the initial part of the request URI. The matching algorithm then tries to match the remainder of the URI based on expressions contained in the Resource1 class.

Here's where the weirdness comes in. Let's say you have the HTTP request OPTIONS /a/b. If you expect that the Resource2.options() method would be invoked, you would be wrong! You would actually get a 405, "Method Not Allowed," error response from the server. This is because the initial part of the request path, /a, matches the Resource1 class best, so Resource1 is used to resolve the rest of the HTTP request. If we change Resource2 as follows, the request would be processed by the options() method:

```
@Path("/a")
public class Resource2 {


    @OPTIONS
    @Path("b")
    public Response options() {}
}
```

If the @Path expressions are the same between two different JAX-RS classes, then they both are used for request matching.

There are also similar ambiguities in subresource locator matching. Take these classes, for example:

```
@Path("/a")
public class Foo {
    @GET
    @Path("b")
    public String get() {...}

    @Path("{id}")
    public Locator locator() { return new Locator(); }
}

public class Locator{
    @PUT
```

```
    public void put() {...}
  }
```

If we did a PUT /a/b request, you would also get a 405 error response. The specification algorithm states that if there is at least one other resource method whose @Path expression matches, then no subresource locator will be traversed to match the request.

In most applications, you will not encounter these maching issues, but it's good to know about them just in case you do. I tried to get these problems fixed in the JAX-RS 2.0 spec, but a few JSR members thought that this would break backward compatibility.

Wrapping Up

In this chapter, we examined the intricacies of the @javax.ws.rs.Path annotation. @Path allows you to define complex URI matching patterns that can map to a Java method. These patterns can be defined using regular expressions and also support encoding. We also discussed subresource locators, which allow you to programmatically perform your own dynamic dispatching of HTTP requests. Finally, we looked at how you can hook into new HTTP operations by using the @HttpMethod annotation. You can test-drive the code in this chapter in Chapter 19.

CHAPTER 5

JAX-RS Injection

A lot of JAX-RS is pulling information from an HTTP request and injecting it into a Java method. You may be interested in a fragment of the incoming URI. You might be interested in a URI query string value. The client might be sending critical HTTP headers or cookie values that your service needs to process the request. JAX-RS lets you grab this information à la carte, as you need it, through a set of injection annotations and APIs.

The Basics

There are a lot of different things JAX-RS annotations can inject. Here is a list of those provided by the specification:

@javax.ws.rs.PathParam
> This annotation allows you to extract values from URI template parameters.

@javax.ws.rs.MatrixParam
> This annotation allows you to extract values from URI matrix parameters.

@javax.ws.rs.QueryParam
> This annotation allows you to extract values from URI query parameters.

@javax.ws.rs.FormParam
> This annotation allows you to extract values from posted form data.

@javax.ws.rs.HeaderParam
> This annotation allows you to extract values from HTTP request headers.

@javax.ws.rs.CookieParam
> This annotation allows you to extract values from HTTP cookies set by the client.

@javax.ws.rs.core.Context

> This class is the all-purpose injection annotation. It allows you to inject various helper and informational objects that are provided by the JAX-RS API.

Usually, these annotations are used on the parameters of a JAX-RS resource method. When the JAX-RS provider receives an HTTP request, it finds a Java method that will service this request. If the Java method has parameters that are annotated with any of these injection annotations, it will extract information from the HTTP request and pass it as a parameter when it invokes the method.

For per-request resources, you may alternatively use these injection annotations on the fields, setter methods, and even constructor parameters of your JAX-RS resource class. Do not try to use these annotations on fields or setter methods if your component model does not follow per-request instantiation. Singletons process HTTP requests concurrently, so it is not possible to use these annotations on fields or setter methods, as concurrent requests will overrun and conflict with each other.

@PathParam

We looked at `@javax.ws.rs.PathParam` a little bit in Chapters 3 and 4. `@PathParam` allows you to inject the value of named URI path parameters that were defined in `@Path` expressions. Let's revisit the `CustomerResource` example that we defined in Chapter 2 and implemented in Chapter 3:

```
@Path("/customers")
public class CustomerResource {

   ...

   @Path("{id}")
   @GET
   @Produces("application/xml")
   public StreamingOutput getCustomer(@PathParam("id") int id) {
      ...
   }
}
```

More Than One Path Parameter

You can reference more than one URI path parameter in your Java methods. For instance, let's say we are using first and last name to identify a customer in our `Customer Resource`:

```
@Path("/customers")
public class CustomerResource {

   ...

   @Path("{first}-{last}")
   @GET
```

```
@Produces("application/xml")
public StreamingOutput getCustomer(@PathParam("first") String firstName,
                                   @PathParam("last") String lastName) {
    ...
  }
}
```

Scope of Path Parameters

Sometimes a named URI path parameter will be repeated by different @Path expressions that compose the full URI matching pattern of a resource method. The path parameter could be repeated by the class's @Path expression or by a subresource locator. In these cases, the @PathParam annotation will always reference the final path parameter. For example:

```
@Path("/customers/{id}")
public class CustomerResource {

    @Path("/address/{id}")
    @Produces("text/plain")
    @GET
    public String getAddress(@PathParam("id") String addressId) {...}
}
```

If our HTTP request was GET /customers/123/address/456, the addressId parameter in the getAddress() method would have the 456 value injected.

PathSegment and Matrix Parameters

@PathParam can not only inject the value of a path parameter, it can also inject instances of javax.ws.rs.core.PathSegment. The PathSegment class is an abstraction of a specific URI path segment:

```
package javax.ws.rs.core;

public interface PathSegment  {

    String getPath();
    MultivaluedMap<String, String> getMatrixParameters();

}
```

The getPath() method is the string value of the actual URI segment minus any matrix parameters. The more interesting method here is getMatrixParameters(). This returns a map of all of the matrix parameters applied to a particular URI segment. In combination with @PathParam, you can get access to the matrix parameters applied to your request's URI. For example:

```
@Path("/cars/{make}")
public class CarResource {
```

```
@GET
@Path("/{model}/{year}")
@Produces("image/jpeg")
public Jpeg getPicture(@PathParam("make") String make,
                       @PathParam("model") PathSegment car,
                       @PathParam("year") String year) {
   String carColor = car.getMatrixParameters().getFirst("color");
   ...
}
```

In this example, we have a CarResource that allows us to get pictures of cars in our database. The getPicture() method returns a JPEG image of cars that match the make, model, and year that we specify. The color of the vehicle is expressed as a matrix parameter of the model. For example:

```
GET /cars/mercedes/e55;color=black/2006
```

Here, our make is mercedes, the model is e55 with a color attribute of black, and the year is 2006. While the make, model, and year information can be injected into our getPicture() method directly, we need to do some processing to obtain information about the color of the vehicle.

Instead of injecting the model information as a Java string, we inject the path parameter as a PathSegment into the car parameter. We then use this PathSegment instance to obtain the color matrix parameter's value.

Matching with multiple PathSegments

Sometimes a particular path parameter matches to more than one URI segment. In these cases, you can inject a list of PathSegments. For example, let's say a model in our Car Resource could be represented by more than one URI segment. Here's how the getPic ture() method might change:

```
@Path("/cars/{make}")
public class CarResource {

   @GET
   @Path("/{model : .+}/year/{year}")
   @Produces("image/jpeg")
   public Jpeg getPicture(@PathParam("make") String make,
                          @PathParam("model") List<PathSegment> car,
                          @PathParam("year") String year) {
   }
}
```

In this example, if our request was GET /cars/mercedes/e55/amg/year/2006, the car parameter would have a list of two PathSegments injected into it, one representing the e55 segment and the other representing the amg segment. We could then query and pull in matrix parameters as needed from these segments.

Programmatic URI Information

All this à la carte injection of path parameter data with the @PathParam annotation is perfect most of the time. Sometimes, though, you need a more general raw API to query and browse information about the incoming request's URI. The interface javax.ws.rs.core.UriInfo provides such an API:

```
public interface UriInfo {
    public String getPath();
    public String getPath(boolean decode);
    public List<PathSegment> getPathSegments();
    public List<PathSegment> getPathSegments(boolean decode);
    public MultivaluedMap<String, String> getPathParameters();
    public MultivaluedMap<String, String> getPathParameters(boolean decode);
    ...
}
```

The getPath() methods allow you to obtain the relative path JAX-RS used to match the incoming request. You can receive the path string decoded or encoded. The get PathSegments() methods break up the entire relative path into a series of PathSeg ment objects. Like getPath(), you can receive this information encoded or decoded. Finally, getPathParameters() returns a map of all the path parameters defined for all matching @Path expressions.

You can obtain an instance of the UriInfo interface by using the @jav ax.ws.rs.core.Context injection annotation. Here's an example:

```
@Path("/cars/{make}")
public class CarResource {

    @GET
    @Path("/{model}/{year}")
    @Produces("image/jpeg")
    public Jpeg getPicture(@Context UriInfo info) {
        String make = info.getPathParameters().getFirst("make");
        PathSegment model = info.getPathSegments().get(1);
        String color = model.getMatrixParameters().getFirst("color");
    ...
    }
}
```

In this example, we inject an instance of UriInfo into the getPicture() method's info parameter. We then use this instance to extract information out of the URI.

@MatrixParam

Instead of injecting and processing PathSegment objects to obtain matrix parameter values, the JAX-RS specification allows you to inject matrix parameter values directly through the @javax.ws.rs.MatrixParam annotation. Let's change our CarResource example from the previous section to reflect using this annotation:

```java
@Path("/{make}")
public class CarResource {

    @GET
    @Path("/{model}/{year}")
    @Produces("image/jpeg")
    public Jpeg getPicture(@PathParam("make") String make,
                           @PathParam("model") String model,
                           @MatrixParam("color") String color) {
        ...
    }
```

Using the @MatrixParam annotation shrinks our code and provides a bit more readability. The only downside of @MatrixParam is that sometimes you might have a repeating matrix parameter that is applied to many different path segments in the URI. For example, what if color shows up multiple times in our car service example?

```
GET /mercedes/e55;color=black/2006/interior;color=tan
```

Here, the color attribute shows up twice: once with the model and once with the interior. Using @MatrixParam("color") in this case would be ambiguous and we would have to go back to processing PathSegments to obtain this matrix parameter.

@QueryParam

The @javax.ws.rs.QueryParam annotation allows you to inject individual URI query parameters into your Java parameters. For example, let's say we wanted to query a customer database and retrieve a subset of all customers in the database. Our URI might look like this:

```
GET /customers?start=0&size=10
```

The start query parameter represents the customer index we want to start with and the size query parameter represents how many customers we want returned. The JAX-RS service that implemented this might look like this:

```java
@Path("/customers")
public class CustomerResource {

    @GET
    @Produces("application/xml")
    public String getCustomers(@QueryParam("start") int start,
                               @QueryParam("size") int size) {
        ...
    }
}
```

Here, we use the @QueryParam annotation to inject the URI query parameters "start" and "size" into the Java parameters start and size. As with other annotation injection, JAX-RS automatically converts the query parameter's string into an integer.

Programmatic Query Parameter Information

You may have the need to iterate through all query parameters defined on the request URI. The javax.ws.rs.core.UriInfo interface has a getQueryParameters() method that gives you a map containing all query parameters:

```
public interface UriInfo {
...
   public MultivaluedMap<String, String> getQueryParameters();
   public MultivaluedMap<String, String> getQueryParameters(boolean decode);
...
}
```

You can inject instances of UriInfo using the @javax.ws.rs.core.Context annotation. Here's an example of injecting this class and using it to obtain the value of a few query parameters:

```
@Path("/customers")
public class CustomerResource {

   @GET
   @Produces("application/xml")
   public String getCustomers(@Context UriInfo info) {
      String start = info.getQueryParameters().getFirst("start");
      String size = info.getQueryParameters().getFirst("size");
      ...
   }
}
```

@FormParam

The @javax.ws.rs.FormParam annotation is used to access application/x-www-form-urlencoded request bodies. In other words, it's used to access individual entries posted by an HTML form document. For example, let's say we set up a form on our website to register new customers:

```
<FORM action="http://example.com/customers" method="post">
   <P>
   First name: <INPUT type="text" name="firstname"><BR>
   Last name: <INPUT type="text" name="lastname"><BR>
   <INPUT type="submit" value="Send">
   </P>
</FORM>
```

We could post this form directly to a JAX-RS backend service described as follows:

```
@Path("/customers")
public class CustomerResource {

    @POST
    public void createCustomer(@FormParam("firstname") String first,
                               @FormParam("lastname") String last) {
        ...
    }
}
```

Here, we are injecting `firstname` and `lastname` from the HTML form into the Java parameters `first` and `last`. Form data is URL-encoded when it goes across the wire. When using `@FormParam`, JAX-RS will automatically decode the form entry's value before injecting it.

@HeaderParam

The `@javax.ws.rs.HeaderParam` annotation is used to inject HTTP request header values. For example, what if your application was interested in the web page that referred to or linked to your web service? You could access the HTTP `Referer` header using the `@HeaderParam` annotation:

```
@Path("/myservice")
public class MyService {

    @GET
    @Produces("text/html")
    public String get(@HeaderParam("Referer") String referer) {
        ...
    }
}
```

The `@HeaderParam` annotation is pulling the `Referer` header directly from the HTTP request and injecting it into the referer method parameter.

Raw Headers

Sometimes you need programmatic access to view all headers within the incoming request. For instance, you may want to log them. The JAX-RS specification provides the `javax.ws.rs.core.HttpHeaders` interface for such scenarios.

```
public interface HttpHeaders {
    public List<String> getRequestHeader(String name);
    public MultivaluedMap<String, String> getRequestHeaders();
    ...
}
```

The `getRequestHeader()` method allows you to get access to one particular header, and `getRequestHeaders()` gives you a map that represents all headers.

As with UriInfo, you can use the @Context annotation to obtain an instance of HttpHeaders. Here's an example:

```
@Path("/myservice")
public class MyService {

    @GET
    @Produces("text/html")
    public String get(@Context HttpHeaders headers) {
        String referer = headers.getRequestHeader("Referer").get(0);
        for (String header : headers.getRequestHeaders().keySet())
        {
            System.out.println("This header was set: " + header);
        }
        ...
    }
}
```

@CookieParam

Servers can store state information in cookies on the client, and can retrieve that information when the client makes its next request. Many web applications use cookies to set up a session between the client and the server. They also use cookies to remember identity and user preferences between requests. These cookie values are transmitted back and forth between the client and server via cookie headers.

The @javax.ws.rs.CookieParam annotation allows you to inject cookies sent by a client request into your JAX-RS resource methods. For example, let's say our applications push a customerId cookie to our clients so that we can track users as they invoke and interact with our web services. Code to pull in this information might look like this:

```
@Path("/myservice")
public class MyService {

    @GET
    @Produces("text/html")
    public String get(@CookieParam("customerId") int custId) {
        ...
    }
}
```

The use of @CookieParam here makes the JAX-RS provider search all cookie headers for the customerId cookie value. It then converts it into an int and injects it into the custId parameter.

If you need more information about the cookie other than its base value, you can instead inject a javax.ws.rs.core.Cookie object:

```
@Path("/myservice")
public class MyService {
```

```
@GET
@Produces("text/html")
public String get(@CookieParam("customerId") Cookie custId) {
   ...
   }
}
```

The Cookie class has additional contextual information about the cookie beyond its name and value:

```
package javax.ws.rs.core;

public class Cookie
{
   public String getName() {...}
   public String getValue() {...}
   public int getVersion() {...}
   public String getDomain() {...}
   public String getPath() {...}

   ...
}
```

The getName() and getValue() methods correspond to the string name and value of the cookie you are injecting. The getVersion() method defines the format of the cookie header—specifically, which version of the cookie specification the header follows.[1] The getDomain() method specifies the DNS name that the cookie matched. The get Path() method corresponds to the URI path that was used to match the cookie to the incoming request. All these attributes are defined in detail by the IETF cookie specification.

You can also obtain a map of all cookies sent by the client by injecting a reference to javax.ws.rs.core.HttpHeaders:

```
public interface HttpHeaders {
   ...
   public Map<String, Cookie> getCookies();
}
```

As you saw in the previous section, you use the @Context annotation to get access to HttpHeaders. Here's an example of logging all cookies sent by the client:

```
@Path("/myservice")
public class MyService {

   @GET
   @Produces("text/html")
```

1. For more information, see *http://www.ietf.org/rfc/rfc2109.txt*.

```
    public String get(@Context HttpHeaders headers) {
        for (String name : headers.getCookies().keySet())
        {
            Cookie cookie = headers.getCookies().get(name);
            System.out.println("Cookie: " +
                            name + "=" + cookie.getValue());
        }
        ...
    }
}
```

@BeanParam

The @BeanParam annotation is something new added in the JAX-RS 2.0 specification. It allows you to inject an application-specific class whose property methods or fields are annotated with any of the injection parameters discussed in this chapter. For example, take this class:

```
public class CustomerInput {

    @FormParam("first")
    String firstName;

    @FormParam("list")
    String lastName;

    @HeaderParam("Content-Type")
    String contentType;

    public String getFirstName() {...}
    ....
}
```

Here we have a simple POJO (Plain Old Java Object) that contains the first and last names of a created customer, as well as the content type of that customer. We can have JAX-RS create, initialize, and inject this class using the @BeanParam annotation:

```
@Path("/customers")
public class CustomerResource {

    @POST
    public void createCustomer(@BeanParam CustomerInput newCust) {
        ...
    }
}
```

The JAX-RS runtime will introspect the @BeanParam parameter's type for injection annotations and then set them as appropriate. In this example, the CustomerInput class is interested in two form parameters and a header value. This is a great way to aggregate information instead of having a long list of method parameters.

Common Functionality

Each of these injection annotations has a common set of functionality and attributes. Some can automatically be converted from their string representation within an HTTP request into a specific Java type. You can also define default values for an injection parameter when an item does not exist in the request. Finally, you can work with encoded strings directly, rather than having JAX-RS automatically decode values for you. Let's look into a few of these.

Automatic Java Type Conversion

All the injection annotations described in this chapter reference various parts of an HTTP request. These parts are represented as a string of characters within the HTTP request. You are not limited to manipulating strings within your Java code, though. JAX-RS can convert this string data into any Java type that you want, provided that it matches one of the following criteria:

1. It is a primitive type. The `int`, `short`, `float`, `double`, `byte`, `char`, and `boolean` types all fit into this category.

2. It is a Java class that has a constructor with a single `String` parameter.

3. It is a Java class that has a static method named `valueOf()` that takes a single `String` argument and returns an instance of the class.

4. It is a `java.util.List<T>`, `java.util.Set<T>`, or `java.util.SortedSet<T>`, where T is a type that satisfies criteria 2 or 3 or is a `String`. Examples are `List<Double>`, `Set<String>`, or `SortedSet<Integer>`.

Primitive type conversion

We've already seen a few examples of automatic string conversion into a primitive type. Let's review a simple example again:

```
@GET
@Path("{id}")
public String get(@PathParam("id") int id) {...}
```

Here, we're extracting an integer ID from a string-encoded segment of our incoming request URI.

Java object conversion

Besides primitives, this string request data can be converted into a Java object before it is injected into your JAX-RS method parameter. This object's class must have a constructor or a static method named `valueOf()` that takes a single `String` parameter.

For instance, let's go back to the @HeaderParam example we used earlier in this chapter. In that example, we used @HeaderParam to inject a string that represented the Referer header. Since Referer is a URL, it would be much more interesting to inject it as an instance of java.net.URL:

```
import java.net.URL;

@Path("/myservice")
public class MyService {

    @GET
    @Produces("text/html")
    public String get(@HeaderParam("Referer") URL referer) {
        ...
    }
}
```

The JAX-RS provider can convert the Referer string header into a java.net.URL because this class has a constructor that takes only one String parameter.

This automatic conversion also works well when only a valueOf() method exists within the Java type we want to convert. For instance, let's revisit the @MatrixParam example we used in this chapter. In that example, we used the @MatrixParam annotation to inject the color of our vehicle into a parameter of a JAX-RS method. Instead of representing color as a string, let's define and use a Java enum class:

```
public enum Color {
    BLACK,
    BLUE,
    RED,
    WHITE,
    SILVER
}
```

You cannot allocate Java enums at runtime, but they do have a built-in valueOf() method that the JAX-RS provider can use:

```
public class CarResource {

    @GET
    @Path("/{model}/{year}")
    @Produces("image/jpeg")
    public Jpeg getPicture(@PathParam("make") String make,
                           @PathParam("model") String model,
                           @MatrixParam("color") Color color) {
        ...
    }
```

JAX-RS has made our lives a bit easier, as we can now work with more concrete Java objects rather than doing string conversions ourselves.

ParamConverters

Sometimes a parameter class cannot use the default mechanisms to convert from string values. Either the class has no `String` constructor or no `valueOf()` method, or the ones that exist won't work with your HTTP requests. For this scenario, JAX-RS 2.0 has provided an additional component to help with parameter conversions.

```
package javax.ws.rs.ext;

public interface ParamConverter<T> {
    public T fromString(String value);
    public String toString(T value);
}
```

As you can see from the code, `ParamConverter` is a pretty simple interface. The `from String()` method takes a `String` and converts it to the desired Java type. The `to String()` method does the opposite. Let's go back to our `Color` example. It pretty much requires full uppercase for all `Color` parameters. Instead, let's write a `ParamConverter` that allows a `Color` string to be any case.

```
public class ColorConverter implements ParamConverter<Color> {

    public Color fromString(String value) {
        if (value.equalsIgnoreCase(BLACK.toString())) return BLACK;
        else if (value.equalsIgnoreCase(BLUE.toString())) return BLUE;
        else if (value.equalsIgnoreCase(RED.toString())) return RED;
        else if (value.equalsIgnoreCase(WHITE.toString())) return WHITE;
        else if (value.equalsIgnoreCase(SILVER.toString())) return SILVER;
        throw new IllegalArgumentException("Invalid color: " + value);
    }

    public String toString(Color value) { return value.toString(); }

}
```

We're still not done yet. We also have to implement the `ParamConverterProvider` interface.

```
package javax.ws.rs.ext;
public interface ParamConverterProvider {
    public <T> ParamConverter<T> getConverter(Class<T> rawType,
                                              Type genericType,
                                              Annotation annotations[]);
}
```

This is basically a factory for `ParamConverters` and is the component that must be scanned or registered with your `Application` deployment class.

```
@Provider
public class ColorConverterProvider {

    private final ColorConverter converter = new ColorConverter();
```

```
    public  <T> ParamConverter<T> getConverter(Class<T> rawType,
                                   Type genericType,
                                   Annotation[] annotations) {
        if (!rawType.equals(Color.class)) return null;

        return converter;
    }
}
```

In our implementation here, we check to see if the rawType is a Color. If not, return null. If it is, then return an instance of our ColorConverter implementation. The Annotation[] parameter for the getConverter() method points to whatever parameter annotations are applied to the JAX-RS method parameter you are converting. This allows you to tailor the behavior of your converter based on any additional metadata applied.

Collections

All the parameter types described in this chapter may have multiple values for the same named parameter. For instance, let's revisit the @QueryParam example from earlier in this chapter. In that example, we wanted to pull down a set of customers from a customer database. Let's expand the functionality of this query so that we can order the data sent back by any number of customer attributes:

```
GET /customers?orderBy=last&orderBy=first
```

In this request, the orderBy query parameter is repeated twice with different values. We can let our JAX-RS provider represent these two parameters as a java.util.List and inject this list with one @QueryParam annotation:

```
import java.util.List;

@Path("/customers")
public class CustomerResource {

    @GET
    @Produces("application/xml")
    public String getCustomers(
                    @QueryParam("start") int start,
                    @QueryParam("size") int size,
                    @QueryParam("orderBy") List<String> orderBy) {

        ...
    }
}
```

You must define the generic type the List will contain; otherwise, JAX-RS won't know which objects to fill it with.

Conversion failures

If the JAX-RS provider fails to convert a string into the Java type specified, it is considered a client error. If this failure happens during the processing of an injection for an `@Ma trixParam`, `@QueryParam`, or `@PathParam`, an error status of 404, "Not Found," is sent back to the client. If the failure happens with `@HeaderParam` or `@CookieParam`, an error response code of 400, "Bad Request," is sent.

@DefaultValue

In many types of JAX-RS services, you may have parameters that are optional. When a client does not provide this optional information within the request, JAX-RS will, by default, inject a null value for object types and a zero value for primitive types.

Many times, though, a null or zero value may not work as a default value for your injection. To solve this problem, you can define your own default value for optional parameters by using the `@javax.ws.rs.DefaultValue` annotation.

For instance, let's look back again at the `@QueryParam` example given earlier in this chapter. In that example, we wanted to pull down a set of customers from a customer database. We used the `start` and `size` query parameters to specify the beginning index and the number of customers desired. While we do want to control the amount of customers sent back as a response, we do not want to require the client to send these query parameters when making a request. We can use `@DefaultValue` to set a base index and dataset size:

```
import java.util.List;

@Path("/customers")
public class CustomerResource {

    @GET
    @Produces("application/xml")
    public String getCustomers(@DefaultValue("0") @QueryParam("start") int start,
                               @DefaultValue("10") @QueryParam("size") int size) {
        ...
    }
}
```

Here, we've used `@DefaultValue` to specify a default start index of 0 and a default dataset size of 10. JAX-RS will use the string conversion rules to convert the string value of the `@DefaultValue` annotation into the desired Java type.

@Encoded

URI template, matrix, query, and form parameters must all be encoded by the HTTP specification. By default, JAX-RS decodes these values before converting them into the desired Java types. Sometimes, though, you may want to work with the raw encoded values. Using the `@javax.ws.rs.Encoded` annotation gives you the desired effect:

```
@GET
@Produces("application/xml")
public String get(@Encoded @QueryParam("something") String str) {...}
```

Here, we've used the `@Encoded` annotation to specify that we want the encoded value of the `something` query parameter to be injected into the `str` Java parameter. If you want to work solely with encoded values within your Java method or even your entire class, you can annotate the method or class with `@Encoded` and only encoded values will be used.

Wrapping Up

In this chapter, we examined how to use JAX-RS injection annotations to insert bits and pieces of an HTTP request à la carte into your JAX-RS resource method parameters. While data is represented as strings within an HTTP request, JAX-RS can automatically convert this data into the Java type you desire, provided that the type follows certain constraints. These features allow you to write compact, easily understandable code and avoid a lot of the boilerplate code you might need if you were using other frameworks like the servlet specification. You can test-drive the code in this chapter by flipping to Chapter 20.

CHAPTER 6

JAX-RS Content Handlers

In the last chapter, we focused on injecting information from the header of an HTTP request. In this chapter, we will focus on the message body of an HTTP request and response. In the examples in previous chapters, we used low-level streaming to read in requests and write out responses. To make things easier, JAX-RS also allows you to marshal message bodies to and from specific Java types. It has a number of built-in providers, but you can also write and plug in your own providers. Let's look at them all.

Built-in Content Marshalling

JAX-RS has a bunch of built-in handlers that can marshal to and from a few different specific Java types. While most are low-level conversions, they can still be useful to your JAX-RS classes.

javax.ws.rs.core.StreamingOutput

We were first introduced to `StreamingOutput` back in Chapter 3. `StreamingOutput` is a simple callback interface that you implement when you want to do raw streaming of response bodies:

```
public interface StreamingOutput  {
    void write(OutputStream output) throws IOException,
                                    WebApplicationException;
}
```

You allocate implemented instances of this interface and return them from your JAX-RS resource methods. When the JAX-RS runtime is ready to write the response body of the message, the `write()` method is invoked on the `StreamingOutput` instance. Let's look at an example:

```
@Path("/myservice")
public class MyService {
```

```
@GET
@Produces("text/plain")
StreamingOutput get() {
   return new StreamingOutput() {
      public void write(OutputStream output) throws IOException,
                                        WebApplicationException {
         output.write("hello world".getBytes());
      }
   };
}
```

Here, we're getting access to the raw `java.io.OutputStream` through the `write()` method and outputting a simple string to the stream. I like to use an anonymous inner class implementation of the `StreamingOutput` interface rather than creating a separate public class. Since the `StreamingOutput` interface is so tiny, I think it's beneficial to keep the output logic embedded within the original JAX-RS resource method so that the code is easier to follow. Usually, you're not going to reuse this logic in other methods, so it doesn't make much sense to create a specific class.

You may be asking yourself, "Why not just inject an `OutputStream` directly? Why have a callback object to do streaming output?" That's a good question! The reason for having a callback object is that it gives the JAX-RS implementation freedom to handle output however it wants. For performance reasons, it may sometimes be beneficial for the JAX-RS implementation to use a different thread other than the calling thread to output responses. More importantly, many JAX-RS implementations have an interceptor model that abstracts things out like automatic GZIP encoding or response caching. Streaming directly can usually bypass these architectural constructs. Finally, the Servlet 3.0 specification has introduced the idea of asynchronous responses. The callback model fits in very nicely with the idea of asynchronous HTTP within the Servlet 3.0 specification.

java.io.InputStream, java.io.Reader

For reading request message bodies, you can use a raw `InputStream` or `Reader` for inputting any media type. For example:

```
@Path("/")
public class MyService {

   @PUT
   @Path("/stuff")
   public void putStuff(InputStream is) {
      byte[] bytes = readFromStream(is);
      String input = new String(bytes);
      System.out.println(input);
   }

   private byte[] readFromStream(InputStream stream)
```

```
        throws IOException
{
    ByteArrayOutputStream baos = new ByteArrayOutputStream();

    byte[] buffer = new byte[1000];
    int wasRead = 0;
    do {
        wasRead = stream.read(buffer);
        if (wasRead > 0) {
            baos.write(buffer, 0, wasRead);
        }
    } while (wasRead > -1);
    return baos.toByteArray();
}
```

Here, we're reading the full raw bytes of the `java.io.InputStream` available and using them to create a `String` that we output to the screen:

```
@PUT
@Path("/morestuff")
public void putMore(Reader reader) {
    LineNumberReader lineReader = new LineNumberReader(reader);
    do {
        String line = lineReader.readLine();
        if (line != null) System.out.println(line);
    } while (line != null);
}
```

For this example, we're creating a `java.io.LineNumberReader` that wraps our injected `Reader` object and prints out every line in the request body.

You are not limited to using `InputStream` and `Reader` for reading input request message bodies. You can also return these as response objects. For example:

```
@Path("/file")
public class FileService {

    private static final String basePath = "...";
    @GET
    @Path("{filepath: .*}")
    @Produces("text/plain")
    public InputStream getFile(@PathParam("filepath") String path) {
        FileInputStream is = new FileInputStream(basePath + path);
        return is;
    }
}
```

Here, we're using an injected `@PathParam` to create a reference to a real file that exists on our disk. We create a `java.io.FileInputStream` based on this path and return it as our response body. The JAX-RS implementation will read from this input stream into a buffer and write it back out incrementally to the response output stream. We must specify the @Produces annotation so that the JAX-RS implementation knows how to set the Content-Type header.

java.io.File

Instances of java.io.File can also be used for input and output of any media type. Here's an example for returning a reference to a file on disk:

```
@Path("/file")
public class FileService {

    private static final String basePath = "...";
    @GET
    @Path("{filepath: .*}")
    @Produces("text/plain")
    public File getFile(@PathParam("filepath") String path) {
        return new File(basePath + path);
    }
}
```

In this example, we're using an injected @PathParam to create a reference to a real file that exists on our disk. We create a java.io.File based on this path and return it as our response body. The JAX-RS implementation will open up an InputStream based on this file reference and stream into a buffer that is written back incrementally to the response's output stream. We must specify the @Produces annotation so that the JAX-RS implementation knows how to set the Content-Type header.

You can also inject java.io.File instances that represent the incoming request response body. For example:

```
@POST
@Path("/morestuff")
public void post(File file) {
    Reader reader = new Reader(new FileInputStream(file));
    LineNumberReader lineReader = new LineNumberReader(reader);
    do {
        String line = lineReader.readLine();
        if (line != null) System.out.println(line);
    } while (line != null);
}
```

The way this works is that the JAX-RS implementation creates a temporary file for input on disk. It reads from the network buffer and saves the bytes read into this temporary file. In our example, we create a java.io.FileInputStream from the java.io.File object that was injected by the JAX-RS runtime. We then use this input stream to create a LineNumberReader and output the posted data to the console.

byte[]

A raw array of bytes can be used for the input and output of any media type. Here's an example:

```
@Path("/")
public class MyService {

   @GET
   @Produces("text/plain")
   public byte[] get() {
      return "hello world".getBytes();
   }

   @POST
   @Consumes("text/plain")
   public void post(byte[] bytes) {
      System.out.println(new String(bytes));
   }
}
```

For JAX-RS resource methods that return an array of bytes, you must specify the @Produces annotation so that JAX-RS knows what media to use to set the Content-Type header.

String, char[]

Most of the data formats on the Internet are text based. JAX-RS can convert any text-based format to and from either a String or an array of characters. For example:

```
@Path("/")
public class MyService {

   @GET
   @Produces("application/xml")
   public String get() {
      return "<customer><name>Bill Burke</name></customer>";
   }

   @POST
   @Consumes("text/plain")
   public void post(String str) {
      System.out.println(str);
   }
}
```

For JAX-RS resource methods that return a String or an array of characters, you must specify the @Produces annotation so that JAX-RS knows what media to use to set the Content-Type header.

The JAX-RS specification does require that implementations be sensitive to the character set specified by the Content-Type when creating an injected String. For example, here's a client HTTP POST request that is sending some text data to our service:

```
POST /data
Content-Type: application/xml;charset=UTF-8

<customer>...</customer>
```

The Content-Type of the request is application/xml, but it is also stating the character encoding is UTF-8. JAX-RS implementations will make sure that the created Java String is encoded as UTF-8 as well.

MultivaluedMap<String, String> and Form Input

HTML forms are a common way to post data to web servers. Form data is encoded as the application/x-www-form-urlencoded media type. In Chapter 5, we saw how you can use the @FormParam annotation to inject individual form parameters from the request. You can also inject a MultivaluedMap<String, String> that represents all the form data sent with the request. For example:

```
@Path("/")
public class MyService {

    @POST
    @Consumes("application/x-www-form-urlencoded")
    @Produces("application/x-www-form-urlencoded")
    public MultivaluedMap<String,String> post(
                            MultivaluedMap<String, String> form) {

        return form;
    }
}
```

Here, our post() method accepts POST requests and receives a Multivalued Map<String, String> containing all our form data. You may also return a Mul tivaluedMap of form data as your response. We do this in our example.

The JAX-RS specification does not say whether the injected MultivaluedMap should contain encoded strings or not. Most JAX-RS implementations will automatically decode the map's string keys and values. If you want it encoded, you can use the @jav ax.ws.rs.Encoded annotation to notify the JAX-RS implementation that you want the data in its raw form.

javax.xml.transform.Source

The javax.xml.transform.Source interface represents XML input or output. It is usually used to perform XSLT transformations on input documents. Here's an example:

```
@Path("/transform")
public class TransformationService {

    @POST
    @Consumes("application/xml")
    @Produces("application/xml")
    public String post(Source source) {

        javax.xml.transform.TransformerFactory tFactory =
                javax.xml.transform.TransformerFactory.newInstance();

        javax.xml.transform.Transformer transformer =
            tFactory.newTransformer(
                new javax.xml.transform.stream.StreamSource("foo.xsl"));

        StringWriter writer = new StringWriter();
        transformer.transform(source,
                new javax.xml.transform.stream.StreamResult(writer));

        return writer.toString();
    }
```

In this example, we're having JAX-RS inject a `javax.xml.transform.Source` instance that represents our request body and we're transforming it using an XSLT transformation.

Except for JAXB, `javax.xml.transform.Source` is the only XML-based construct that the specification requires implementers to support. I find it a little strange that you can't automatically inject and marshal `org.w3c.dom.Document` objects. This was probably just forgotten in the writing of the specification.

JAXB

JAXB is an older Java specification and is not defined by JAX-RS. JAXB is an annotation framework that maps Java classes to XML and XML schema. It is extremely useful because instead of interacting with an abstract representation of an XML document, you can work with real Java objects that are closer to the domain you are modeling. JAX-RS has built-in support for JAXB, but before we review these handlers, let's get a brief overview of the JAXB framework.

Intro to JAXB

A whole book could be devoted to explaining the intricacies of JAXB, but I'm only going to focus here on the very basics of the framework. If you want to map an existing Java class to XML using JAXB, there are a few simple annotations you can use. Let's look at an example:

```
@XmlRootElement(name="customer")
@XmlAccessorType(XmlAccessType.FIELD)
public class Customer {

    @XmlAttribute
    protected int id;

    @XmlElement
    protected String fullname;

    public Customer() {}

    public int getId() { return this.id; }
    public void setId(int id) { this.id = id; }

    public String getFullName() { return this.fullname; }
    public void setFullName(String name} { this.fullname = name; }
}
```

The @javax.xml.bind.annotation.XmlRootElement annotation is put on Java classes
to denote that they are XML elements. The name() attribute of @XmlRootElement specifies the string to use for the name of the XML element. In our example, the annotation
@XmlRootElement specifies that our Customer objects should be marshalled into an XML
element named <customer>.

The @javax.xml.bind.annotation.XmlAttribute annotation was placed on the id
field of our Customer class. This annotation tells JAXB to map the field to an id attribute
on the main <Customer> element of the XML document. The @XmlAttribute annotation also has a name() attribute that allows you to specify the exact name of the XML
attribute within the XML document. By default, it is the same name as the annotated
field.

In our example, the @javax.xml.bind.annotation.XmlElement annotation was placed
on the fullname field of our Customer class. This annotation tells JAXB to map the field
to a <fullname> element within the main <Customer> element of the XML document.
@XmlElement does have a name() attribute, so you can specify the exact string of the
XML element. By default, it is the same name as the annotated field.

If we were to output an instance of our Customer class that had an id of 42 and a name
of "Bill Burke," the outputted XML would look like this:

```
<customer id="42">
    <fullname>Bill Burke</fullname>
</customer>
```

You can also use the @XmlElement annotation to embed other JAXB-annotated classes.
For example, let's say we wanted to add an Address class to our Customer class:

```
@XmlRootElement(name="address")
@XmlAccessorType(XmlAccessType.FIELD)
```

```
public class Address  {

    @XmlElement
    protected String street;

    @XmlElement
    protected String city;

    @XmlElement
    protected String state;

    @XmlElement
    protected String zip;

    // getters and setters

    ...
}
```

We would simply add a field to `Customer` that was of type `Address` as follows:

```
@XmlRootElement(name="customer")
@XmlAccessorType(XmlAccessType.FIELD)
public class Customer {

    @XmlAttribute
    protected int id;

    @XmlElement
    protected String name;

    @XmlElement
    protected Address address;

    public Customer() {}

    public int getId() { return this.id; }
    public void setId(int id) { this.id = id; }
    ...
}
```

If we were to output an instance of our new `Customer` class that had an `id` of 42, a `name` of "Bill Burke," a `street` of "200 Marlborough Street," a `city` of "Boston," a `state` of "MA," and a `zip` of "02115," the outputted XML would look like this:

```
<customer id="42">
    <name>Bill Burke</name>
    <address>
        <street>200 Marlborough Street</street>
        <city>Boston</city>
        <state>MA</state>
        <zip>02115</zip>
```

```
    </address>
  </customer>
```

There are a number of other annotations and settings that allow you to do some more complex Java-to-XML mappings. JAXB implementations are also required to have command-line tools that can automatically generate JAXB-annotated Java classes from XML schema documents. If you need to integrate with an existing XML schema, these autogeneration tools are the way to go.

To marshal Java classes to and from XML, you need to interact with the `javax.xml.bind.JAXBContext` class. `JAXBContext` instances introspect your classes to understand the structure of your annotated classes. They are used as factories for the `javax.xml.bind.Marshaller` and `javax.xml.bind.Unmarshaller` interfaces. `Marshaller` instances are used to take Java objects and output them as XML. `Unmarshaller` instances are used to take XML input and create Java objects out of it. Here's an example of using JAXB to write an instance of the `Customer` class we defined earlier into XML and then to take that XML and re-create the `Customer` object:

```
Customer customer = new Customer();
customer.setId(42);
customer.setName("Bill Burke");

JAXBContext ctx = JAXBContext.newInstance(Customer.class);
StringWriter writer = new StringWriter();

ctx.createMarshaller().marshal(customer, writer);

String custString = writer.toString();

customer = (Customer)ctx.createUnmarshaller()
                .unmarshal(new StringReader(custString));
```

We first create an initialized instance of a `Customer` class. We then initialize a `JAXBContext` to understand how to deal with `Customer` classes. We use a `Marshaller` instance created by the method `JAXBContext.createMarshaller()` to write the `Customer` object into a Java string. Next we use the `Unmarshaller` created by the `JAXBContext.createUnmarshaller()` method to re-create the `Customer` object with the XML string we just created.

Now that we have a general idea of how JAXB works, let's look at how JAX-RS integrates with it.

JAXB JAX-RS Handlers

The JAX-RS specification requires implementations to automatically support the marshalling and unmarshalling of classes that are annotated with `@XmlRootElement` or

@XmlType as well as objects wrapped inside `javax.xml.bind.JAXBElement` instances. Here's an example that interacts using the `Customer` class defined earlier:

```
@Path("/customers")
public class CustomerResource {

    @GET
    @Path("{id}")
    @Produces("application/xml")
    public Customer getCustomer(@PathParam("id") int id) {

        Customer cust = findCustomer(id);
        return cust;
    }

    @POST
    @Consumes("application/xml")
    public void createCustomer(Customer cust) {
        ...
    }
}
```

As you can see, once you've applied JAXB annotations to your Java classes, it is very easy to exchange XML documents between your client and web services. The built-in JAXB handlers will handle any JAXB-annotated class for the `application/xml`, `text/xml`, or `application/*+xml` media types. By default, they will also manage the creation and initialization of `JAXBContext` instances. Because the creation of `JAXBContext` instances can be expensive, JAX-RS implementations usually cache them after they are first initialized.

Managing your own JAXBContexts with ContextResolvers

If you are already familiar with JAXB, you'll know that many times you need to configure your `JAXBContext` instances a certain way to get the output you desire. The JAX-RS built-in JAXB provider allows you to plug in your own `JAXBContext` instances. The way it works is that you have to implement a factory-like interface called `javax.ws.rs.ext.ContextResolver` to override the default `JAXBContext` creation:

```
public interface ContextResolver<T> {

    T getContext(Class<?> type);
}
```

`ContextResolvers` are pluggable factories that create objects of a specific type, for a certain Java type, and for a specific media type. To plug in your own `JAXBContext`, you will have to implement this interface. Here's an example of creating a specific JAXBContext for our `Customer` class:

```
@Provider
@Produces("application/xml")
public class CustomerResolver
                    implements ContextResolver<JAXBContext> {
   private JAXBContext ctx;

   public CustomerResolver() {
      this.ctx = ...; // initialize it the way you want
   }


   public JAXBContext getContext(Class<?> type) {
      if (type.equals(Customer.class)) {
         return ctx;
      } else {
         return null;
      }
   }
}
```

Your resolver class must implement ContextResolver with the parameterized type of JAXBContext. The class must also be annotated with the @javax.ws.rs.ext.Provid er annotation to identify it as a JAX-RS component. In our example, the Customer Resolver constructor initializes a JAXBContext specific to our Customer class.

You register your ContextResolver using the javax.ws.rs.core.Application API discussed in Chapters 3 and 14. The built-in JAXB handler will see if there are any registered ContextResolvers that can create JAXBContext instances. It will iterate through them, calling the getContext() method passing in the Java type it wants a JAXBContext created for. If the getContext() method returns null, it will go on to the next ContextResolver in the list. If the getContext() method returns an instance, it will use that JAXBContext to handle the request. If there are no ContextResolvers found, it will create and manage its own JAXBContext. In our example, the Customer Resolver.getContext() method checks to see if the type is a Customer class. If it is, it returns the JAXBContext we initialized in the constructor; otherwise, it returns null.

The @Produces annotation on your CustomerResolver implementation is optional. It allows you to specialize a ContextResolver for a specific media type. You'll see in the next section that you can use JAXB to output to formats other than XML. This is a way to create JAXBContext instances for each individual media type in your system.

JAXB and JSON

JAXB is flexible enough to support formats other than XML. The Jettison[1] open source project has written a JAXB adapter that can input and output the JSON format. JSON is a text-based format that can be directly interpreted by JavaScript. It is the preferred exchange format for Ajax applications. Although not required by the JAX-RS specification, many JAX-RS implementations use Jettison to support marshalling JAXB annotated classes to and from JSON.

JSON is a much simpler format than XML. Objects are enclosed in curly brackets, "{}", and contain key/value pairs. Values can be quoted strings, Booleans (true or false), numeric values, or arrays of these simple types. Here's an example:

```
{
  "id" : 42,
  "name" : "Bill Burke",
  "married" : true,
  "kids" : [ "Molly", "Abby" ]
}
```

Key and value pairs are separated by a colon character and delimited by commas. Arrays are enclosed in brackets, "[]." Here, our object has four properties—id, name, married, and kids—with varying values.

XML to JSON using BadgerFish

As you can see, JSON is a much simpler format than XML. While XML has elements, attributes, and namespaces, JSON only has name/value pairs. There has been some work in the JSON community to produce a mapping between XML and JSON so that one XML schema can output documents of both formats. The de facto standard, Badger-Fish, is a widely used XML-to-JSON mapping and is available in most JAX-RS implementations that have JAXB/JSON support. Let's go over this mapping:

1. XML element names become JSON object properties and the text values of these elements are contained within a nested object that has a property named "$." So, if you had the XML `<customer>Bill Burke</customer>`, it would map to { "customer" : { "$" : "Bill Burke" }}.

2. XML elements become properties of their base element. Suppose you had the following XML:

```
<customer>
   <first>Bill</first>
   <last>Burke</last>
</customer>
```

---

1. For more information, see *http://jettison.codehaus.org*.

The JSON mapping would look like:

```
{ "customer" :
   { "first" : { "$" : "Bill"},
     "last" : { "$" : "Burke" }
   }
}
```

3. Multiple nested elements of the same name would become an array value. So, the XML:

```
<customer>
   <phone>978-666-5555</phone>
   <phone>978-555-2233</phone>
</customer
```

would look like the following in JSON:

```
{ "customer" :
   { "phone" : [ { "$", "978-666-5555"}, { "$", "978-555-2233"} ] }
}
```

4. XML attributes become JSON properties prefixed with the @ character. So, if you had the XML:

```
<customer id="42">
   <name>Bill Burke</name>
</customer>
```

the JSON mapping would look like the following:

```
{ "customer" :
   { "@id" : 42,
     "name" : "Bill Burke"
   }
}
```

5. Active namespaces are contained in an @xmlns JSON property of the element. The "$" represents the default namespace. All nested elements and attributes would use the namespace prefix as part of their names. So, if we had the XML:

```
<customer xmlns="urn:cust" xmlns:address="urn:address">
   <name>Bill Burke</name>
   <address:zip>02115</address:zip>
</customer>
```

the JSON mapping would be the following:

```
{ "customer" :
   { "@xmlns" : { "$" : "urn:cust",
                   "address" : "urn:address" } ,
     "name" : { "$" : "Bill Burke",
                 "@xmlns" : { "$" : "urn:cust",
                              "address" : "urn:address" } },
     "address:zip" : { "$" : "02115",
                        "@xmlns" : { "$" : "urn:cust",
```

```
                              "address" : "urn:address" }}
              }
       }
```

BadgerFish is kind of unnatural when writing JavaScript, but if you want to unify your formats under XML schema, it's the way to go.

JSON and JSON Schema

The thing with using XML schema and the BadgerFish mapping to define your JSON data structures is that it is very weird for JavaScript programmers to consume. If you do not need to support XML clients or if you want to provide a cleaner and simpler JSON representation, there are some options available for you.

It doesn't make much sense to use XML schema to define JSON data structures. The main reason is that JSON is a richer data format that supports things like maps, lists, and numeric, Boolean, and string data. It is a bit quirky modeling these sorts of simple data structures with XML schema. To solve this problem, the JSON community has come up with JSON schema. Here's an example of what it looks like when you define a JSON data structure representing our customer example:

```
{
  "description":"A customer",
  "type":"object",

  "properties":
    {"first": {"type": "string"},
     "last" : {"type" : "string"}
    }
}
```

The `description` property defines the description for the schema. The `type` property defines what is being described. Next, you define a list of properties that make up your object. I won't go into a lot of detail about JSON schema, so you should visit *http://www.json-schema.org* to get more information on this subject.

If you do a Google search on Java and JSON, you'll find a plethora of frameworks that help you marshal and unmarshal between Java and JSON. One particularly good one is the Jackson[2] framework. It has a prewritten JAX-RS content handler that can automatically convert Java beans to and from JSON. It can also generate JSON schema documents from a Java object model.

The way it works by default is that it introspects your Java class, looking for properties, and maps them into JSON. For example, if we had the Java class:

---

2. *http://jackson.codehaus.org/*

```
public class Customer {
    private int id;
    private String firstName;
    private String lastName;

    public int getId() {
        return id;
    }

    public void setId(int id) {
        this.id = id;
    }

    public String getFirstName() {
        return firstName;
    }

    public void setFirstName(String firstName) {
        this.firstName = firstName;
    }

    public String getLastName() {
        return lastName;
    }

    public void setLastName(String lastName) {
        this.lastName = lastName;
    }
}
```

and sample data:

```
{
    "id" : 42,
    "firstName" : "Bill",
    "lastName" : "Burke"
}
```

reading in the data to create a Customer object would be as easy as this:

```
ObjectMapper mapper = new ObjectMapper();
Customer cust = mapper.readValue(inputStream, Customer.class);
```

Writing the data would be as easy as this:

```
ObjectMapper mapper = new ObjectMapper();
mapper.writeValue(outputStream, customer);
```

The Jackson framework's JAX-RS integration actually does all this work for you, so all you have to do in your JAX-RS classes is specify the output and input format as appli cation/json when writing your JAX-RS methods.

Custom Marshalling

So far in this chapter, we've focused on built-in JAX-RS handlers that can marshal and unmarshal message content. Unfortunately, there are hundreds of data formats available on the Internet, and the built-in JAX-RS handlers are either too low level to be useful or may not match the format you need. Luckily, JAX-RS allows you to write your own handlers and plug them into the JAX-RS runtime.

To illustrate how to write your own handlers, we're going to pretend that there is no built-in JAX-RS JAXB support and instead write one ourselves using JAX-RS APIs.

MessageBodyWriter

The first thing we're going to implement is JAXB-marshalling support. To automatically convert Java objects into XML, we have to create a class that implements the `javax.ws.rs.ext.MessageBodyWriter` interface:

```
public interface MessageBodyWriter<T> {

    boolean isWriteable(Class<?> type, Type genericType,
                        Annotation annotations[],
                                    MediaType mediaType);


    long getSize(T t, Class<?> type, Type genericType,
                 Annotation annotations[], MediaType mediaType);


    void writeTo(T t, Class<?> type, Type genericType,
                 Annotation annotations[],
                 MediaType mediaType,
                 MultivaluedMap<String, Object> httpHeaders,
                 OutputStream entityStream)
                         throws IOException, WebApplicationException;
}
```

The `MessageBodyWriter` interface has only three methods. The `isWriteable()` method is called by the JAX-RS runtime to determine if the writer supports marshalling the given type. The `getSize()` method is called by the JAX-RS runtime to determine the `Content-Length` of the output. Finally, the `writeTo()` method does all the heavy lifting and writes the content out to the HTTP response buffer. Let's implement this interface to support JAXB:

```
@Provider
@Produces("application/xml")
public class JAXBMarshaller implements MessageBodyWriter {

    public boolean isWriteable(Class<?> type, Type genericType,
                        Annotation annotations[], MediaType mediaType) {
```

```
        return type.isAnnotationPresent(XmlRootElement.class);
    }
```

We start off the implementation of this class by annotating it with the @jav
ax.ws.rs.ext.Provider annotation. This tells JAX-RS that this is a deployable JAX-
RS component. We must also annotate it with @Produces to tell JAX-RS which media
types this MessageBodyWriter supports. Here, we're saying that our JAXBMarshaller
class supports application/xml.

The isWriteable() method is a callback method that tells the JAX-RS runtime whether
or not the class can handle writing out this type. JAX-RS follows this algorithm to find
an appropriate MessageBodyWriter to write out a Java object into the HTTP response:

1. First, JAX-RS calculates a list of MessageBodyWriters by looking at each writer's
   @Produces annotation to see if it supports the media type that the JAX-RS resource
   method wants to output.

2. This list is sorted, with the best match for the desired media type coming first. In
   other words, if our JAX-RS resource method wants to output application/xml
   and we have three MessageBodyWriters (one produces application/*, one supports anything */*, and the last supports application/xml), the one producing
   application/xml will come first.

3. Once this list is calculated, the JAX-RS implementation iterates through the list in
   order, calling the MessageBodyWriter.isWriteable() method. If the invocation
   returns true, that MessageBodyWriter is used to output the data.

The isWriteable() method takes four parameters. The first one is a java.lang.Class
that is the type of the object that is being marshalled. We determine the type by calling
the getClass() method of the object. In our example, we use this parameter to find out
if our object's class is annotated with the @XmlRootElement annotation.

The second parameter is a java.lang.reflect.Type. This is generic type information
about the object being marshalled. We determine it by introspecting the return type of
the JAX-RS resource method. We don't use this parameter in our JAXBMarshaller.is
Writeable() implementation. This parameter would be useful, for example, if we
wanted to know the type parameter of a java.util.List generic type.

The third parameter is an array of java.lang.annotation.Annotation objects. These
annotations are applied to the JAX-RS resource method we are marshalling the response
for. Some MessageBodyWriters may be triggered by JAX-RS resource method annotations rather than class annotations. In our JAXBMarshaller class, we do not use this
parameter in our isWriteable() implementation.

The fourth parameter is the media type that our JAX-RS resource method wants to
produce.

Let's examine the rest of our `JAXBMarshaller` implementation:

```
public long getSize(Object obj, Class<?> type, Type genericType,
                    Annotation[] annotations, MediaType mediaType)
{
    return -1;
}
```

The `getSize()` method is responsible for determining the `Content-Length` of the response. If you cannot easily determine the length, just return –1. The underlying HTTP layer (i.e., a servlet container) will handle populating the `Content-Length` in this scenario or use the chunked transfer encoding.

The first parameter of `getSize()` is the actual object we are outputting. The rest of the parameters serve the same purpose as the parameters for the `isWriteable()` method.

Finally, let's look at how we actually write the JAXB object as XML:

```
public void writeTo(Object target,
                    Class<?> type,
                    Type genericType,
                    Annotation[] annotations,
                    MediaType mediaType,
                    MultivaluedMap<String, Object> httpHeaders,
                    OutputStream outputStream) throws IOException
{
    try {
        JAXBContext ctx = JAXBContext.newInstance(type);
        ctx.createMarshaller().marshal(target, outputStream);
    } catch (JAXBException ex) {
        throw new RuntimeException(ex);
    }
}
```

The `target`, `type`, `genericType`, `annotations`, and `mediaType` parameters of the `write To()` method are the same information passed into the `getSize()` and `isWriteable()` methods. The `httpHeaders` parameter is a `javax.ws.rs.core.MultivaluedMap` that represents the HTTP response headers. You may modify this map and add, remove, or change the value of a specific HTTP header as long as you do this before outputting the response body. The `outputStream` parameter is a `java.io.OutputStream` and is used to stream out the data.

Our implementation simply creates a `JAXBContext` using the `type` parameter. It then creates a `javax.xml.bind.Marshaller` and converts the Java object to XML.

Adding pretty printing

By default, JAXB outputs XML without any whitespace or special formatting. The XML output is all one line of text with no new lines or indentation. We may have human clients looking at this data, so we want to give our JAX-RS resource methods the option to pretty-print the output XML. We will provide this functionality using an @Pretty annotation. For example:

```
@Path("/customers")
public class CustomerService {

    @GET
    @Path("{id}")
    @Produces("application/xml")
    @Pretty
    public Customer getCustomer(@PathParam("id") int id) {...}
}
```

Since the writeTo() method of our MessageBodyWriter has access to the getCustomer() method's annotations, we can implement this easily. Let's modify our JAXB Marshaller class:

```
public void writeTo(Object target,
                    Class<?> type,
                    Type genericType,
                    Annotation[] annotations,
                    MediaType mediaType,
                    MultivaluedMap<String, Object> httpHeaders,
                    OutputStream outputStream) throws IOException
{
    try {
        JAXBContext ctx = JAXBContext.newInstance(type);
        Marshaller m = ctx.createMarshaller();

        boolean pretty = false;
        for (Annotation ann : annotations) {
            if (ann.annotationType().equals(Pretty.class)) {
                pretty = true;
                break;
            }
        }
        if (pretty) {
            marshaller.setProperty(Marshaller.JAXB_FORMATTED_OUTPUT, true);
        }

        m.marshal(target, outputStream);
    } catch (JAXBException ex) {
        throw new RuntimeException(ex);
    }
}
```

Here, we iterate over the annotations parameter to see if any of them are the @Pretty annotation. If @Pretty has been set, we set the JAXB_FORMATTED_OUTPUT property on the Marshaller so that it will format the XML with line breaks and indentation strings.

Pluggable JAXBContexts using ContextResolvers

Earlier in this chapter, we saw how you could plug in your own JAXBContext using the ContextResolver interface. Let's look at how we can add this functionality to our JAXB Marshaller class.

First, we need a way to locate a ContextResolver that can provide a custom JAXBContext. We do this through the javax.ws.rs.ext.Providers interface:

```
public interface Providers {

    <T> ContextResolver<T> getContextResolver(Class<T> contextType,
                                              MediaType mediaType);

    <T> MessageBodyReader<T>
    getMessageBodyReader(Class<T> type, Type genericType,
                         Annotation annotations[], MediaType mediaType);


    <T> MessageBodyWriter<T>
    getMessageBodyWriter(Class<T> type, Type genericType,
                         Annotation annotations[], MediaType mediaType);


    <T extends Throwable> ExceptionMapper<T>
    getExceptionMapper(Class<T> type);

}
```

We use the Providers.getContextResolver() method to find a ContextResolver. We inject a reference to a Providers object using the @Context annotation. Let's modify our JAXBMarshaller class to add this new functionality:

```
@Context
protected Providers providers;

public void writeTo(Object target,
                    Class<?> type,
                    Type genericType,
                    Annotation[] annotations,
                    MediaType mediaType,
                    MultivaluedMap<String, Object> httpHeaders,
                    OutputStream outputStream) throws IOException
{
    try {
        JAXBContext ctx = null;
        ContextResolver<JAXBContext> resolver =
            providers.getContextResolver(JAXBContext.class, mediaType);
        if (resolver != null) {
            ctx = resolver.getContext(type);
        }
        if (ctx == null) {
```

```
      // create one ourselves
      ctx = JAXBContext.newInstance(type);
    }
    ctx.createMarshaller().marshal(target, outputStream);
  } catch (JAXBException ex) {
    throw new RuntimeException(ex);
  }
}
```

In our writeTo() method, we now use the Providers interface to find a ContextResolv
er that can give us a custom JAXBContext. If one exists, we call resolver.getCon
text(), passing in the type of the object we want a JAXBContext for.

The ContextResolver returned by Providers.getContextResolver() is actually a
proxy that sits in front of a list of ContextResolvers that can provide JAXBContext
instances. When getContextResolver() is invoked, the proxy iterates on this list, re-
calling getContextResolver() on each individual resolver in the list. If it returns a
JAXBContext instance, it returns that to the original caller; otherwise, it tries the next
resolver in this list.

MessageBodyReader

Now that we have written a MessageBodyWriter to convert a Java object into XML and
output it as the HTTP response body, let's write an unmarshaller that knows how to
convert HTTP XML request bodies back into a Java object. To do this, we need to use
the javax.ws.rs.ext.MessageBodyReader interface:

```
public interface MessageBodyReader<T> {

   boolean isReadable(Class<?> type, Type genericType,
                      Annotation annotations[], MediaType mediaType);

   T readFrom(Class<T> type, Type genericType,
             Annotation annotations[], MediaType mediaType,
             MultivaluedMap<String, String> httpHeaders,
             InputStream entityStream)
                    throws IOException, WebApplicationException;

}
```

The MessageBodyReader interface has only two methods. The isReadable() method
is called by the JAX-RS runtime when it is trying to find a MessageBodyReader to unmarshal the message body of an HTTP request. The readFrom() method is responsible
for creating a Java object from the HTTP request body.

Implementing a MessageBodyReader is very similar to writing a MessageBodyWriter.
Let's look at how we would implement one:

```
@Provider
@Consumes("application/xml")
public class JAXBUnmarshaller implements MessageBodyReader {

    public boolean isReadable(Class<?> type, Type genericType,
                    Annotation annotations[], MediaType mediaType) {
        return type.isAnnotationPresent(XmlRootElement.class);
    }
```

Our JAXBUnmarshaller class is annotated with @Provider and @Consumes. The latter annotation tells the JAX-RS runtime which media types it can handle. The matching rules for finding a MessageBodyReader are the same as the rules for matching Message BodyWriter. The difference is that the @Consumes annotation is used instead of the @Produces annotation to correlate media types.

Let's now look at how we read and convert our HTTP message into a Java object:

```
Object readFrom(Class<Object>, Type genericType,
                Annotation annotations[], MediaType mediaType,
                MultivaluedMap<String, String> httpHeaders,
                InputStream entityStream)
                        throws IOException, WebApplicationException {

    try {
        JAXBContext ctx = JAXBContext.newInstance(type);
        return ctx.createUnmarshaller().unmarshal(entityStream);
    } catch (JAXBException ex) {
        throw new RuntimeException(ex);
    }
}
```

The readFrom() method gives us access to the HTTP headers of the incoming request as well as a java.io.InputStream that represents the request message body. Here, we just create a JAXBContext based on the Java type we want to create and use a jav ax.xml.bind.Unmarshaller to extract it from the stream.

Life Cycle and Environment

By default, only one instance of each MessageBodyReader, MessageBodyWriter, or ContextResolver is created per application. If JAX-RS is allocating instances of these components (see Chapter 14), the classes of these components must provide a public constructor for which the JAX-RS runtime can provide all the parameter values. A public constructor may only include parameters annotated with the @Context annotation. For example:

```
@Provider
@Consumes("application/json")
public class MyJsonReader implements MessageBodyReader {

    public MyJsonReader(@Context Providers providers) {
```

```
            this.providers = providers;
    }
}
```

Whether or not the JAX-RS runtime is allocating the component instance, JAX-RS will perform injection into properly annotated fields and setter methods. Again, you can only inject JAX-RS objects that are found using the @Context annotation.

Wrapping Up

In this chapter, you learned that JAX-RS can automatically convert Java objects to a specific data type format and write it out as an HTTP response. It can also automatically read in HTTP request bodies and create specific Java objects that represent the request. JAX-RS has a number of built-in handlers, but you can also write your own custom marshallers and unmarshallers. Chapter 21 walks you through some sample code that you can use to test-drive many of the concepts and APIs introduced in this chapter.

CHAPTER 7

Server Responses and Exception Handling

So far, the examples given in this book have been very clean and tidy. The JAX-RS resource methods we have written have looked like regular vanilla Java methods with JAX-RS annotations. We haven't talked a lot about the default behavior of JAX-RS resource methods, particularly around HTTP response codes in success and failure scenarios. Also, in the real world, you can't always have things so neat and clean. Many times you need to send specific response headers to deal with complex error conditions. This chapter first discusses the default response codes that vanilla JAX-RS resource methods give. It then walks you through writing complex responses using JAX-RS APIs. Finally, it goes over how exceptions can be handled within JAX-RS.

Default Response Codes

The default response codes that JAX-RS uses are pretty straightforward. There is pretty much a one-to-one relationship to the behavior described in the HTTP 1.1 Method Definition specification.[1].] Let's examine what the response codes would be for both success and error conditions for the following JAX-RS resource class:

```
@Path("/customers")
public class CustomerResource {

    @Path("{id}")
    @GET
    @Produces("application/xml")
    public Customer getCustomer(@PathParam("id") int id) {...}

    @POST
    @Produces("application/xml")
    @Consumes("application/xml")
```

1. For more information, see *http://www.w3.org/Protocols/rfc2616/rfc2616-sec9.html*

```
    public Customer create(Customer newCust) {...}

    @PUT
    @Path("{id}")
    @Consumes("application/xml")
    public void update(@PathParam("id") int id, Customer cust) {...}

    @Path("{id}")
    @DELETE
    public void delete(@PathParam("id") int id) {...}
}
```

Successful Responses

Successful HTTP response code numbers range from 200 to 399. For the create() and getCustomer() methods of our CustomerResource class, they will return a response code of 200, "OK," if the Customer object they are returning is not null. If the return value is null, a successful response code of 204, "No Content," is returned. The 204 response is not an error condition. It just tells the client that everything went OK, but that there is no message body to look for in the response. If the JAX-RS resource method's return type is void, a response code of 204, "No Content," is returned. This is the case with our update() and delete() methods.

The HTTP specification is pretty consistent for the PUT, POST, GET, and DELETE methods. If a successful HTTP response contains a message body, 200, "OK," is the response code. If the response doesn't contain a message body, 204, "No Content," must be returned.

Error Responses

In our CustomerResource example, error responses are mostly driven by application code throwing an exception. We will discuss this exception handling later in this chapter. There are some default error conditions that we can talk about right now, though.

Standard HTTP error response code numbers range from 400 to 599. In our example, if a client mistypes the request URI, for example, to customers, it will result in the server not finding a JAX-RS resource method that can service the request. In this case, a 404, "Not Found," response code will be sent back to the client.

For our getCustomer() and create() methods, if the client requests a text/html response, the JAX-RS implementation will automatically return a 406, "Not Acceptable," response code with no response body. This means that JAX-RS has a relative URI path that matches the request, but doesn't have a JAX-RS resource method that can produce the client's desired response media type. (Chapter 9 talks in detail about how clients can request certain formats from the server.)

If the client invokes an HTTP method on a valid URI to which no JAX-RS resource method is bound, the JAX-RS runtime will send an error code of 405, "Method Not Allowed." So, in our example, if our client does a PUT, GET, or DELETE on the /custom ers URI, it will get a 405 response because POST is the only supported method for that URI. The JAX-RS implementation will also return an Allow response header back to the client that contains a list of HTTP methods the URI supports. So, if our client did a GET /customers in our example, the server would send this response back:

```
HTTP/1.1 405, Method Not Allowed
Allow: POST
```

The exception to this rule is the HTTP HEAD and OPTIONS methods. If a JAX-RS resource method isn't available that can service HEAD requests for that particular URI, but there does exist a method that can handle GET, JAX-RS will invoke the JAX-RS resource method that handles GET and return the response from that minus the request body. If there is no existing method that can handle OPTIONS, the JAX-RS implementation is required to send back some meaningful, automatically generated response along with the Allow header set.

Complex Responses

Sometimes the web service you are writing can't be implemented using the default request/response behavior inherent in JAX-RS. For the cases in which you need to explicitly control the response sent back to the client, your JAX-RS resource methods can return instances of javax.ws.rs.core.Response:

```
public abstract class Response {

    public abstract Object getEntity();
    public abstract int getStatus();
    public abstract MultivaluedMap<String, Object> getMetadata();
    ...
}
```

The Response class is an abstract class that contains three simple methods. The getEn tity() method returns the Java object you want converted into an HTTP message body. The getStatus() method returns the HTTP response code. The getMetadata() method is a MultivaluedMap of response headers.

Response objects cannot be created directly; instead, they are created from jav ax.ws.rs.core.Response.ResponseBuilder instances returned by one of the static helper methods of Response:

```
public abstract class Response {
    ...
    public static ResponseBuilder status(Status status) {...}
    public static ResponseBuilder status(int status) {...}
```

```
    public static ResponseBuilder ok() {...}
    public static ResponseBuilder ok(Object entity) {...}
    public static ResponseBuilder ok(Object entity, MediaType type) {...}
    public static ResponseBuilder ok(Object entity, String type) {...}
    public static ResponseBuilder ok(Object entity, Variant var) {...}
    public static ResponseBuilder serverError() {...}
    public static ResponseBuilder created(URI location) {...}
    public static ResponseBuilder noContent() {...}
    public static ResponseBuilder notModified() {...}
    public static ResponseBuilder notModified(EntityTag tag) {...}
    public static ResponseBuilder notModified(String tag) {...}
    public static ResponseBuilder seeOther(URI location) {...}
    public static ResponseBuilder temporaryRedirect(URI location) {...}
    public static ResponseBuilder notAcceptable(List<Variant> variants) {...}
    public static ResponseBuilder fromResponse(Response response) {...}
  ...
}
```

If you want an explanation of each and every static helper method, the JAX-RS Javadocs are a great place to look. They generally center on the most common use cases for creating custom responses. For example:

```
public static ResponseBuilder ok(Object entity, MediaType type) {...}
```

The ok() method here takes the Java object you want converted into an HTTP response and the Content-Type of that response. It returns a preinitialized ResponseBuilder with a status code of 200, "OK." The other helper methods work in a similar way, setting appropriate response codes and sometimes setting up response headers automatically.

The ResponseBuilder class is a factory that is used to create one individual Response instance. You store up state you want to use to create your response and when you're finished, you have the builder instantiate the Response:

```
public static abstract class ResponseBuilder {

    public abstract Response build();
    public abstract ResponseBuilder clone();

    public abstract ResponseBuilder status(int status);
    public ResponseBuilder status(Status status) {...}

    public abstract ResponseBuilder entity(Object entity);
    public abstract ResponseBuilder type(MediaType type);
    public abstract ResponseBuilder type(String type);

    public abstract ResponseBuilder variant(Variant variant);
    public abstract ResponseBuilder variants(List<Variant> variants);

    public abstract ResponseBuilder language(String language);
    public abstract ResponseBuilder language(Locale language);

    public abstract ResponseBuilder location(URI location);
```

```
    public abstract ResponseBuilder contentLocation(URI location);

    public abstract ResponseBuilder tag(EntityTag tag);
    public abstract ResponseBuilder tag(String tag);

    public abstract ResponseBuilder lastModified(Date lastModified);
    public abstract ResponseBuilder cacheControl(CacheControl cacheControl);

    public abstract ResponseBuilder expires(Date expires);
    public abstract ResponseBuilder header(String name, Object value);

    public abstract ResponseBuilder cookie(NewCookie... cookies);
}
```

As you can see, `ResponseBuilder` has a lot of helper methods for initializing various response headers. I don't want to bore you with all the details, so check out the JAX-RS Javadocs for an explanation of each one. I'll be giving examples using many of them throughout the rest of this book.

Now that we have a rough idea about creating custom responses, let's look at an example of a JAX-RS resource method setting some specific response headers:

```
@Path("/textbook")
public class TextBookService {

    @GET
    @Path("/restfuljava")
    @Produces("text/plain")
    public Response getBook() {

        String book = ...;
        ResponseBuilder builder = Response.ok(book);
        builder.language("fr")
               .header("Some-Header", "some value");

        return builder.build();
    }
}
```

Here, our `getBook()` method is returning a plain-text string that represents a book our client is interested in. We initialize the response body using the `Response.ok()` method. The status code of the `ResponseBuilder` is automatically initialized with 200. Using the `ResponseBuilder.language()` method, we then set the `Content-Language` header to French. We then use the `ResponseBuilder.header()` method to set a custom response header. Finally, we create and return the `Response` object using the `ResponseBuild er.build()` method.

One interesting thing to note about this code is that we never set the `Content-Type` of the response. Because we have already specified an `@Produces` annotation, the JAX-RS runtime will set the media type of the response for us.

Returning Cookies

JAX-RS also provides a simple class to represent new cookie values. This class is javax.ws.rs.core.NewCookie:

```
public class NewCookie extends Cookie {

    public static final int DEFAULT_MAX_AGE = -1;

    public NewCookie(String name, String value) {}

    public NewCookie(String name, String value, String path,
                     String domain, String comment,
                       int maxAge, boolean secure) {}

    public NewCookie(String name, String value, String path,
                     String domain, int version, String comment,
                       int maxAge, boolean secure) {}

    public NewCookie(Cookie cookie) {}

    public NewCookie(Cookie cookie, String comment,
                     int maxAge, boolean secure) {}

    public static NewCookie valueOf(String value)
                     throws IllegalArgumentException {}

    public String getComment() {}
    public int getMaxAge() {}
    public boolean isSecure() {}
    public Cookie toCookie() {}
}
```

The NewCookie class extends the Cookie class discussed in Chapter 5. To set response cookies, create instances of NewCookie and pass them to the method ResponseBuild er.cookie(). For example:

```
@Path("/myservice")
public class MyService {

    @GET
    public Response get() {

        NewCookie cookie = new NewCookie("key", "value");
        ResponseBuilder builder = Response.ok("hello", "text/plain");
        return builder.cookie(cookie).build();
    }
}
```

Here, we're just setting a cookie named key to the value value.

The Status Enum

Generally, developers like to have constant variables represent raw strings or numeric values within. For instance, instead of using a numeric constant to set a `Response` status code, you may want a static final variable to represent a specific code. The JAX-RS specification provides a Java enum called `javax.ws.rs.core.Response.Status` for this very purpose:

```
public enum Status {
    OK(200, "OK"),
    CREATED(201, "Created"),
    ACCEPTED(202, "Accepted"),
    NO_CONTENT(204, "No Content"),
    MOVED_PERMANENTLY(301, "Moved Permanently"),
    SEE_OTHER(303, "See Other"),
    NOT_MODIFIED(304, "Not Modified"),
    TEMPORARY_REDIRECT(307, "Temporary Redirect"),
    BAD_REQUEST(400, "Bad Request"),
    UNAUTHORIZED(401, "Unauthorized"),
    FORBIDDEN(403, "Forbidden"),
    NOT_FOUND(404, "Not Found"),
    NOT_ACCEPTABLE(406, "Not Acceptable"),
    CONFLICT(409, "Conflict"),
    GONE(410, "Gone"),
    PRECONDITION_FAILED(412, "Precondition Failed"),
    UNSUPPORTED_MEDIA_TYPE(415, "Unsupported Media Type"),
    INTERNAL_SERVER_ERROR(500, "Internal Server Error"),
    SERVICE_UNAVAILABLE(503, "Service Unavailable");

    public enum Family {
        INFORMATIONAL, SUCCESSFUL, REDIRECTION,
        CLIENT_ERROR, SERVER_ERROR, OTHER
    }

    public Family getFamily()

    public int getStatusCode()

    public static Status fromStatusCode(final int statusCode)
}
```

Each `Status` enum value is associated with a specific family of HTTP response codes. These families are identified by the `Status.Family` Java enum. Codes in the 100 range are considered *informational*. Codes in the 200 range are considered *successful*. Codes in the 300 range are success codes, but fall under the *redirection* category. Error codes are in the 400 to 500 ranges. The 400s are *client errors* and 500s are *server errors*.

Both the `Response.status()` and `ResponseBuilder.status()` methods can accept a `Status` enum value. For example:

```
@DELETE
Response delete() {
    ...

    return Response.status(Status.GONE).build();
}
```

Here, we're telling the client that the thing we want to delete is already gone (410).

javax.ws.rs.core.GenericEntity

When we're dealing with returning `Response` objects, we do have a problem with `Mes sageBodyWriters` that are sensitive to generic types. For example, what if our built-in JAXB `MessageBodyWriter` can handle lists of JAXB objects? The `isWriteable()` method of our JAXB handler needs to extract parameterized type information of the generic type of the response entity. Unfortunately, there is no easy way in Java to obtain generic type information at runtime. To solve this problem, JAX-RS provides a helper class called `javax.ws.rs.core.GenericEntity`. This is best explained with an example:

```
@GET
@Produces("application/xml")
public Response getCustomerList() {
    List<Customer> list = new ArrayList<Customer>();
    list.add(new Customer(...));

    GenericEntity entity = new GenericEntity<List<Customer>>(list){};
    return Response.ok(entity).build();
}
```

The `GenericEntity` class is a Java generic template. What you do here is create an anonymous class that extends `GenericEntity`, initializing the `GenericEntity`'s template with the generic type you're using. If this looks a bit magical, it is. The creators of Java generics made things a bit difficult, so we're stuck with this solution.

Exception Handling

Errors can be reported to a client either by creating and returning the appropriate `Response` object or by throwing an exception. Application code is allowed to throw any checked (classes extending `java.lang.Exception`) or unchecked (classes extending `java.lang.RuntimeException`) exceptions they want. Thrown exceptions are handled by the JAX-RS runtime if you have registered an exception mapper. Exception mappers can convert an exception to an HTTP response. If the thrown exception is not handled by a mapper, it is propagated and handled by the container (i.e., servlet) JAX-RS is running within. JAX-RS also provides the `javax.ws.rs.WebApplicationException`. This can be thrown by application code and automatically processed by JAX-RS without

having to write an explicit mapper. Let's look at how to use the WebApplicationExcep
tion first. We'll then examine how to write your own specific exception mappers.

javax.ws.rs.WebApplicationException

JAX-RS has a built-in unchecked exception that applications can throw. This exception
is preinitialized with either a Response or a particular status code:

```
public class WebApplicationException extends RuntimeException {

    public WebApplicationException() {...}
    public WebApplicationException(Response response) {...}
    public WebApplicationException(int status) {...}
    public WebApplicationException(Response.Status status) {...}
    public WebApplicationException(Throwable cause) {...}
    public WebApplicationException(Throwable cause,
                                   Response response) {...}
    public WebApplicationException(Throwable cause, int status) {...}
    public WebApplicationException(Throwable cause,
                                   Response.Status status) {...}

    public Response getResponse() {...]
}
```

When JAX-RS sees that a WebApplicationException has been thrown by application
code, it catches the exception and calls its getResponse() method to obtain a Response
to send back to the client. If the application has initialized the WebApplicationExcep
tion with a status code or Response object, that code or Response will be used to create
the actual HTTP response. Otherwise, the WebApplicationException will return a status code of 500, "Internal Server Error," to the client.

For example, let's say we have a web service that allows clients to query for customers
represented in XML:

```
@Path("/customers")
public class CustomerResource {

    @GET
    @Path("{id}")
    @Produces("application/xml")
    public Customer getCustomer(@PathParam("id") int id) {

        Customer cust = findCustomer(id);
        if (cust == null) {
          throw new WebApplicationException(Response.Status.NOT_FOUND);
        }
        return cust;
    }
}
```

In this example, if we do not find a `Customer` instance with the given ID, we throw a `WebApplicationException` that causes a 404, "Not Found," status code to be sent back to the client.

Exception Mapping

Many applications have to deal with a multitude of exceptions thrown from application code and third-party frameworks. Relying on the underlying servlet container to handle the exception doesn't give us much flexibility. Catching and then wrapping all these exceptions within `WebApplicationException` would become quite tedious. Alternatively, you can implement and register instances of `javax.ws.rs.ext.ExceptionMapper`. These objects know how to map a thrown application exception to a `Response` object:

```
public interface ExceptionMapper<E extends Throwable> {
{
    Response toResponse(E exception);
}
```

For example, one exception that is commonly thrown in Java Persistence API (JPA)–based database applications is `javax.persistence.EntityNotFoundException`. It is thrown when JPA cannot find a particular object in the database. Instead of writing code to handle this exception explicitly, you could write an `ExceptionMapper` to handle this exception for you. Let's do that:

```
@Provider
public class EntityNotFoundMapper
        implements ExceptionMapper<EntityNotFoundException> {

    public Response toResponse(EntityNotFoundException e) {
        return Response.status(Response.Status.NOT_FOUND).build();
    }
}
```

Our `ExceptionMapper` implementation must be annotated with the `@Provider` annotation. This tells the JAX-RS runtime that it is a component. The class implementing the `ExceptionMapper` interface must provide the parameterized type of the `Exception Mapper`. JAX-RS uses this generic type information to match up thrown exceptions to `ExceptionMappers`. Finally, the `toResponse()` method receives the thrown exception and creates a `Response` object that will be used to build the HTTP response.

JAX-RS supports exception inheritance as well. When an exception is thrown, JAX-RS will first try to find an `ExceptionMapper` for that exception's type. If it cannot find one, it will look for a mapper that can handle the exception's superclass. It will continue this process until there are no more superclasses to match against.

Finally, ExceptionMappers are registered with the JAX-RS runtime using the deployment APIs discussed in Chapter 14.

Exception Hierarchy

JAX-RS 2.0 has added a nice exception hierarchy for various HTTP error conditions. So, instead of creating an instance of WebApplicationException and initializing it with a specific status code, you can use one of these exceptions instead. We can change our previous example to use javax.ws.rs.NotFoundException:

```
@Path("/customers")
public class CustomerResource {

    @GET
    @Path("{id}")
    @Produces("application/xml")
    public Customer getCustomer(@PathParam("id") int id) {

        Customer cust = findCustomer(id);
        if (cust == null) {
          throw new NotFoundException());
        }
        return cust;
    }
}
```

Like the other exceptions in the exception hierarchy, NotFoundException inherits from WebApplicationException. If you looked at the code, you'd see that in its constructor it is initializing the status code to be 404. Table 7-1 lists some other exceptions you can use for error conditions that are under the javax.ws.rs package.

Table 7-1. JAX-RS exception hierarchy

Exception	Status code	Description
BadRequestException	400	Malformed message
NotAuthorizedException	401	Authentication failure
ForbiddenException	403	Not permitted to access
NotFoundException	404	Couldn't find resource
NotAllowedException	405	HTTP method not supported
NotAcceptableException	406	Client media type requested not supported
NotSupportedException	415	Client posted media type not supported
InternalServerErrorException	500	General server error
ServiceUnavailableException	503	Server is temporarily unavailable or busy

BadRequestException is used when the client sends something to the server that the server cannot interpret. The JAX-RS runtime will actually throw this exception in certain scenarios. The most obvious is when a PUT or POST request has submitted malformed XML or JSON that the `MessageBodyReader` fails to parse. JAX-RS will also throw this exception if it fails to convert a header or cookie value to the desired type. For example:

```
@HeaderParam("Custom-Header") int header;
@CookieParam("myCookie") int cookie;
```

If the HTTP request's `Custom-Header` value or the `myCookie` value cannot be parsed into an integer, `BadRequestException` is thrown.

`NotAuthorizedException` is used when you want to write your own authentication protocols. The 401 HTTP response code this exception represents requires you to send back a challenge header called `WWW-Authenticate`. This header is used to tell the client how it should authenticate with the server. `NotAuthorizedException` has a few convenience constructors that make it easier to build this header automatically:

```
public NotAuthorizedException(Object challenge, Object... moreChallenges) {}
```

For example, if I wanted to tell the client that OAuth Bearer tokens are required for authentication, I would throw this exception:

```
throw new NotAuthorizedException("Bearer");
```

The client would receive this HTTP response:

```
HTTP/1.1 401 Not Authorized
WWW-Authenticate: Bearer
```

`ForbiddenException` is generally used when the client making the invocation does not have permission to access the resource it is invoking on. In Java EE land, this is usually because the authenticated client does not have the specific role mapping required.

`NotFoundException` is used when you want to tell the client that the resource it is requesting does not exist. There are also some error conditions where the JAX-RS runtime will throw this exception automatically. If the JAX-RS runtime fails to inject into an `@PathParam`, `@QueryParam`, or `@MatrixParam`, it will throw this exception. Like in the conditions discussed for `BadRequestException`, this can happen if you are trying to convert to a type the parameter value isn't meant for.

`NotAllowedException` is used when the HTTP method the client is trying to invoke isn't supported by the resource the client is accessing. The JAX-RS runtime will automatically throw this exception if there isn't a JAX-RS method that matches the invoked HTTP method.

`NotAcceptableException` is used when the client is requesting a specific format through the `Accept` header. The JAX-RS runtime will automatically throw this exception if there is not a JAX-RS method with an `@Produces` annotation that is compatible with the client's `Accept` header.

`NotSupportedException` is used when a client is posting a representation that the server does not understand. The JAX-RS runtime will automatically throw this exception if there is no JAX-RS method with an `@Consumes` annotation that matches the `Content-Type` of the posted entity.

`InternalServerErrorException` is a general-purpose error that is thrown by the server. For applications, you would throw this exception if you've reached an error condition that doesn't really fit with the other HTTP error codes. The JAX-RS runtime throws this exception if a `MessageBodyWriter` fails or if there is an exception thrown from an `ExceptionMapper`.

`ServiceUnavailableException` is used when the server is temporarily unavailable or busy. In most cases, it is OK for the client to retry the request at a later time. The HTTP 503 status code is often sent with a `Retry-After` header. This header is a suggestion to the client when it might be OK to retry the request. Its value is in seconds or a formatted date string. `ServiceUnavailableException` has a few convenience constructors to help with initializing this header:

```
public ServiceUnavailableException(Long retryAfter) {}
public ServiceUnavailableException(Date retryAfter) {}
```

Mapping default exceptions

What's interesting about the default error handling for JAX-RS is that you can write an `ExceptionMapper` for these scenarios. For example, if you want to send back a different response to the client when JAX-RS cannot find an `@Produces` match for an `Accept` header, you can write an `ExceptionMapper` for `NotAcceptableException`. This gives you complete control on how errors are handled by your application.

Wrapping Up

In this chapter, you learned that JAX-RS has default response codes for both success and error conditions. For more complex responses, your JAX-RS resource methods can return `javax.ws.rs.core.Response` objects. JAX-RS has a few exception utilities. You can throw instances of `javax.ws.rs.WebApplicationException` or let the underlying servlet container handle the exception. Or, you can write an `ExceptionMapper` that can map a particular exception to an HTTP response. Chapter 22 walks you through some sample code that you can use to test-drive many of the concepts and APIs introduced in this chapter.

CHAPTER 8

JAX-RS Client API

One huge gaping hole in the first version of the JAX-RS specification was the lack of a client API. You could slog through the very difficult-to-use `java.net.URL` set of classes to invoke on remote RESTful services. Or you could use something like Apache HTTP Client, which is not JAX-RS aware, so you would have to do marshalling and unmarshalling of Java objects manually. Finally, you could opt to use one of the proprietary client APIs of one of the many JAX-RS implementations out there. This would, of course, lock you into that vendor's implementation. JAX-RS 2.0 fixed this problem by introducing a new HTTP client API.

Client Introduction

Before I dive into the Client API, let's look at a simple code example that illustrates the basics of the API:

```
Client client = ClientBuilder.newClient();

WebTarget target = client.target("http://commerce.com/customers");

Response response = target.post(Entity.xml(new Customer("Bill", "Burke")));
response.close();

Customer customer = target.queryParam("name", "Bill Burke")
                          .request()
                          .get(Customer.class);
client.close();
```

This example invokes GET and POST requests on a target URL to create and view a Customer object that is represented by XML over the wire. Let's now pull this code apart and examine each of its components in detail.

Bootstrapping with ClientBuilder

The `javax.ws.rs.client.Client` interface is the main entry point into the JAX-RS Client API. `Client` instances manage client socket connections and are pretty heavyweight. Instances of this interface should be reused wherever possible, as it can be quite expensive to create and destroy these objects. `Client` objects are created with the `ClientBuilder` class:

```java
package javax.ws.rs.client;

import java.net.URL;
import java.security.KeyStore;

import javax.ws.rs.core.Configurable;
import javax.ws.rs.core.Configuration;

import javax.net.ssl.HostnameVerifier;
import javax.net.ssl.SSLContext;

public abstract class ClientBuilder implements Configurable<ClientBuilder> {

    public static Client newClient() {...}
    public static Client newClient(final Configuration configuration) {...}

    public static ClientBuilder newBuilder() {...}

    public abstract ClientBuilder sslContext(final SSLContext sslContext);
    public abstract ClientBuilder keyStore(final KeyStore keyStore,
                                      final char[] password);
    public ClientBuilder keyStore(final KeyStore keyStore,
                                      final String password) {}
    public abstract ClientBuilder trustStore(final KeyStore trustStore);
    public abstract ClientBuilder
                        hostnameVerifier(final HostnameVerifier verifier);

    public abstract Client build();
}
```

The easiest way to create a `Client` is to call `ClientBuilder.newClient()`. It instantiates a preinitialized `Client` that you can use right away. To fine-tune the construction of your `Client` interfaces, the `newBuilder()` method creates a `ClientBuilder` instance that allows you to register components and set configuration properties. It inherits these capabilities by implementing the `Configurable` interface:

```java
package javax.ws.rs.core;

public interface Configurable<C extends Configurable> {
    public C property(String name, Object value);

    public C register(Class<?> componentClass);
```

```
    public C register(Object component);

    ...

}
```

The `ClientBuilder` class also has methods to configure SSL. We'll cover this in detail in Chapter 15. Let's take a look at using `ClientBuilder`:

```
Client client = ClientBuilder.newBuilder()
                        .property("connection.timeout", 100)
                        .sslContext(sslContext)
                        .register(JacksonJsonProvider.class)
                        .build();
```

We create a `ClientBuilder` instance by calling the static method `ClientBuilder.new Builder()`. We then set a proprietary, JAX-RS implementation–specific configuration property that controls socket connection timeouts. Next we specify the `sslContext` we want to use to manage HTTPS connections. The RESTful services we're going to interact with are primarily JSON, so we `register()` an `@Provider` that knows how to marshal Java objects to and from JSON. Finally, we call `build()` to create the `Client` instance.

 Always remember to `close()` your `Client` objects. `Client` objects often pool connections for performance reasons. If you do not close them, you are leaking valuable system resources. While most JAX-RS implementations implement a `finalize()` method for `Client`, it is not a good idea to rely on the garbage collector to clean up poorly written code.

Client and WebTarget

Now that we have a `Client`, there's a bunch of stuff we can do with this object. Like `ClientBuilder`, the `Client` interface implements `Configurable`. This allows you to change configuration and register components for the `Client` on the fly as your application executes. The most important purpose of `Client`, though, is to create `WebTar get` instances:

```
package javax.ws.rs.client.Client;

public interface Client extends Configurable<Client> {

    public void close();

    public WebTarget target(String uri);
    public WebTarget target(URI uri);
    public WebTarget target(UriBuilder uriBuilder);
    public WebTarget target(Link link);
```

```
    ...
}
```

The WebTarget interface represents a specific URI you want to invoke on. Through the Client interface, you can create a WebTarget using one of the target() methods:

```
package javax.ws.rs.client.Client;

public interface WebTarget extends Configurable<WebTarget> {
    public URI getUri();
    public UriBuilder getUriBuilder();

    public WebTarget path(String path);
    public WebTarget resolveTemplate(String name, Object value);
    public WebTarget resolveTemplate(String name, Object value,
                                     boolean encodeSlashInPath);
    public WebTarget resolveTemplateFromEncoded(String name, Object value);
    public WebTarget resolveTemplates(Map<String, Object> templateValues);
    public WebTarget resolveTemplates(Map<String, Object> templateValues,
                                      boolean encodeSlashInPath);
    public WebTarget resolveTemplatesFromEncoded(
                                      Map<String, Object> templateValues);
    public WebTarget matrixParam(String name, Object... values);
    public WebTarget queryParam(String name, Object... values);

    ...
}
```

WebTarget has additional methods to extend the URI you originally constructed it with. You can add path segments or query parameters by invoking path() and queryParam(). If the WebTarget represents a URI template, the resolveTemplate() methods can fill in those variables:

```
WebTarget target = client.target("http://commerce.com/customers/{id}")
                         .resolveTemplate("id", "123")
                         .queryParam("verbose", true);
```

In this example, we initialized a WebTarget with a URI template string. The resolveTemplate() method fills in the id expression, and we add another query parameter. If you take a look at the UriBuilder class, you'll see that WebTarget pretty much mirrors it. Instead of building URIs, though, WebTarget is building instances of WebTargets that you can use to invoke HTTP requests.

Building and Invoking Requests

Once you have a WebTarget that represents the exact URI you want to invoke on, you can begin building and invoking HTTP requests through one of its request() methods:

```
public interface WebTarget extends Configurable<WebTarget> {
    ...
```

```
    public Invocation.Builder request();
    public Invocation.Builder request(String... acceptedResponseTypes);
    public Invocation.Builder request(MediaType... acceptedResponseTypes);
}
```

The `Invocation.Builder` interface hierarchy is a bit convoluted, so I'll explain how to build requests using examples and code fragments:

```
package javax.ws.rs.client;

public interface Invocation {
...
    public interface Builder extends SyncInvoker, Configurable<Builder> {
        ...
        public Builder accept(String... types);
        public Builder accept(MediaType... types
        public Builder acceptLanguage(Locale... locales);
        public Builder acceptLanguage(String... locales);
        public Builder acceptEncoding(String... encodings);
        public Builder cookie(Cookie cookie);
        public Builder cookie(String name, String value);
        public Builder cacheControl(CacheControl cacheControl);
        public Builder header(String name, Object value);
        public Builder headers(MultivaluedMap<String, Object> headers);
    }
}
```

`Invocation.Builder` has a bunch of methods that allow you to set different types of request headers. The various `acceptXXX()` methods are for content negotiation (see Chapter 9). The `cookie()` methods allow you to set HTTP cookies you want to return to the server. And then there are the more generic `header()` and `headers()` methods that cover the more esoteric HTTP headers and any custom ones your application might have.

After setting the headers the request requires, you can then invoke a specific HTTP method to get back a response from the server. GET requests have two flavors:

```
    <T> T get(Class<T> responseType);
    <T> T get(GenericType<T> responseType);

    Response get();
```

The first two generic `get()` methods will convert successful HTTP requests to specific Java types. Let's look at these in action:

```
Customer customer = client.target("http://commerce.com/customers/123")
                        .request().accept("application/json")
                        .get(Customer.class);

List<Customer> customer = client.target("http://commerce.com/customers")
```

```
                        .request().accept("application/xml")
                        .get(new GenericType<List<Customer>>() {});
```

In the first request we want JSON from the server, so we set the Accept header with the accept() method. We want the JAX-RS client to grab this JSON from the server and convert it to a Customer Java type using one of the registered MessageBodyReader components.

The second request is a little more complicated. We have a special MessageBodyRead er that knows how to convert XML into List<Customer>. The reader is very sensitive to the generic type of the Java object, so it uses the javax.ws.rs.core.GenericType class to obtain information about the type. GenericType is a sneaky trick that bypasses Java type erasure to obtain generic type information at runtime. To use it, you create an anonymous inner class that implements GenericType and fill in the Java generic type you want to pass information about to the template parameter. I know this is a little weird, but there's no other way around the Java type system.

 WebTarget has additional request() methods whose parameters take one or more String or MediaType parameters. These parameters are media types you want to include in an Accept header. I think it makes the code more readable if you use the Invocation.Builder.ac cept() method instead. But this generally is a matter of personal preference.

There's also a get() method that returns a Response object. This is the same Re sponse class that is used on the server side. This gives you more fine-grained control of the HTTP response on the client side. Here's an example:

```
import javax.ws.rs.core.Response;

Response response = client.target("http://commerce.com/customers/123")
                          .accept("application/json")
                          .get();
try {
   if (response.getStatus() == 200) {
      Customer customer = response.readEntity(Customer.class);
   }
} finally {
   response.close();
}
```

In this example, we invoke an HTTP GET to obtain a Response object. We check that the status is OK and if so, extract a Customer object from the returned JSON document by invoking Response.readEntity(). The readEntity() method matches up the re quested Java type and the response content with an appropriate MessageBodyReader.

This method can be invoked only once unless you buffer the response with the `buffer Entity()` method. For example:

```
Response response = client.target("http://commerce.com/customers/123")
                          .accept("application/json")
                          .get();
try {
   if (response.getStatus() == 200) {
      response.bufferEntity();
      Customer customer = response.readEntity(Customer.class);
      Map rawJson = response.readEntity(Map.class);
   }
} finally {
   response.close();
}
```

In this example, the call to `bufferEntity()` allows us to extract the HTTP response content into different Java types, the first type being a `Customer` and the second a `java.util.Map` that represents raw JSON data. If we didn't buffer the entity, the second `readEntity()` call would result in an `IllegalStateException`.

 Always remember to `close()` your `Response` objects. `Response` objects reference open socket streams. If you do not close them, you are leaking system resources. While most JAX-RS implementations implement a `finalize()` method for `Response`, it is not a good idea to rely on the garbage collector to clean up poorly written code. The default behavior of the RESTEasy JAX-RS implementation actually only lets you have one open `Response` per `Client` instance. This forces you to write responsible client code.

So far we haven't discussed PUT and POST requests that submit a representation to the server. These types of requests have similar method styles to GET but also specify an entity parameter:

```
<T> T put(Entity<?> entity, Class<T> responseType);
<T> T put(Entity<?> entity, GenericType<T> responseType);
<T> T post(Entity<?> entity, Class<T> responseType);
<T> T post(Entity<?> entity, GenericType<T> responseType);

Response post(Entity<?> entity);
Response put(Entity<?> entity);
```

The `Entity` class encapsulates the Java object we want to send with the POST or GET request:

```
package javax.ws.rs.client;

public final class Entity<T> {
    public Variant getVariant() {}
```

```
        public MediaType getMediaType() {
        public String getEncoding() {
        public Locale getLanguage() {
        public T getEntity() {
        public Annotation[] getAnnotations() { }
    ...
}
```

The Entity class does not have a public constructor. You instead have to invoke one of the static convenience methods to instantiate one:

```
package javax.ws.rs.client;

import javax.ws.rs.core.Form;

public final class Entity<T> {
    public static <T> Entity<T> xml(final T entity) { }
    public static <T> Entity<T> json(final T entity) { }
    public static Entity<Form> form(final Form form) { }
    ...
}
```

The xml() method takes a Java object as a parameter. It sets the MediaType to applica tion/xml. The json() method acts similarly, except with JSON. The form() method deals with form parameters and application/x-www-form-urlencoded, and requires using the Form type. There's a few other helper methods, but for brevity we won't cover them here.

Let's look at two different examples that use the POST create pattern to create two different customer resources on the server. One will use JSON, while the other will use form parameters:

```
Customer customer = new Customer("Bill", "Burke");
Response response = client.target("http://commerce.com/customers")
                          .request().
                          .post(Entity.json(customer));
response.close();
```

Here we pass in an Entity instance to the post() method using the Entity.json() method. This method will automatically set the Content-Type header to application/ json.

To submit form parameters, we must use the Form class:

```
package javax.ws.rs.core;

public class Form {
    public Form() { }
    public Form(final String parameterName, final String parameterValue) { }
    public Form(final MultivaluedMap<String, String> store) { }
    public Form param(final String name, final String value) { }
```

```
        public MultivaluedMap<String, String> asMap() { }
    }
```

This class represents `application/x-www-form-urlencoded` in a request. Here's an example of it in use:

```
    Form form = new Form().param("first", "Bill")
                          .param("last", "Burke");
    response = client.target("http://commerce.com/customers")
                     .request().
                     .post(Entity.form(form));
    response.close();
```

Invocation

The previous examples are how you're going to typically interact with the Client API. JAX-RS has an additional invocation model that is slightly different. You can create full `Invocation` objects that represent the entire HTTP request without invoking it. There's a few additional methods on `Invocation.Builder` that help you do this:

```
    public interface Invocation {
    ...
        public interface Builder extends SyncInvoker, Configurable<Builder> {
            Invocation build(String method);
            Invocation build(String method, Entity<?> entity);
            Invocation buildGet();
            Invocation buildDelete();
            Invocation buildPost(Entity<?> entity);
            Invocation buildPut(Entity<?> entity);
            ...
        }
    }
```

The `buildXXX()` methods fill in the HTTP method you want to use and finish up building the request by returning an `Invocation` instance. You can then execute the HTTP request by calling one of the `invoke()` methods:

```
    package javax.ws.rs.client;

    public interface Invocation {
        public Response invoke();
        public <T> T invoke(Class<T> responseType);
        public <T> T invoke(GenericType<T> responseType);
    ...
    }
```

So what is the use of this invocation style? For one, the same `Invocation` object can be used for multiple requests. Just prebuild your `Invocation` instances and reuse them as needed. Also, since `invoke()` is a generic method, you could queue up `Invocation` instances or use them with the execute pattern. Let's see an example:

```
Invocation generateReport = client.target("http://commerce.com/orders/report")
                                  .queryParam("start", "now - 5 minutes")
                                  .queryParam("end", "now")
                                  .request()
                                  .accept("application/json")
                                  .buildGet();

while (true) {
   Report report = generateReport.invoke(Report.class);
   renderReport(report);
   Thread.sleep(300000);
}
```

The example code prebuilds a GET Invocation that will fetch a JSON report summary
of orders made in the last five minutes. We then loop every five minutes and reexecute
the invocation. Sure, this example is a little bit contrived, but I think you get the idea.

Exception Handling

One thing we didn't discuss is what happens if an error occurs when you use an invocation style that automatically unmarshalls the response. Consider this example:

```
Customer customer = client.target("http://commerce.com/customers/123")
                          .accept("application/json")
                          .get(Customer.class);
```

In this scenario, the client framework converts any HTTP error code into one of the
exception hierarchy exceptions discussed in "Exception Hierarchy" on page 109. You
can then catch these exceptions in your code to handle them appropriately:

```
try {
    Customer customer = client.target("http://commerce.com/customers/123")
                              .accept("application/json")
                              .get(Customer.class);
} catch (NotAcceptableException notAcceptable) {
   ...
} catch (NotFoundException notFound) {
   ...
}
```

If the server responds with an HTTP error code not covered by a specific JAX-RS exception, then a general-purpose exception is thrown. ClientErrorException covers
any error code in the 400s. ServerErrorException covers any error code in the 500s.

This invocation style will not automatically handle server redirects—that is, when the
server sends one of the HTTP 3xx redirection response codes. Instead, the JAX-RS
Client API throws a RedirectionException from which you can obtain the Location
URL to do the redirect yourself. For example:

```
WebTarget target = client.target("http://commerce.com/customers/123");
boolean redirected = false;
```

```
Customer customer = null;
do {
    try {
        customer = target.accept("application/json")
                         .get(Customer.class);
    } catch (RedirectionException redirect) {
        if (redirected) throw redirect;
        redirected = true;
        target = client.target(redirect.getLocation());
    }

} while (customer == null);
```

In this example, we loop if we receive a redirect from the server. The code makes sure
that we allow only one redirect by checking a flag in the catch block. We change the
WebTarget in the catch block to the Location header provided in the server's response.
You might want to massage this code a little bit to handle other error conditions, but
hopefully you get the concepts I'm trying to get across.

Configuration Scopes

If you look at the declarations of ClientBuilder, Client, WebTarget, Invocation, and
Invocation.Builder, you'll notice that they all implement the Configurable interface.
Each one of these interfaces has its own scope of properties and registered components
that it inherits from wherever it was created from. You can also override or add registered
components or properties for each one of these components. For example:

```
Client client = ClientBuilder.newBuilder()
                             .property("authentication.mode", "Basic")
                             .property("username", "bburke")
                             .property("password", "geheim")
                             .build();

WebTarget target1 = client.target("http://facebook.com");
WebTarget target2 = client.target("http://google.com")
                          .property("username", "wburke")
                          .register(JacksonJsonProvider.class);
```

If you viewed the properties of target1 you'd find the same properties as those defined
on the client instances, as WebTargets inherit their configuration from the Client or
WebTarget they were created from. The target2 variable overrides the username property and registers a provider specifically for target2. So, target2's configuration properties and registered components will be a little bit different than target1's. This way
of configuration scoping makes it much easier for you to share initialization code so
you can avoid creating a lot of extra objects you don't need and reduce the amount of
code you have to write.

Wrapping Up

In this chapter, we learned about the JAX-RS Client API. `Client` interfaces manage global configuration and the underlying socket connections you'll use to communicate with a service. `WebTarget` represents a URI that you can build and invoke HTTP requests from. If you want to see the Client API in action, check out the numerous examples in Part II. They all use the Client API in some form or another.

CHAPTER 9

HTTP Content Negotiation

Within any meaningfully sized organization or on the Internet, SOA (service-oriented architecture) applications need to be flexible enough to handle and integrate with a variety of clients and platforms. RESTful services have an advantage in this area because most programming languages can communicate with the HTTP protocol. This is not enough, though. Different clients need different formats in order to run efficiently. Java clients might like their data within an XML format. Ajax clients work a lot better with JSON. Ruby clients prefer YAML. Clients may also want internationalized data so that they can provide translated information to their English, Chinese, Japanese, Spanish, or French users. Finally, as our RESTful applications evolve, older clients need a clean way to interact with newer versions of our web services.

HTTP does have facilities to help with these types of integration problems. One of its most powerful features is a client's capability to specify to a server how it would like its responses formatted. The client can negotiate the content type of the message body, how it is encoded, and even which human language it wants the data translated into. This protocol is called HTTP Content Negotiation, or *conneg* for short. In this chapter, I'll explain how conneg works, how JAX-RS supports it, and most importantly how you can leverage this feature of HTTP within your RESTful web services.

Conneg Explained

The first part of HTTP Content Negotiation is that clients can request a specific media type they would like returned when querying a server for information. Clients set an Accept request header that is a comma-delimited list of preferred formats. For example:

```
GET http://example.com/stuff
Accept: application/xml, application/json
```

In this example request, the client is asking the server for /stuff formatted in either XML or JSON. If the server is unable to provide the desired format, it will respond with a status code of 406, "Not Acceptable." Otherwise, the server chooses one of the media types and sends a response in that format back to the client.

Wildcards and media type properties can also be used within the `Accept` header listing. For example:

```
GET http://example.com/stuff
Accept: text/*, text/html;level=1
```

The `text/*` media type means any text format.

Preference Ordering

The protocol also has both implicit and explicit rules for choosing a media type to respond with. The implicit rule is that more specific media types take precedence over less specific ones. Take this example:

```
GET http://example.com/stuff
Accept: text/*, text/html;level=1, */*, application/xml
```

The server assumes that the client always wants a concrete media type over a wildcard one, so the server would interpret the client preference as follows:

1. `text/html;level=1`
2. `application/xml`
3. `text/*`
4. `*/*`

The `text/html;level=1` type would come first because it is the most specific. The `application/xml` type would come next because it does not have any MIME type properties like `text/html;level=1` does. After this would come the wildcard types, with `text/*` coming first because it is obviously more concrete than the match-all qualifier `*/*`.

Clients can also be more specific on their preferences by using the q MIME type property. This property is a numeric value between 0.0 and 1.0, with 1.0 being the most preferred. For example:

```
GET http://example.com/stuff
Accept: text/*;q=0.9, */*;q=0.1, audio/mpeg, application/xml;q=0.5
```

If no q qualifier is given, then a value of 1.0 must be assumed. So, in our example request, the preference order is as follows:

1. `audio/mpeg`
2. `text/*`

3. application/xml

4. */*

The audio/mpeg type is chosen first because it has an implicit qualifier of 1.0. Text types come next, as text/* has a qualifier of 0.9. Even though application/xml is more specific, it has a lower preference value than text/*, so it follows in the third spot. If none of those types matches the formats the server can offer, anything can be passed back to the client.

Language Negotiation

HTTP Content Negotiation also has a simple protocol for negotiating the desired human language of the data sent back to the client. Clients use the Accept-Language header to specify which human language they would like to receive. For example:

```
GET http://example.com/stuff
Accept-Language: en-us, es, fr
```

Here, the client is asking for a response in English, Spanish, or French. The Accept-Language header uses a coded format. Two digits represent a language identified by the ISO-639 standard.[1] You can further specialize the code by following the two-character language code with an ISO-3166 two-character country code.[2] In the previous example, en-us represents US English.

The Accept-Language header also supports preference qualifiers:

```
GET http://example.com/stuff
Accept-Language: fr;q=1.0, es;q=1.0, en=0.1
```

Here, the client prefers French or Spanish, but would accept English as the default translation.

Clients and servers use the Content-Language header to specify the human language for message body translation.

Encoding Negotiation

Clients can also negotiate the encoding of a message body. To save on network bandwidth, encodings are generally used to compress messages before they are sent. The most common algorithm for encoding is GZIP compression. Clients use the Accept-Encoding header to specify which encodings they support. For example:

---

1. For more information, see the w3 website (*http://www.w3.org/wai/er/ig/ert/iso639.htm*).

2. For more information, see the ISO website (*http://bit.ly/17iOukB*).

```
GET http://example.com/stuff
Accept-Encoding: gzip, deflate
```

Here, the client is saying that it wants its response either compressed using GZIP or uncompressed (`deflate`).

The `Accept-Encoding` header also supports preference qualifiers:

```
GET http://example.com/stuff
Accept-Encoding: gzip;q=1.0, compress;0.5; deflate;q=0.1
```

Here, `gzip` is desired first, then `compress`, followed by `deflate`. In practice, clients use the `Accept-Encoding` header to tell the server which encoding formats they support, and they really don't care which one the server uses.

When a client or server encodes a message body, it must set the `Content-Encoding` header. This tells the receiver which encoding was used.

JAX-RS and Conneg

The JAX-RS specification has a few facilities that help you manage conneg. It does method dispatching based on `Accept` header values. It allows you to view this content information directly. It also has complex negotiation APIs that allow you to deal with multiple decision points. Let's look into each of these.

Method Dispatching

In previous chapters, we saw how the `@Produces` annotation denotes which media type a JAX-RS method should respond with. JAX-RS also uses this information to dispatch requests to the appropriate Java method. It matches the preferred media types listed in the `Accept` header of the incoming request to the metadata specified in `@Produces` annotations. Let's look at a simple example:

```
@Path("/customers")
public class CustomerResource {

    @GET
    @Path("{id}")
    @Produces("application/xml")
    public Customer getCustomerXml(@PathParam("id") int id) {...}

    @GET
    @Path("{id}")
    @Produces("text/plain")
    public String getCustomerText(@PathParam("id") int id) {...}

    @GET
    @Path("{id}")
    @Produces("application/json")
```

```
        public Customer getCustomerJson(@PathParam("id") int id) {...}
}
```

Here, we have three methods that all service the same URI but produce different data formats. JAX-RS can pick one of these methods based on what is in the Accept header. For example, let's say a client made this request:

```
GET http://example.com/customers/1
Accept: application/json;q=1.0, application/xml;q=0.5
```

The JAX-RS provider would dispatch this request to the getCustomerJson() method.

Leveraging Conneg with JAXB

In Chapter 6, I showed you how to use JAXB annotations to map Java objects to and from XML and JSON. If you leverage JAX-RS integration with conneg, you can implement one Java method that can service both formats. This can save you from writing a whole lot of boilerplate code:

```
@Path("/service")
public class MyService {

    @GET
    @Produces({"application/xml", "application/json"})
    public Customer getCustomer(@PathParam("id") int id) {...}
}
```

In this example, our getCustomer() method produces either XML or JSON, as denoted by the @Produces annotation applied to it. The returned object is an instance of a Java class, Customer, which is annotated with JAXB annotations. Since most JAX-RS implementations support using JAXB to convert to XML or JSON, the information contained within our Accept header can pick which MessageBodyWriter to use to marshal the returned Java object.

Complex Negotiation

Sometimes simple matching of the Accept header with a JAX-RS method's @Produces annotation is not enough. Different JAX-RS methods that service the same URI may be able to deal with different sets of media types, languages, and encodings. Unfortunately, JAX-RS does not have the notion of either an @ProduceLanguages or @ProduceEncodings annotation. Instead, you must code this yourself by looking at header values directly or by using the JAX-RS API for managing complex conneg. Let's look at both.

Viewing Accept headers

In Chapter 5, you were introduced to javax.ws.rs.core.HttpHeaders, the JAX-RS utility interface. This interface contains some preprocessed conneg information about the incoming HTTP request:

```
public interface HttpHeaders {

    public List<MediaType> getAcceptableMediaTypes();

    public List<Locale> getAcceptableLanguages();
    ...
}
```

The getAcceptableMediaTypes() method contains a list of media types defined in the HTTP request's Accept header. It is preparsed and represented as a javax.ws.rs.core.MediaType. The returned list is also sorted based on the "q" values (explicit or implicit) of the preferred media types, with the most desired listed first.

The getAcceptableLanguages() method processes the HTTP request's Accept-Language header. It is preparsed and represented as a list of java.util.Locale objects. As with getAcceptableMediaTypes(), the returned list is sorted based on the "q" values of the preferred languages, with the most desired listed first.

You inject a reference to HttpHeaders using the @javax.ws.rs.core.Context annotation. Here's how your code might look:

```
@Path("/myservice")
public class MyService {

    @GET
    public Response get(@Context HttpHeaders headers) {

        MediaType type = headers.getAcceptableMediaTypes().get(0);
        Locale language = headers.getAcceptableLanguages().get(0);

        Object responseObject = ...;

        Response.ResponseBuilder builder = Response.ok(responseObject, type);
        builder.language(language);
        return builder.build();
    }
}
```

Here, we create a Response with the ResponseBuilder interface, using the desired media type and language pulled directly from the HttpHeaders injected object.

Variant processing

JAX-RS also has an API to deal with situations in which you have multiple sets of media types, languages, and encodings you have to match against. You can use the interface javax.ws.rs.core.Request and the class javax.ws.rs.core.Variant to perform these complex mappings. Let's look at the Variant class first:

```
package javax.ws.rs.core.Variant

public class Variant {

    public Variant(MediaType mediaType, Locale language, String encoding) {...}

    public Locale getLanguage() {...}

    public MediaType getMediaType() {...}

    public String getEncoding() {...}
}
```

The Variant class is a simple structure that contains one media type, one language, and one encoding. It represents a single set that your JAX-RS resource method supports. You build a list of these objects to interact with the Request interface:

```
package javax.ws.rs.core.Request

public interface Request {

    Variant selectVariant(List<Variant> variants) throws IllegalArgumentException;
    ...
}
```

The selectVariant() method takes in a list of Variant objects that your JAX-RS method supports. It examines the Accept, Accept-Language, and Accept-Encoding headers of the incoming HTTP request and compares them to the Variant list you provide to it. It picks the variant that best matches the request. More explicit instances are chosen before less explicit ones. The method will return null if none of the listed variants matches the incoming accept headers. Here's an example of using this API:

```
@Path("/myservice")
public class MyService {

    @GET
    Response getSomething(@Context Request request) {

        List<Variant> variants = new ArrayList<Variant>();
        variants.add(new Variant(
                    MediaType.APPLICATION_XML_TYPE,
                    "en", "deflate"));

        variants.add(new Variant(
                    MediaType.APPLICATION_XML_TYPE,
                    "es", "deflate"));
        variants.add(new Variant(
                    MediaType.APPLICATION_JSON_TYPE,
                    "en", "deflate"));

        variants.add(new Variant(
                    MediaType.APPLICATION_JSON_TYPE,
```

```
                        "es", "deflate"));
        variants.add(new Variant(
                        MediaType.APPLICATION_XML_TYPE,
                        "en", "gzip"));

        variants.add(new Variant(
                        MediaType.APPLICATION_XML_TYPE,
                        "es", "gzip"));
        variants.add(new Variant(
                        MediaType.APPLICATION_JSON_TYPE,
                        "en", "gzip"));

        variants.add(new Variant(
                        MediaType.APPLICATION_JSON_TYPE,
                        "es", "gzip"));

        // Pick the variant
        Variant v = request.selectVariant(variants);
        Object entity = ...; // get the object you want to return

        ResponseBuilder builder = Response.ok(entity);
        builder.type(v.getMediaType())
                .language(v.getLanguage())
                .header("Content-Encoding", v.getEncoding());

        return builder.build();
    }
```

That's a lot of code to say that the getSomething() JAX-RS method supports XML,
JSON, English, Spanish, deflated, and GZIP encodings. You're almost better off not using
the selectVariant() API and doing the selection manually. Luckily, JAX-RS offers the
javax.ws.rs.core.Variant.VariantListBuilder class to make writing these complex selections easier:

```
public static abstract class VariantListBuilder {

    public static VariantListBuilder newInstance() {...}

    public abstract VariantListBuilder mediaTypes(MediaType... mediaTypes);

    public abstract VariantListBuilder languages(Locale... languages);

    public abstract VariantListBuilder encodings(String... encodings);

    public abstract List<Variant> build();

    public abstract VariantListBuilder add();
}
```

The VariantListBuilder class allows you to add a series of media types, languages,
and encodings to it. It will then automatically create a list of variants that contains every

possible combination of these objects. Let's rewrite our previous example using a Var
iantListBuilder:

```
@Path("/myservice")
public class MyService {

    @GET
    Response getSomething(@Context Request request) {

        Variant.VariantListBuilder vb = Variant.VariantListBuilder.newInstance();
        vb.mediaTypes(MediaType.APPLICATION_XML_TYPE,
                        MediaType.APPLICATION_JSON_TYPE)
          .languages(new Locale("en"), new Locale("es"))
          .encodings("deflate", "gzip").add();

        List<Variant> variants = vb.build();

        // Pick the variant
        Variant v = request.selectVariant(variants);
        Object entity = ...; // get the object you want to return

        ResponseBuilder builder = Response.ok(entity);
        builder.type(v.getMediaType())
                .language(v.getLanguage())
                .header("Content-Encoding", v.getEncoding());

        return builder.build();
    }
```

You interact with VariantListBuilder instances by calling the mediaTypes(), lan
guages(), and encodings() methods. When you are done adding items, you invoke
the build() method and it generates a Variant list containing all the possible combinations of items you built it with.

You might have the case where you want to build two or more different combinations
of variants. The VariantListBuilder.add() method allows you to delimit and differentiate between the combinatorial sets you are trying to build. When invoked, it generates a Variant list internally based on the current set of items added to it. It also clears
its builder state so that new things added to the builder do not combine with the original
set of data. Let's look at another example:

```
Variant.VariantListBuilder vb = Variant.VariantListBuilder.newInstance();
vb.mediaTypes(MediaType.APPLICATION_XML_TYPE,
                MediaType.APPLICATION_JSON_TYPE)
  .languages(new Locale("en"), new Locale("es"))
  .encodings("deflate", "gzip")
  .add()
  .mediaTypes(MediaType.TEXT_PLAIN_TYPE)
  .languages(new Locale("en"), new Locale("es"), new Locale("fr"))
  .encodings("compress");
```

In this example, we want to add another set of variants that our JAX-RS method supports. Our JAX-RS resource method will now also support text/plain with English, Spanish, or French, but only the compress encoding. The add() method delineates between our original set and our new one.

You're not going to find a lot of use for the Request.selectVariant() API in the real world. First of all, content encodings are not something you're going to be able to easily work with in JAX-RS. If you wanted to deal with content encodings portably, you'd have to do all the streaming yourself. Most JAX-RS implementations have automatic support for encodings like GZIP anyway, and you don't have to write any code for this.

Second, most JAX-RS services pick the response media type automatically based on the @Produces annotation and Accept header. I have never seen a case in which a given language is not supported for a particular media type. In most cases, you're solely interested in the language desired by the client. You can obtain this information easily through the HttpHeaders.getAcceptableLanguages() method.

Negotiation by URI Patterns

Conneg is a powerful feature of HTTP. The problem is that some clients, specifically browsers, do not support it. For example, the Firefox browser hardcodes the Accept header it sends to the web server it connects to as follows:

```
text/html,application/xhtml+xml,application/xml;q=0.9,*/*;q=0.8
```

If you wanted to view a JSON representation of a specific URI through your browser, you would not be able to if JSON is not one of the preferred formats that your browser is hardcoded to accept.

A common pattern to support such clients is to embed conneg information within the URI instead of passing it along within an Accept header. Two examples are:

```
/customers/en-US/xml/3323
/customers/3323.xml.en-US
```

The content information is embedded within separate paths of the URI or as filename suffixes. In these examples, the client is asking for XML translated into English. You could model this within your JAX-RS resource methods by creating simple path parameter patterns within your @Path expressions. For example:

```
@Path("/customers/{id}.{type}.{language}")
@GET
public Customer getCustomer(@PathParam("id") int id,
                    @PathParam("type") String type,
                    @PathParam("language") String language) {...}
```

Before the JAX-RS specification went final, a facility revolving around the filename suffix pattern was actually defined as part of the specification. Unfortunately, the expert group could not agree on the full semantics of the feature, so it was removed. Many JAX-RS implementations still support this feature, so I think it is important to go over how it works.

The way the specification worked and the way many JAX-RS implementations now work is that you define a mapping between file suffixes, media types, and languages. An xml suffix maps to application/xml. An en suffix maps to en-US. When a request comes in, the JAX-RS implementation extracts the suffix and uses that information as the conneg data instead of any incoming Accept or Accept-Language header. Consider this JAX-RS resource class:

```
@Path("/customers")
public class CustomerResource {

    @GET
    @Produces("application/xml")
    public Customer getXml() {...}

    @GET
    @Produces("application/json")
    public Customer getJson() {...}
}
```

For this CustomerService JAX-RS resource class, if a request of GET /custom ers.json came in, the JAX-RS implementation would extract the .json suffix and remove it from the request path. It would then look in its media type mappings for a media type that matched json. In this case, let's say json mapped to application/json. It would use this information instead of the Accept header and dispatch this request to the getJson() method.

Leveraging Content Negotiation

Most of the examples so far in this chapter have used conneg simply to differentiate between well-known media types like XML and JSON. While this is very useful to help service different types of clients, it's not the main purpose of conneg. Your web services will evolve over time. New features will be added. Expanded datasets will be offered. Data formats will change and evolve. How do you manage these changes? How can you manage older clients that can only work with older versions of your services? Modeling your application design around conneg can address a lot of these issues. Let's discuss some of the design decisions you must make to leverage conneg when designing and building your applications.

Creating New Media Types

An important principle of REST is that the complexities of your resources are encapsulated within the data formats you are exchanging. While location information (URIs) and protocol methods remain fixed, data formats can evolve. This is a very important thing to remember and consider when you are planning how your web services are going to handle versioning.

Since complexity is confined to your data formats, clients can use media types to ask for different format versions. A common way to address this is to design your applications to define their own new media types. The convention is to combine a vnd prefix, the name of your new format, and a concrete media type suffix delimited by the "+" character. For example, let's say the company Red Hat had a specific XML format for its customer database. The media type name might look like this:

```
application/vnd.rht.customers+xml
```

The vnd prefix stands for vendor. The rht string in this example represents Red Hat and, of course, the customers string represents our customer database format. We end it with +xml to let users know that the format is XML based. We could do the same with JSON as well:

```
application/vnd.rht.customers+json
```

Now that we have a base media type name for the Red Hat format, we can append versioning information to it so that older clients can still ask for older versions of the format:

```
application/vnd.rht.customers+xml;version=1.0
```

Here, we've kept the subtype name intact and used media type properties to specify version information. Specifying a version property within a custom media type is a common pattern to denote versioning information. As this customer data format evolves over time, we can bump the version number to support newer clients without breaking older ones.

Flexible Schemas

Using media types to version your web services and applications is a great way to mitigate and manage change as your web services and applications evolve over time. While embedding version information within the media type is extremely useful, it shouldn't be the primary way you manage change. When defining the initial and newer versions of your data formats, you should pay special attention to backward compatibility.

Take , for instance, your initial schema should allow for extended or custom elements and attributes within each and every schema type in your data format definition. Here's the initial definition of a customer data XML schema:

```
<schema targetNamespace="http://www.example.org/customer"
        xmlns="http://www.w3.org/2001/XMLSchema">
   <element name="customer" type="customerType"/>
   <complexType name="customerType">
      <attribute name="id" use="required" type="string"/>
      <anyAttribute/>
      <element name="first" type="string" minOccurs="1"/>
      <element name="last" type="string" minOccurs="1"/>
      <any/>
   </complexType>
</schema>
```

In this example, the schema allows for adding any arbitrary attribute to the customer element. It also allows documents to contain any XML element in addition to the first and last elements. If new versions of the customer XML data format retain the initial data structure, clients that use the older version of the schema can still validate and process newer versions of the format as they receive them.

As the schema evolves, new attributes and elements can be added, but they should be made optional. For example:

```
<schema targetNamespace="http://www.example.org/customer"
        xmlns="http://www.w3.org/2001/XMLSchema">
   <element name="customer" type="customerType"/>
   <complexType name="customerType">
      <attribute name="id" use="required" type="string"/>
      <anyAttribute/>
      <element name="first" type="string" minOccurs="1"/>
      <element name="last" type="string" minOccurs="1"/>
      <element name="street" type="string" minOccurs="0"/>
      <element name="city" type="string" minOccurs="0"/>
      <element name="state" type="string" minOccurs="0"/>
      <element name="zip" type="string" minOccurs="0"/>
      <any/>
   </complexType>
</schema>
```

Here, we have added the street, city, state, and zip elements to our schema, but have made them optional. This allows older clients to still PUT and POST older, yet valid, versions of the data format.

If you combine flexible, backward-compatible schemas with media type versions, you truly have an evolvable system of data formats. Clients that are version-aware can use the media type version scheme to request specific versions of your data formats. Clients that are not version-aware can still request and send the version of the format they understand.

Wrapping Up

In this chapter, you learned how HTTP Content Negotiation works and how you can write JAX-RS-based web services that take advantage of this feature. You saw how clients can provide a list of preferences for data format, language, and encoding. You also saw that JAX-RS has implicit and explicit ways for dealing with conneg. Finally, we discussed general architectural guidelines for modeling your data formats and defining your own media types. You can test-drive the code in this chapter by flipping to Chapter 23.

CHAPTER 10

HATEOAS

The Internet is commonly referred to as "the Web" because information is connected together through a series of hyperlinks embedded within HTML documents. These links create threads between interrelated websites on the Internet. Because of this, humans can "surf" the Web for interesting tidbits of related information by clicking through these links with their browsers. Search engines can crawl these links and create huge indexes of searchable data. Without them, the Internet would never have scaled. There would have been no way to easily index information, and registering websites would have been a painful manual process.

Besides links, another key feature of the Internet is HTML . Sometimes a website wants you to fill out information to buy something or register for some service. The server is telling you, the client, what information it needs to complete an action described on the web page you are viewing. The browser renders the web page into a format that you can easily understand. You read the web page and fill out and submit the form. An HTML form is an interesting data format because it is a self-describing interaction between the client and server.

The architectural principle that describes linking and form submission is called HATEOAS. HATEOAS stands for Hypermedia As The Engine Of Application State. It is a bit of a weird name for a key architecture principle, but we're stuck with it (my editor actually thought I was making the acronym up). The idea of HATEOAS is that your data format provides extra information on how to change the state of your application. On the Web, HTML links allow you to change the state of your browser. When you're reading a web page, a link tells you which possible documents (states) you can view next. When you click a link, your browser's state changes as it visits and renders a new web page. HTML forms, on the other hand, provide a way for you to change the state of a specific resource on your server. When you buy something on the Internet through an HTML form, you are creating two new resources on the server: a credit card transaction and an order entry.

HATEOAS and Web Services

How does HATEOAS relate to web services? When you're applying HATEOAS to web services, the idea is to embed links within your XML or JSON documents. While this can be as easy as inserting a URL as the value of an element or attribute, most XML-based RESTful applications use syntax from the Atom Syndication Format as a means to implement HATEOAS.[1] From the Atom RFC:

> Atom is an XML-based document format that describes lists of related information known as "feeds." Feeds are composed of a number of items, known as "entries," each with an extensible set of attached metadata.

Think of Atom as the next evolution of RSS. It is generally used to publish blog feeds on the Internet, but a few data structures within the format are particularly useful for web services, particularly Atom links.

Atom Links

The Atom link XML type is a very simple yet standardized way of embedding links within your XML documents. Let's look at an example:

```
<customers>
   <link rel="next"
        href="http://example.com/customers?start=2&size=2"
        type="application/xml"/>
   <customer id="123">
      <name>Bill Burke</name>
   </customer>
   <customer id="332">
      <name>Roy Fielding</name>
   </customer>
</customers>
```

The Atom link is just a simple XML element with a few specific attributes.

The rel *attribute*

The rel attribute is used for link relationships. It is the logical, simple name used to reference the link. This attribute gives meaning to the URL you are linking to, much in the same way that text enclosed in an HTML <a> element gives meaning to the URL you can click in your browser.

The href *attribute*

This is the URL you can traverse in order to get new information or change the state of your application.

---

1. For more information, see the w3 website (*http://www.w3.org/2005/atom*).

The type *attribute*
This is the exchanged media type of the resource the URL points to.

The hreflang *attribute*
Although not shown in the example, this attribute represents the language the data format is translated into. Some examples are French, English, German, and Spanish.

When a client receives a document with embedded Atom links, it looks up the relationship it is interested in and invokes the URI embedded within the href link attribute.

Advantages of Using HATEOAS with Web Services

It is pretty obvious why links and forms have done so much to make the Web so prevalent. With one browser, we have a window to a wide world of information and services. Search engines crawl the Internet and index websites, so all that data is at our fingertips. This is all possible because the Web is self-describing. We get a document and we know how to retrieve additional information by following links. We know how to purchase something from Amazon because the HTML form tells us how.

Machine-based clients are a little different, though. Other than browsers, there aren't a lot of generic machine-based clients that know how to interpret self-describing documents. They can't make decisions on the fly like humans can. They require programmers to tell them how to interpret data received from a service and how to transition to other states in the interaction between client and server. So, does that make HATEOAS useless to machine-based clients? Not at all. Let's look at some of the advantages.

Location transparency

One feature that HATEOAS provides is location transparency. In a RESTful system that leverages HATEOAS, very few URIs are published to the outside world. Services and information are represented within links embedded in the data formats returned by accessing these top-level URIs. Clients need to know the logical link names to look for, but don't have to know the actual network locations of the linked services.

For those of you who have written EJBs, this isn't much different than using the Java Naming and Directory Interface (JNDI). Like a naming service, links provide a level of indirection so that underlying services can change their locations on the network without breaking client logic and code. HATEOAS has an additional advantage in that the top-level web service has control over which links are transferred.

Decoupling interaction details

Consider a request that gives us a list of customers in a customer database: GET /custom ers. If our database has thousands and thousands of entries, we do not want to return them all with one basic query. What we could do is define a view into our database using URI query parameters:

```
/customers?start={startIndex}&size={numberReturned}
```

The start query parameter identifies the starting index for our customer list. The size parameter specifies how many customers we want returned from the query.

This is all well and good, but what we've just done is increased the amount of predefined knowledge the client must have to interact with the service beyond a simple URI of /customers. Let's say in the future, the server wanted to change how view sets are queried. For instance, maybe the customer database changes rather quickly and a start index isn't enough information anymore to calculate the view. If the service changes the interface, we've broken older clients.

Instead of publishing this RESTful interface for viewing our database, what if, instead, we embedded this information within the returned document?

```xml
<customers>
    <link rel="next"
          href="http://example.com/customers?start=2&size=2"
          type="application/xml"/>
    <customer id="123">
        <name>Bill Burke</name>
    </customer>
    <customer id="332">
        <name>Roy Fielding</name>
    </customer>
</customers>
```

By embedding an Atom link within a document, we've given a logical name to a state transition. The state transition here is the next set of customers within the database. We are still requiring the client to have predefined knowledge about how to interact with the service, but the knowledge is much simpler. Instead of having to remember which URI query parameters to set, all that's needed is to follow a specific named link. The client doesn't have to do any bookkeeping of the interaction. It doesn't have to remember which section of the database it is currently viewing.

Also, this returned XML is self-contained. What if we were to hand off this document to a third party? We would have to tell the third party that it is only a partial view of the database and specify the start index. Since we now have a link, this information is all a part of the document.

By embedding an Atom link, we've decoupled a specific interaction between the client and server. We've made our web service a little more transparent and change-resistant because we've simplified the predefined knowledge the client must have to interact with the service. Finally, the server has the power to guide the client through interactions by providing links.

Reduced state transition errors

Links are not used only as a mechanism to aggregate and navigate information. They can also be used to change the state of a resource. Consider an order in an ecommerce website obtained by traversing the URI /orders/333:

```
<order id="333">
  <customer id="123">...</customer>
  <amount>$99.99</amount>
  <order-entries>
    ...
  </order-entries>
</order>
```

Let's say a customer called up and wanted to cancel her order. We could simply do an HTTP DELETE on /orders/333. This isn't always the best approach, as we usually want to retain the order for data warehousing purposes. So, instead, we might PUT a new representation of the order with a cancelled element set to true:

```
PUT /orders/333 HTTP/1.1
Content-Type: application/xml

<order id="333">
  <customer id="123">...</customer>
  <amount>$99.99</amount>
  <cancelled>true</cancelled>
  <order-entries>
    ...
  </order-entries>
</order>
```

But what happens if the order can't be cancelled? We may be at a certain state in our order process where such an action is not allowed. For example, if the order has already been shipped, it cannot be cancelled. In this case, there really isn't a good HTTP status code to send back that represents the problem. A better approach would be to embed a cancel link:

```
<order id="333">
  <customer id="123">...</customer>
  <amount>$99.99</amount>
  <cancelled>false</cancelled>
  <link rel="cancel"
        href="http://example.com/orders/333/cancelled"/>
  <order-entries>
    ...
  </order-entries>
</order>
```

The client would do a GET /orders/333 and get the XML document representing the order. If the document contains the cancel link, the client is allowed to change the order status to "cancelled" by doing an empty POST or PUT to the URI referenced in the link.

If the document doesn't contain the link, the client knows that this operation is not possible. This allows the web service to control how the client is able to interact with it in real time.

W3C standardized relationships

An interesting thing that is happening in the REST community is an effort to define, register, and standardize a common set of link relationship names and their associated behaviors.[2] Some examples are given in Table 10-1.

Table 10-1. W3C standard relationship names

Relationship	Description
previous	A URI that refers to the immediately preceding document in a series of documents.
next	A URI that refers to the immediately following document in a series of documents.
edit	A URI that can be retrieved, updated, and deleted.
payment	A URI where payment is accepted. It is meant as a general way to facilitate acts of payment.

This is not an exhaustive list, but hopefully you get the general idea where this registry is headed. Registered relationships can go a long way to help make data formats even more self-describing and intuitive to work with.

Link Headers Versus Atom Links

While Atom links have become very popular for publishing links in RESTful systems, there is an alternative. Instead of embedding a link directly in your document, you can instead use Link response headers.[3] This is best explained with an example.

Consider the order cancellation example described in the previous section. An Atom link is used to specify whether or not the cancelling of an order is allowed and which URL to use to do a POST that will cancel the order. Instead of using an Atom link embedded within the order XML document, let's use a Link header. So, if a user submits GET /orders/333, he will get back the following HTTP response:

```
HTTP/1.1 200 OK
Content-Type: application/xml
Link: <http://example.com/orders/333/cancelled>; rel=cancel

<order id="333">
  ...
</order>
```

---

2. For more information, see *http://www.iana.org/assignments/link-relations/link-relations.xhtml*.

3. For more information, see 9 Method Definitions (*http://tools.ietf.org/html/rfc5988*).

The Link header has all the same characteristics as an Atom link. The URI is enclosed within <> followed by one or more attributes delimited by semicolons. The rel attribute is required and means the same thing as the corresponding Atom attribute of the same name. This part isn't shown in the example, but you may also specify a media type via the type attribute.

Personally, I really like Link headers as an alternative to embedding Atom links. Many times, I find that my client isn't interested in the resource representation and is only interested in the link relations. You shouldn't have to parse a whole XML or JSON document just to find the URL you're interested in invoking on. Another nice thing is that instead of doing a GET invocation, you can do a HEAD invocation and avoid getting the XML document entirely. In general, I like to use Atom links for data aggregation and Link headers for everything else.

HATEOAS and JAX-RS

JAX-RS doesn't have many facilities to help with HATEOAS. HATEOAS is defined by the application, so there's not much a framework can add. What it does have, though, are helper classes that you can use to build the URIs that you link to in your data formats.

Building URIs with UriBuilder

One such helper class is javax.ws.rs.core.UriBuilder. The UriBuilder class allows you to construct a URI piece by piece and is also sensitive to template parameters:

```java
public abstract class UriBuilder {
    public static UriBuilder fromUri(URI uri)
                              throws IllegalArgumentException
    public static UriBuilder fromUri(String uri)
                              throws IllegalArgumentException
    public static UriBuilder fromPath(String path)
                              throws IllegalArgumentException
    public static UriBuilder fromResource(Class<?> resource)
                              throws IllegalArgumentException
    public static UriBuilder fromLink(Link link)
                              throws IllegalArgumentException
```

UriBuilder instances can only be instantiated from the static helper methods listed. They can be initialized by a URI, path, or the @Path annotation of a JAX-RS resource class:

```java
    public abstract UriBuilder clone();
    public abstract UriBuilder uri(URI uri)
                              throws IllegalArgumentException;
    public abstract UriBuilder scheme(String scheme)
                              throws IllegalArgumentException;
    public abstract UriBuilder schemeSpecificPart(String ssp)
                              throws IllegalArgumentException;
```

```
public abstract UriBuilder userInfo(String ui);
public abstract UriBuilder host(String host)
                            throws IllegalArgumentException;
public abstract UriBuilder port(int port)
                            throws IllegalArgumentException;
public abstract UriBuilder replacePath(String path);
public abstract UriBuilder path(String path)
                            throws IllegalArgumentException;
public abstract UriBuilder path(Class resource)
                            throws IllegalArgumentException;
public abstract UriBuilder path(Class resource, String method)
                            throws IllegalArgumentException;
public abstract UriBuilder path(Method method)
                            throws IllegalArgumentException;
public abstract UriBuilder segment(String... segments)
                            throws IllegalArgumentException;
public abstract UriBuilder replaceMatrix(String matrix)
                            throws IllegalArgumentException;
public abstract UriBuilder matrixParam(String name, Object... vals)
                            throws IllegalArgumentException;
public abstract UriBuilder replaceMatrixParam(String name,
            Object... values) throws IllegalArgumentException;
public abstract UriBuilder replaceQuery(String query)
                            throws IllegalArgumentException;
public abstract UriBuilder queryParam(String name, Object... values)
                            throws IllegalArgumentException;
public abstract UriBuilder replaceQueryParam(String name,
            Object... values) throws IllegalArgumentException;
public abstract UriBuilder fragment(String fragment);
```

These methods are used to piece together various parts of the URI. You can set the values of a specific part of a URI directly or by using the @Path annotation values declared on JAX-RS resource methods. Both string values and @Path expressions are allowed to contain template parameters:

```
public abstract URI buildFromMap(Map<String, ? extends Object> values)
        throws IllegalArgumentException, UriBuilderException;
public abstract URI buildFromEncodedMap(
            Map<String, ? extends Object> values)
        throws IllegalArgumentException, UriBuilderException;
public abstract URI build(Object... values)
        throws IllegalArgumentException, UriBuilderException;
public abstract URI buildFromEncoded(Object... values)
        throws IllegalArgumentException, UriBuilderException;
}
```

The build() methods create the actual URI. Before building the URI, though, any template parameters you have defined must be filled in. The build() methods take either a map of name/value pairs that can match up to named template parameters or you can provide a list of values that will replace template parameters as they appear in the templated URI. These values can either be encoded or decoded values, your choice. Let's look at a few examples:

```
UriBuilder builder = UriBuilder.fromPath("/customers/{id}");
builder.scheme("http")
       .host("{hostname}")
       .queryParam("param={param}");
```

In this code block, we have defined a URI pattern that looks like this:

```
http://{hostname}/customers/{id}?param={param}
```

Since we have template parameters, we need to initialize them with values passed to one of the build arguments to create the final URI. If you want to reuse this builder, you should clone() it before calling a build() method, as the template parameters will be replaced in the internal structure of the object:

```
UriBuilder clone = builder.clone();
URI uri = clone.build("example.com", "333", "value");
```

This code would create a URI that looks like this:

```
http://example.com/customers/333?param=value
```

We can also define a map that contains the template values:

```
Map<String, Object> map = new HashMap<String, Object>();
map.put("hostname", "example.com");
map.put("id", 333);
map.put("param", "value");

UriBuilder clone = builder.clone();
URI uri = clone.buildFromMap(map);
```

Another interesting example is to create a URI from the @Path expressions defined in a JAX-RS annotated class. Here's an example of a JAX-RS resource class:

```
@Path("/customers")
public class CustomerService {

    @Path("{id}")
    public Customer getCustomer(@PathParam("id") int id) {...}
}
```

We can then reference this class and the getCustomer() method within our UriBuild er initialization to define a new template:

```
UriBuilder builder = UriBuilder.fromResource(CustomerService.class);
builder.host("{hostname}")
builder.path(CustomerService.class, "getCustomer");
```

This builder code defines a URI template with a variable hostname and the patterns defined in the @Path expressions of the CustomerService class and the getCusto mer() method. The pattern would look like this in the end:

```
http://{hostname}/customers/{id}
```

You can then build a URI from this template using one of the build() methods discussed earlier.

There's also a few peculiarities with this interface. The build(Object..) and build(Map<String, ?>) methods automatically encode / characters. Take this, for example:

```
URI uri = UriBuilder.fromUri("/{id}").build("a/b");
```

This expression would result in:

```
/a%2Fb
```

Oftentimes, you may not want to encode the / character. So, two new build() methods were introduced in JAX-RS 2.0:

```
public abstract URI build(Object[] values, boolean encodeSlashInPath)
        throws IllegalArgumentException, UriBuilderException
public abstract URI buildFromMap(Map<String, ?> values, boolean encodeSlashInPath)
        throws IllegalArgumentException, UriBuilderException
```

If you set the encodeSlashInPath to false, then the / character will not be encoded.

Finally, you may also want to use UriBuilder to create template strings. These are often embedded within Atom links. A bunch of new resolveTemplate() methods were added to UriBuilder in JAX-RS 2.0:

```
public abstract UriBuilder resolveTemplate(String name, Object value);
public abstract UriBuilder resolveTemplate(String name, Object value,
                                           boolean encodeSlashInPath);
public abstract UriBuilder resolveTemplateFromEncoded(String name,
                                                      Object value);
public abstract UriBuilder resolveTemplates(Map<String, Object>
                                            templateValues);
public abstract UriBuilder resolveTemplates(Map<String, Object>
                                            templateValues, boolean
                                            encodeSlashInPath)
        throws IllegalArgumentException;
public abstract UriBuilder resolveTemplatesFromEncoded(Map<String, Object>
                                                       templateValues);
```

These work similarly to their build() counterparts and are used to partially resolve URI templates. Each of them returns a new UriBuilder instance that resolves any of the supplied URI template parameters. You can then use the toTemplate() method to obtain the template as a String. Here's an example:

```
String original = "http://{host}/{id}";
String newTemplate = UriBuilder.fromUri(original)
                    .resolveTemplate("host", "localhost")
                    .toTemplate();
```

Relative URIs with UriInfo

When you're writing services that distribute links, there's certain information that you cannot know at the time you write your code. Specifically, you will probably not know the hostnames of the links. Also, if you are linking to other JAX-RS services, you may not know the base paths of the URIs, as you may be deployed within a servlet container.

While there are ways to write your applications to get this base URI information from configuration data, JAX-RS provides a cleaner, simpler way through the use of the `javax.ws.rs.core.UriInfo` interface. You were introduced to a few features of this interface in Chapter 5. Besides basic path information, you can also obtain `UriBuild er` instances preinitialized with the base URI used to define all JAX-RS services or the URI used to invoke the current HTTP request:

```
public interface UriInfo {
    public URI getRequestUri();
    public UriBuilder getRequestUriBuilder();
    public URI getAbsolutePath();
    public UriBuilder getAbsolutePathBuilder();
    public URI getBaseUri();
    public UriBuilder getBaseUriBuilder();
```

For example, let's say you have a JAX-RS service that exposes the customers in a customer database. Instead of having a base URI that returns all customers in a document, you want to embed previous and next links so that you can navigate through subsections of the database (I described an example of this earlier in this chapter). You will want to create these link relations using the URI to invoke the request:

```
@Path("/customers")
public class CustomerService {

    @GET
    @Produces("application/xml")
    public String getCustomers(@Context UriInfo uriInfo) {

        UriBuilder nextLinkBuilder = uriInfo.getAbsolutePathBuilder();
        nextLinkBuilder.queryParam("start", 5);
        nextLinkBuilder.queryParam("size", 10);
        URI next = nextLinkBuilder.build();

        ... set up the rest of the document ...
    }
```

To get access to a `UriInfo` instance that represents the request, we use the `@jav ax.ws.rs.core.Context` annotation to inject it as a parameter to the JAX-RS resource method `getCustomers()`. Within `getCustomers()`, we call `uriInfo.getAbsolutePath Builder()` to obtain a preinitialized `UriBuilder`. Depending on how this service was deployed, the URI created might look like this:

```
http://example.com/jaxrs/customers?start=5&size=10
```

UriInfo also allows you to relativize a URI based on the current request URI.

```
public URI relativize(URI uri);
```

So, for example, if the current request was `http://localhost/root/a/b/c` and you passed `a/d/e` as a parameter to the `relativize()` method, then the returned URI would be `../../d/e`. The `root` segment is the context root of your JAX-RS deployment. Relativization is based off of this root.

You can also resolve URIs with respect to the base URI of your JAX-RS deployment using the `resolve()` method:

```
public URI resolve(URI uri);
```

Invoking this method is the same as calling `uriInfo.getBaseURI().resolve(uri)`.

There are other interesting tidbits available for building your URIs. In Chapter 4, I talked about the concept of subresource locators and subresources. Code running within a subresource can obtain partial URIs for each JAX-RS class and method that matches the incoming requests. It can get this information from the following methods on `UriInfo`:

```
public interface UriInfo {
...
    public List<String> getMatchedURIs();
    public List<String> getMatchedURIs(boolean decode);
}
```

So, for example, let's reprint the subresource locator example in Chapter 4:

```
@Path("/customers")
public class CustomerDatabaseResource {

    @Path("{database}-db")
    public CustomerResource getDatabase(@PathParam("database") String db) {
        Map map = ...; // find the database based on the db parameter
        return new CustomerResource(map);
    }
}
```

`CustomerDatabaseResource` is the subresource locator. Let's also reprint the subresource example from Chapter 4 with a minor change using these `getMatchedURIs()` methods:

```
public class CustomerResource {
    private Map customerDB;

    public CustomerResource(Map db) {
        this.customerDB = db;
    }

    @GET
```

```
@Path("{id}")
@Produces("application/xml")
public StreamingOutput getCustomer(@PathParam("id") int id,
                                   @Context UriInfo uriInfo) {

   for(String uri : uriInfo.getMatchedURIs()) {
     System.out.println(uri);
   }
   ...
}
}
```

If the request is GET *http://example.com/customers/usa-db/333*, the output of the
for loop in the getCustomer() method would print out the following:

```
http://example.com/customers
http://example.com/customers/usa-db
http://example.com/customers/usa-db/333
```

The matched URIs correspond to the @Path expressions on the following:

- CustomerDatabaseResource
- CustomerDatabaseResource.getDatabase()
- CustomerResource.getCustomer()

Honestly, I had a very hard time coming up with a use case for the getMatchedURIs()
methods, so I can't really tell you why you might want to use them.

The final method of this category in UriInfo is the getMatchedResources() method:

```
public interface UriInfo {
...
   public List<Object> getMatchedResources();
}
```

This method returns a list of JAX-RS resource objects that have serviced the request.
Let's modify our CustomerResource.getCustomer() method again to illustrate how
this method works:

```
public class CustomerResource {
  private Map customerDB;

  public CustomerResource(Map db) {
     this.customerDB = db;
  }

  @GET
  @Path("{id}")
  @Produces("application/xml")
  public StreamingOutput getCustomer(@PathParam("id") int id,
                                     @Context UriInfo uriInfo) {
```

```
        for(Object match : uriInfo.getMatchedResources()) {
          System.out.println(match.getClass().getName());
        }
        ...
      }
    }
```

The for loop in getCustomer() prints out the class names of the JAX-RS resource objects that were used to process the request. If the request is GET *http://example.com/ customers/usa-db/333*, the output of the for loop would be:

```
com.acme.CustomerDatabaseResource
com.acme.CustomerResource
```

Again, I'm hard-pressed to find a use case for this method, but it's in the specification and you should be aware of it.

Building Links and Link Headers

JAX-RS 2.0 added some support to help you build Link headers and to embed links in your XML documents through the Link and Link.Builder classes:

```
package javax.ws.rs.core;

public abstract class Link {
    public abstract URI getUri();
    public abstract UriBuilder getUriBuilder();
    public abstract String getRel();
    public abstract List<String> getRels();
    public abstract String getTitle();
    public abstract String getType();
    public abstract Map<String, String> getParams();
    public abstract String toString();
}
```

Link is an abstract class that represents all the metadata contained in either a Link header or Atom link. The getUri() method pertains to the href attribute of your Atom link. getRel() pertains to the rel attribute, and so on. You can also reference any of these attributes as well as any proprietary extension attributes through the getParams() method. The toString() method will convert the Link instance into a Link header.

Link instances are built through a Link.Builder, which is created by one of these methods:

```
public abstract class Link {
    public static Builder fromUri(URI uri)
    public static Builder fromUri(String uri)
    public static Builder fromUriBuilder(UriBuilder uriBuilder)
    public static Builder fromLink(Link link)
```

```
public static Builder fromPath(String path)
public static Builder fromResource(Class<?> resource)
public static Builder fromMethod(Class<?> resource, String method)
```

All these fromXXX() methods work similarly to the UriBuilder.fromXXX() methods. They initialize an underlying UriBuilder that is used to build the href of the link.

The link(), uri(), and uriBuilder() methods allow you to override the underlying URI of the link you are creating:

```
public abstract class Link {
    interface Builder {
        public Builder link(Link link);
        public Builder link(String link);
        public Builder uri(URI uri);
        public Builder uri(String uri);
        public Builder uriBuilder(UriBuilder uriBuilder);
    ...
```

As you can probably guess, the following methods allow you to set various attributes on the link you are building:

```
public Builder rel(String rel);
public Builder title(String title);
public Builder type(String type);
public Builder param(String name, String value);
```

Finally, there's the build() method that will create the link:

```
public Link build(Object... values);
```

The Link.Builder has an underlying UriBuilder. The values passed into the build() method are passed along to this UriBuilder to create the URI for the Link. Let's look at an example:

```
Link link = Link.fromUri("http://{host}/root/customers/{id}")
               .rel("update").type("text/plain")
               .build("localhost", "1234");
```

Calling toString() on the link instance will result in:

```
<http://localhost/root/customers/1234>; rel="update"; type="text/plain"
```

You can also build relativized links using the buildRelativized() method:

```
public Link buildRelativized(URI uri, Object... values);
```

This method will build the link instance with a relativized URI based on the underlying URI of the Link.Builder and the passed-in uri parameter. For example:

```
Link link = Link.fromUri("a/d/e")
               .rel("update").type("text/plain")
               .buildRelativized(new URI("a"));
```

The URI is calculated internally like this:

```
URI base = new URI("a");
URI supplied = new URI("a/d/e");
URI result = base.relativize(supplied);
```

So, the `String` representation of the `link` variable from the example would be:

```
<d/e>; rel="update"; type="text/plain"
```

You can also use the `baseUri()` methods to specific a base URI to prefix your link's URI. Take this, for example:

```
Link link = Link.fromUri("a/d/e")
            .rel("update").type("text/plain")
            .baseUri("http://localhost/")
            .buildRelativized(new URI("http://localhost/a"));
```

This example code would also output:

```
<d/e>; rel="update"; type="text/plain"
```

Writing Link Headers

Built `Link` instances can be used to create `Link` headers. Here's an example:

```
@Path
@GET
Response get() {
   Link link = Link.fromUri("a/b/c").build();
   Response response = Response.noContent()
                               .links(link)
                               .build();

   return response;
}
```

Just build your `Link` and add it as a header to your `Response`.

Embedding Links in XML

The `Link` class also contains a JAXB `XmlAdapter` so that you can embed links within a JAXB class. For example, let's take our familiar `Customer` domain class and enable it to add one or more embedded links:

```
import javax.ws.rs.core.Link;

@XmlRootElement
public class Customer {
   private String name;
   private List<Link> links = new ArrayList<Link>();

      @XmlElement
      public String getName()
```

```
        {
            return name;
        }

        public void setName(String name)
        {
            this.name = name;
        }

        @XmlElement(name = "link")
        XmlJavaTypeAdapter(Link.JaxbAdapter.class)
        public List<Link> getLinks()
        {
            return links;
        }
    }
```

You can now build any links you want and add them to the `Customer` domain class. They will be converted into XML elements.

Wrapping Up

In this chapter, we discussed how links and forms have allowed the Web to scale. You learned the advantages of applying HATEOAS to RESTful web service design. Finally, you saw some JAX-RS utilities that can help make enabling HATEOAS in your JAX-RS services easier. Chapter 24 contains some code you can use to test-drive many of the concepts in this chapter.

CHAPTER 11

Scaling JAX-RS Applications

When studying the Web, one can't help but notice how massively scalable it is. There are hundreds of thousands of websites and billions of requests per day traveling across it. Terabytes of data are downloaded from the Internet every hour. Websites like Amazon and Bank of America process millions of transactions per day. In this chapter, I'll discuss some features of the Web, specifically within HTTP, that make it more scalable and how you can take advantage of these features within JAX-RS applications.

Caching

Caching is one of the more important features of the Web. When you visit a website for the first time, your browser stores images and static text in memory and on disk. If you revisit the site within minutes, hours, days, or even months, your browser doesn't have to reload the data over the network and can instead pick it up locally. This greatly speeds up the rendering of revisited web pages and makes the browsing experience much more fluid. Browser caching not only helps page viewing, it also cuts down on server load. If the browser is obtaining images or text locally, it is not eating up scarce server bandwidth or CPU cycles.

Besides browser caching, there are also proxy caches. Proxy caches are pseudo–web servers that work as middlemen between browsers and websites. Their sole purpose is to ease the load on master servers by caching static content and serving it to clients directly, bypassing the main servers. Content delivery networks (CDNs) like Akamai have made multimillion-dollar businesses out of this concept. These CDNs provide you with a worldwide network of proxy caches that you can use to publish your website and scale to hundreds of thousand of users.

If your web services are RESTful, there's no reason you can't leverage the caching semantics of the Web within your applications. If you have followed the HTTP constrained interface religiously, any service URI that can be reached with an HTTP GET is a candidate for caching, as they are, by definition, read-only and idempotent.

So when do you cache? Any service that provides static unchanging data is an obvious candidate. Also, if you have more dynamic data that is being accessed concurrently, you may also want to consider caching, even if your data is valid for only a few seconds or minutes. For example, consider the free stock quote services available on many websites. If you read the fine print, you'll see that these stock quotes are between 5 and 15 minutes old. Caching is viable in this scenario because there is a high chance that a given quote is accessed more than once within the small window of validity. So, even if you have dynamic web services, there's still a good chance that web caching is viable for these services.

HTTP Caching

Before we can leverage web caching, proxy caches, and CDNs for our web services, we need to understand how caching on the Web works. The HTTP protocol defines a rich set of built-in caching semantics. Through the exchange of various request and response headers, the HTTP protocol gives you fine-grained control over the caching behavior of both browser and proxy caches. The protocol also has validation semantics to make managing caches much more efficient. Let's dive into the specifics.

Expires Header

How does a browser know when to cache? In HTTP 1.0, a simple response header called Expires tells the browser that it can cache and for how long. The value of this header is a date in the future when the data is no longer valid. When this date is reached, the client should no longer use the cached data and should retrieve the data again from the server. For example, if a client submitted GET /customers/123, an example response using the Expires header would look like this:

```
HTTP/1.1 200 OK
Content-Type: application/xml
Expires: Tue, 15 May 2014 16:00 GMT

<customer id="123">...</customers>
```

This cacheable XML data is valid until Tuesday, May 15, 2014.

We can implement this within JAX-RS by using a javax.ws.rs.core.Response object. For example:

```
@Path("/customers")
public class CustomerResource {

    @Path("{id}")
    @GET
```

```
@Produces("application/xml")
public Response getCustomer(@PathParam("id") int id) {
    Customer cust = findCustomer(id);
    ResponseBuilder builder = Response.ok(cust, "application/xml");
    Date date = Calendar.getInstance(TimeZone.getTimeZone("GMT"))
                      .set(2010, 5, 15, 16, 0);
    builder.expires(date);
    return builder.build();
}
```

In this example, we initialize a `java.util.Date` object and pass it to the `Response Builder.expires()` method. This method sets the `Expires` header to the string date format the header expects.

Cache-Control

HTTP caching semantics were completely redone for the HTTP 1.1 specification. The specification includes a much richer feature set that has more explicit controls over browser and CDN/proxy caches. The idea of cache revalidation was also introduced. To provide all this new functionality, the `Expires` header was deprecated in favor of the `Cache-Control` header. Instead of a date, `Cache-Control` has a variable set of comma-delimited directives that define who can cache, how, and for how long. Let's take a look at them:

private

> The `private` directive states that no shared intermediary (proxy or CDN) is allowed to cache the response. This is a great way to make sure that the client, and only the client, caches the data.

public

> The `public` directive is the opposite of `private`. It indicates that the response may be cached by any entity within the request/response chain.

no-cache

> Usually, this directive simply means that the response should not be cached. If it is cached anyway, the data should not be used to satisfy a request unless it is revalidated with the server (more on revalidation later).

no-store

> A browser will store cacheable responses on disk so that they can be used after a browser restart or computer reboot. You can direct the browser or proxy cache to not store cached data on disk by using the `no-store` directive.

no-transform

> Some intermediary caches have the option to automatically transform their cached data to save memory or disk space or to simply reduce network traffic. An example

is compressing images. For some applications, you might want to disallow this using the no-transform directive.

max-age

> This directive is how long (in seconds) the cache is valid. If both an Expires header and a max-age directive are set in the same response, the max-age always takes precedence.

s-maxage

> The s-maxage directive is the same as the max-age directive, but it specifies the maximum time a shared, intermediary cache (like a proxy) is allowed to hold the data. This directive allows you to have different expiration times than the client.

Let's take a look at a simple example of a response to see Cache-Control in action:

```
HTTP/1.1 200 OK
Content-Type: application/xml
Cache-Control: private, no-store, max-age=300

<customers>...</customers>
```

In this example, the response is saying that only the client may cache the response. This response is valid for 300 seconds and must not be stored on disk.

The JAX-RS specification provides javax.ws.rs.core.CacheControl, a simple class to represent the Cache-Control header:

```
public class CacheControl {
    public CacheControl() {...}

    public static CacheControl valueOf(String value)
            throws IllegalArgumentException {...}
    public boolean isMustRevalidate() {...}
    public void setMustRevalidate(boolean mustRevalidate) {...}
    public boolean isProxyRevalidate() {...}
    public void setProxyRevalidate(boolean proxyRevalidate) {...}
    public int getMaxAge() {...}
    public void setMaxAge(int maxAge) {...}
    public int getSMaxAge() {...}
    public void setSMaxAge(int sMaxAge) {...}
    public List<String> getNoCacheFields() {...}
    public void setNoCache(boolean noCache) {...}
    public boolean isNoCache() {...}
    public boolean isPrivate() {...}
    public List<String> getPrivateFields() {...}
    public void setPrivate(boolean _private) {...}
    public boolean isNoTransform() {...}
    public void setNoTransform(boolean noTransform) {...}
    public boolean isNoStore() {...}
    public void setNoStore(boolean noStore) {...}
```

```
    public Map<String, String> getCacheExtension() {...}
}
```

The `ResponseBuilder` class has a method called `cacheControl()` that can accept a `CacheControl` object:

```
@Path("/customers")
public class CustomerResource {

    @Path("{id}")
    @GET
    @Produces("application/xml")
    public Response getCustomer(@PathParam("id") int id) {
        Customer cust = findCustomer(id);

        CacheControl cc = new CacheControl();
        cc.setMaxAge(300);
        cc.setPrivate(true);
        cc.setNoStore(true);
        ResponseBuilder builder = Response.ok(cust, "application/xml");
        builder.cacheControl(cc);
        return builder.build();
    }
}
```

In this example, we initialize a `CacheControl` object and pass it to the `ResponseBuild er.cacheControl()` method to set the `Cache-Control` header of the response. Unfortunately, JAX-RS doesn't yet have any nice annotations to do this for you automatically.

Revalidation and Conditional GETs

One interesting aspect of the caching protocol is that when the cache is stale, the cacher can ask the server if the data it is holding is still valid. This is called *revalidation*. To be able to perform revalidation, the client needs some extra information from the server about the resource it is caching. The server will send back a `Last-Modified` and/or an `ETag` header with its initial response to the client.

Last-Modified

The `Last-Modified` header represents a timestamp of the data sent by the server. Here's an example response:

```
HTTP/1.1 200 OK
Content-Type: application/xml
Cache-Control: max-age=1000
Last-Modified: Tue, 15 May 2013 09:56 EST

<customer id="123">...</customer>
```

This initial response from the server is stating that the XML returned is valid for 1,000 seconds and has a timestamp of Tuesday, May 15, 2013, 9:56 AM EST. If the client supports revalidation, it will store this timestamp along with the cached data. After 1,000 seconds, the client may opt to revalidate its cache of the item. To do this, it does a *conditional* GET request by passing a request header called If-Modified-Since with the value of the cached Last-Modified header. For example:

```
GET /customers/123 HTTP/1.1
If-Modified-Since: Tue, 15 May 2013 09:56 EST
```

When a service receives this GET request, it checks to see if its resource has been modified since the date provided within the If-Modified-Since header. If it has been changed since the timestamp provided, the server will send back a 200, "OK," response with the new representation of the resource. If it hasn't been changed, the server will respond with 304, "Not Modified," and return no representation. In both cases, the server should send an updated Cache-Control and Last-Modified header if appropriate.

ETag

The ETag header is a pseudounique identifier that represents the version of the data sent back. Its value is any arbitrary quoted string and is usually an MD5 hash. Here's an example response:

```
HTTP/1.1 200 OK
Content-Type: application/xml
Cache-Control: max-age=1000
ETag: "3141271342554322343200"

<customer id="123">...</customer>
```

Like the Last-Modified header, when the client caches this response, it should also cache the ETag value. When the cache expires after 1,000 seconds, the client performs a revalidation request with the If-None-Match header that contains the value of the cached ETag. For example:

```
GET /customers/123 HTTP/1.1
If-None-Match: "3141271342554322343200"
```

When a service receives this GET request, it tries to match the current ETag hash of the resource with the one provided within the If-None-Match header. If the tags don't match, the server will send back a 200, "OK," response with the new representation of the resource. If it hasn't been changed, the server will respond with 304, "Not Modified," and return no representation. In both cases, the server should send an updated Cache-Control and ETag header if appropriate.

One final thing about ETags is they come in two flavors: strong and weak. A strong ETag should change whenever any bit of the resource's representation changes. A weak ETag changes only on semantically significant events. Weak `ETags` are identified with a `W/` prefix. For example:

```
HTTP/1.1 200 OK
Content-Type: application/xml
Cache-Control: max-age=1000
ETag: W/"3141271342554322343200"

<customer id="123">...</customer>
```

Weak `ETags` give applications a bit more flexibility to reduce network traffic, as a cache can be revalidated when there have been only minor changes to the resource.

JAX-RS has a simple class called `javax.ws.rs.core.EntityTag` that represents the `ETag` header:

```
public class EntityTag {

    public EntityTag(String value) {...}
    public EntityTag(String value, boolean weak) {...}
    public static EntityTag valueOf(String value)
                throws IllegalArgumentException {...}
    public boolean isWeak() {...}
    public String getValue() {...}
}
```

It is constructed with a string value and optionally with a flag telling the object if it is a weak `ETag` or not. The `getValue()` and `isWeak()` methods return these values on demand.

JAX-RS and conditional GETs

To help with conditional GETs, JAX-RS provides an injectable helper class called `jav ax.ws.rs.core.Request`:

```
public interface Request {
    ...

    ResponseBuilder evaluatePreconditions(EntityTag eTag);
    ResponseBuilder evaluatePreconditions(Date lastModified);
    ResponseBuilder evaluatePreconditions(Date lastModified, EntityTag eTag);
}
```

The overloaded `evaluatePreconditions()` methods take a `javax.ws.rs.core.Enti tyTag`, a `java.util.Date` that represents the last modified timestamp, or both. These values should be current, as they will be compared with the values of the `If-Modified-Since`, `If-Unmodified-Since`, or `If-None-Match` headers sent with the request. If these headers don't exist or if the request header values don't pass revalidation, this method returns null and you should send back a 200, "OK," response with the new representation

of the resource. If the method does not return null, it returns a preinitialized instance
of a `ResponseBuilder` with the response code preset to 304. For example:

```
@Path("/customers")
public class CustomerResource {

    @Path("{id}")
    @GET
    @Produces("application/xml")
    public Response getCustomer(@PathParam("id") int id,
                                @Context Request request) {
        Customer cust = findCustomer(id);
        EntityTag tag = new EntityTag(
                                Integer.toString(cust.hashCode()));

        CacheControl cc = new CacheControl();
        cc.setMaxAge(1000);

        ResponseBuilder builder = request.evaluatePreconditions(tag);
        if (builder != null) {
            builder.cacheControl(cc);
            return builder.build();
        }

        // Preconditions not met!

        builder = Response.ok(cust, "application/xml");
        builder.cacheControl(cc);
        builder.tag(tag);
        return builder.build();
    }
}
```

In this example, we have a `getCustomer()` method that handles GET requests for
the /customers/\{id} URI pattern. An instance of `javax.ws.rs.core.Request` is injected into the method using the `@Context` annotation. We then find a `Customer` instance
and create a current `ETag` value for it from the hash code of the object (this isn't the best
way to create the `EntityTag`, but for simplicity's sake, let's keep it that way). We then
call `Request.evaluatePreconditions()`, passing in the up-to-date tag. If the tags
match, we reset the client's cache expiration by sending a new `Cache-Control` header
and return. If the tags don't match, we build a `Response` with the new, current version
of the `ETag` and `Customer`.

Concurrency

Now that we have a good idea of how to boost the performance of our JAX-RS services
using HTTP caching, we need to look at how to scale applications that update resources
on our server. The way RESTful updates work is that the client fetches a representation
of a resource through a GET request. It then modifies the representation locally and

PUTs or POSTs the modified representation back to the server. This is all fine and dandy if there is only one client at a time modifying the resource, but what if the resource is being modified concurrently? Because the client is working with a snapshot, this data could become stale if another client modifies the resource while the snapshot is being processed.

The HTTP specification has a solution to this problem through the use of conditional PUTs or POSTs. This technique is very similar to how cache revalidation and conditional GETs work. The client first starts out by fetching the resource. For example, let's say our client wants to update a customer in a RESTful customer directory. It would first start off by submitting GET /customers/123 to pull down the current representation of the specific customer it wants to update. The response might look something like this:

```
HTTP/1.1 200 OK
Content-Type: application/xml
Cache-Control: max-age=1000
ETag: "3141271342554322343200"
Last-Modified: Tue, 15 May 2013 09:56 EST

<customer id="123">...</customer>
```

In order to do a conditional update, we need either an ETag or Last-Modified header. This information tells the server which snapshot version we have modified when we perform our update. It is sent along within the If-Match or If-Unmodified-Since header when we do our PUT or POST request. The If-Match header is initialized with the ETag value of the snapshot. The If-Unmodified-Since header is initialized with the value of Last-Modified header. So, our update request might look like this:

```
PUT /customers/123 HTTP/1.1
If-Match: "3141271342554322343200"
If-Unmodified-Since: Tue, 15 May 2013 09:56 EST
Content-Type: application/xml

<customer id="123">...</customer>
```

You are not required to send both the If-Match and If-Unmodified-Since headers. One or the other is sufficient to perform a conditional PUT or POST. When the server receives this request, it checks to see if the current ETag of the resource matches the value of the If-Match header and also to see if the timestamp on the resource matches the If-Unmodified-Since header. If these conditions are not met, the server will return an error response code of 412, "Precondition Failed." This tells the client that the representation it is updating was modified concurrently and that it should retry. If the conditions are met, the service performs the update and sends a success response code back to the client.

JAX-RS and Conditional Updates

To do conditional updates with JAX-RS, you use the `Request.evaluatePrecondi` `tions()` method again. Let's look at how we can implement it within Java code:

```
@Path("/customers")
public class CustomerResource {

    @Path("{id}")
    @PUT
    @Consumes("application/xml")
    public Response updateCustomer(@PathParam("id") int id,
                                   @Context Request request,
                                   Customer update ) {
        Customer cust = findCustomer(id);
        EntityTag tag = new EntityTag(
                                    Integer.toString(cust.hashCode()));
        Date timestamp = ...; // get the timestamp

        ResponseBuilder builder =
                        request.evaluatePreconditions(timestamp, tag);

        if (builder != null) {
            // Preconditions not met!
            return builder.build();
        }

        ... perform the update ...

        builder = Response.noContent();
        return builder.build();
    }
}
```

The `updateCustomer()` method obtains a customer ID and an instance of `jav` `ax.ws.rs.core.Request` from the injected parameters. It then locates an instance of a `Customer` object in some application-specific way (for example, from a database). From this current instance of `Customer`, it creates an `EntityTag` from the hash code of the object. It also finds the current timestamp of the `Customer` instance in some application-specific way. The `Request.evaluatePreconditions()` method is then called with `time` `stamp` and `tag` variables. If these values do not match the values within the `If-Match` and `If-Unmodified-Since` headers sent with the request, `evaluatePreconditions()` sends back an instance of a `ResponseBuilder` initialized with the error code 412, "Precondition Failed." A `Response` object is built and sent back to the client. If the preconditions are met, the service performs the update and sends back a success code of 204, "No Content."

With this code in place, we can now worry less about concurrent updates of our resources. One interesting thought is that we did not have to come up with this scheme

---

ourselves. It is already defined within the HTTP specification. This is one of the beauties of REST, in that it fully leverages the HTTP protocol.

Wrapping Up

In this chapter, you learned that HTTP has built-in facilities to help scale the performance of our distributed systems. HTTP caching is a rich protocol that gives us a lot of control over browser, proxy, and client caches. It helps tremendously in reducing network traffic and speeding up response times for applications. Besides caching, distributed systems also have the problem of multiple clients trying to update the same resource. The HTTP protocol again comes to the rescue with well-defined semantics for handling concurrent updates. For both caching and concurrent updates, JAX-RS provides some helper classes to make it easier to enable these features in your Java applications. Chapter 25 contains some code you can use to test-drive many of the concepts in this chapter.

CHAPTER 12

Filters and Interceptors

Filters and interceptors are objects that are able to interpose themselves on client or server request processing. They allow you to encapsulate common behavior that cuts across large parts of your application. This behavior is usually infrastructure- or protocol-related code that you don't want to pollute your business logic with. While most JAX-RS features are applied by application developers, filters and interceptors are targeted more toward middleware and systems developers. They are also often used to write portable extensions to the JAX-RS API. This chapter teaches you how to write filters and interceptors using real-world examples.

Server-Side Filters

On the server side there are two different types of filters: *request filters* and *response filters*. Request filters execute before a JAX-RS method is invoked. Response filters execute after the JAX-RS method is finished. By default they are executed for all HTTP requests, but can be bound to a specific JAX-RS method too. Internally, the algorithm for executing an HTTP on the server side looks something like this:

```
for (filter : preMatchFilters) {
   filter.filter(request);
}

jaxrs_method = match(request);

for (filter : postMatchFilters) {
   filter.filter(request);
}

response = jaxrs_method.invoke();

for (filter : responseFilters) {
```

```
        filter.filter(request, response);
    }
```

For those of you familiar with the Servlet API, JAX-RS filters are quite different. JAX-RS breaks up its filters into separate request and response interfaces, while servlet filters wrap around servlet processing and are run in the same Java call stack. Because JAX-RS has an asynchronous API, JAX-RS filters cannot run in the same Java call stack. Each request filter runs to completion before the JAX-RS method is invoked. Each response filter runs to completion only after a response becomes available to send back to the client. In the asynchronous case, response filters run after `resume()`, `cancel()`, or a timeout happens. See Chapter 13 for more details on the asynchronous API.

Server Request Filters

Request filters are implementations of the `ContainerRequestFilter` interface:

```
package javax.ws.rs.container;

public interface ContainerRequestFilter {
    public void filter(ContainerRequestContext requestContext)
                    throws IOException;
}
```

`ContainerRequestFilters` come in two flavors: prematching and postmatching. Prematching `ContainerRequestFilters` are designated with the `@PreMatching` annotation and will execute before the JAX-RS resource method is matched with the incoming HTTP request. Prematching filters often are used to modify request attributes to change how they match to a specific resource. For example, some firewalls do not allow PUT and/or DELETE invocations. To circumvent this limitation, many applications tunnel the HTTP method through the HTTP header `X-Http-Method-Override`:

```
import javax.ws.rs.container.ContainerRequestFilter;
import javax.ws.rs.container.ContainerRequestContext;

@Provider
@PreMatching
public class HttpMethodOverride implements ContainerRequestFilter {
    public void filter(ContainerRequestContext ctx) throws IOException {
        String methodOverride = ctx.getHeaderString("X-Http-Method-Override");
        if (methodOverride != null) ctx.setMethod(methodOverride);
    }
}
```

This `HttpMethodOverride` filter will run before the HTTP request is matched to a specific JAX-RS method. The `ContainerRequestContext` parameter passed to the `filter()` method provides information about the request like headers, the URI, and so on. The `filter()` method uses the `ContainerRequestContext` parameter to check the value of the `X-Http-Method-Override` header. If the header is set in the request, the filter overrides the request's HTTP method by calling `ContainerRequestFilter.setMe thod()`. Filters can modify pretty much anything about the incoming request through methods on `ContainerRequestContext`, but once the request is matched to a JAX-RS method, a filter cannot modify the request URI or HTTP method.

Another great use case for request filters is implementing custom authentication protocols. For example, OAuth 2.0 has a token protocol that is transmitted through the `Authorization` HTTP header. Here's what an implementation of that might look like:

```java
import javax.ws.rs.container.ContainerRequestFilter;
import javax.ws.rs.container.ContainerRequestContext;
import javax.ws.rs.NotAuthorizedException;

@Provider
@PreMatching
public class BearerTokenFilter implements ContainerRequestFilter {
    public void filter(ContainerRequestContext ctx) throws IOException {
        String authHeader = request.getHeaderString(HttpHeaders.AUTHORIZATION);
        if (authHeader == null) throw new NotAuthorizedException("Bearer");
        String token = parseToken(authHeader);
        if (verifyToken(token) == false) {
            throw new NotAuthorizedException("Bearer error=\"invalid_token\"");
        }
    }

    private String parseToken(String header) {...}
    private boolean verifyToken(String token) {...}
}
```

In this example, if there is no `Authorization` header or it is invalid, the request is aborted with a `NotAuthorizedException`. The client receives a 401 response with a `WWW-Authenticate` header set to the value passed into the constructor of `NotAuthorizedEx ception`. If you want to avoid exception mapping, then you can use the `ContainerRe questContext.abortWith()` method instead. Generally, however, I prefer to throw exceptions.

Server Response Filters

Response filters are implementations of the `ContainerResponseFilter` interface:

```java
package javax.ws.rs.container;

public interface ContainerResponseFilter {
    public void filter(ContainerRequestContext requestContext,
                       ContainerResponseContext responseContext)
            throws IOException;
}
```

Generally, you use these types of filters to decorate the response by adding or modifying response headers. One example is if you wanted to set a default Cache-Control header for each response to a GET request. Here's what it might look like:

```java
import javax.ws.rs.container.ContainerResponseFilter;
import javax.ws.rs.container.ContainerRequestContext;
import javax.ws.rs.container.ContainerResponseContext;
import javax.ws.rs.core.CacheControl;

@Provider
public class CacheControlFilter implements ContainerResponseFilter {
    public void filter(ContainerRequestContext req, ContainerResponseContext res)
        throws IOException
    {
      if (req.getMethod().equals("GET")) {
        CacheControl cc = new CacheControl();
        cc.setMaxAge(100);
        res.getHeaders().add("Cache-Control", cc);
      }
    }
}
```

The ContainerResponseFilter.filter() method has two parameters. The Contain erRequestContext parameter gives you access to information about the request. Here we're checking to see if the request was a GET. The ContainerResponseContext parameter allows you to view, add, and modify the response before it is marshalled and sent back to the client. In the example, we use the ContainerResponseContext to set a Cache-Control response header.

Reader and Writer Interceptors

While filters modify request or response headers, reader and writer interceptors deal with message bodies. They work in conjunction with a MessageBodyReader or Messa geBodyWriter and are usable on both the client and server. Reader interceptors implement the ReaderInterceptor interface. Writer interceptors implement the WriterIn terceptor interface.

```java
package javax.ws.rs.ext;

public interface ReaderInterceptor {
    public Object aroundReadFrom(ReaderInterceptorContext context)
            throws java.io.IOException, javax.ws.rs.WebApplicationException;
}

public interface WriterInterceptor {
    void aroundWriteTo(WriterInterceptorContext context)
            throws java.io.IOException, javax.ws.rs.WebApplicationException;
}
```

These interceptors are only triggered when a `MessageBodyReader` or `MessageBodyWrit`er is needed to unmarshal or marshal a Java object to and from the HTTP message body. They also are invoked in the same Java call stack. In other words, a `ReaderIntercep`tor wraps around the invocation of `MessageBodyReader.readFrom()` and a `WriterIn`terceptor wraps around the invocation of `MessageBodyWWriter.writeTo()`.

A simple example that illustrates these interfaces in action is adding compression to your input and output streams through content encoding. While most JAX-RS implementations support GZIP encoding, let's look at how you might add support for it using a `ReaderInterceptor` and `WriterInterceptor`:

```
@Provider
public class GZIPEncoder implements WriterInterceptor {

    public void aroundWriteTo(WriterInterceptorContext ctx)
                    throws IOException, WebApplicationException {
        GZIPOutputStream os = new GZIPOutputStream(ctx.getOutputStream());
        ctx.getHeaders().putSingle("Content-Encoding", "gzip");
        ctx.setOutputStream(os);
        ctx.proceed();
        return;
    }
}
```

The `WriterInterceptorContext` parameter allows you to view and modify the HTTP headers associated with this invocation. Since interceptors can be used on both the client and server side, these headers represent either a client request or a server response. In the example, our `aroundWriteTo()` method uses the `WriterInterceptorContext` to get and replace the `OutputStream` of the HTTP message body with a `GZipOutputStream`. We also use it to add a `Content-Encoding` header. The call to `WriterInterceptorCon`text.proceed() will either invoke the next registered `WriterInterceptor`, or if there aren't any, invoke the underlying `MessageBodyWriter.writeTo()` method.

Let's now implement the `ReaderInterceptor` counterpart to this encoding example:

```
@Provider
public class GZIPDecoder implements ReaderInterceptor {
    public Object aroundReadFrom(ReaderInterceptorContext ctx)
                            throws IOException {
        String encoding = ctx.getHeaders().getFirst("Content-Encoding");
        if (!"gzip".equalsIgnoreCase(encoding)) {
            return ctx.proceed();
        }
        GZipInputStream is = new GZipInputStream(ctx.getInputStream());
        ctx.setInputStream(is);
        return ctx.proceed(is);
    }
}
```

The `ReaderInterceptorContext` parameter allows you to view and modify the HTTP headers associated with this invocation. Since interceptors can be used on both the client and server side, these headers represent either a client response or a server request. In the example, our `aroundReadFrom()` method uses the `ReaderInterceptorContext` to first check to see if the message body is GZIP encoded. If not, it returns with a call to `ReaderInterceptorContext.proceed()`. The `ReaderInterceptorContext` is also used to get and replace the `InputStream` of the HTTP message body with a `GZipInput Stream`. The call to `ReaderInterceptorContext.proceed()` will either invoke the next registered `ReaderInterceptor`, or if there aren't any, invoke the underlying `MessageBo dyReader.readFrom()` method. The value returned by `proceed()` is whatever was returned by `MessageBodyReader.readFrom()`. You can change this value if you want, by returning a different value from your `aroundReadFrom()` method.

There's a lot of other use cases for interceptors that I'm not going to go into detail with. For example, the RESTEasy project uses interceptors to digitally sign and/or encrypt message bodies into a variety of Internet formats. You could also use a `WriterInter ceptor` to add a JSONP wrapper to your JSON content. A `ReaderInterceptor` could augment the unmarshalled Java object with additional data pulled from the request or response. The rest is up to your imagination.

Client-Side Filters

The JAX-RS Client API also has its own set of request and response filter interfaces:

```
package javax.ws.rs.client;

public interface ClientRequestFilter {
    public void filter(ClientRequestContext requestContext) throws IOException;
}

public interface ClientResponseFilter {
    public void filter(ClientRequestContext requestContext,
                       ClientResponseContext responseContext)
            throws IOException;
}
```

Let's use these two interfaces to implement a client-side cache. We want this cache to behave like a browser's cache. This means we want it to honor the `Cache-Control` semantics discussed in Chapter 11. We want cache entries to expire based on the metadata within `Cache-Control` response headers. We want to perform conditional GETs if the client is requesting an expired cache entry. Let's implement our `ClientRequest Filter` first:

```
import javax.ws.rs.client.ClientRequestFilter;
import javax.ws.rs.client.ClientRequestContext;
```

```java
public class ClientCacheRequestFilter implements ClientRequestFilter {
   private Cache cache;

   public ClientCacheRequestFilter(Cache cache) {
      this.cache = cache;
   }

   public void filter(ClientRequestContext ctx) throws IOException {
      if (!ctx.getMethod().equalsIgnoreCase("GET")) return;

      CacheEntry entry = cache.getEntry(request.getUri());
      if (entry == null) return;

      if (!entry.isExpired()) {
         ByteArrayInputStream is = new ByteArrayInputStream(entry.getContent());
         Response response = Response.ok(is)
                                   .type(entry.getContentType()).build();
         ctx.abortWith(response);
         return;
      }

      String etag = entry.getETagHeader();
      String lastModified = entry.getLastModified();

      if (etag != null) {
         ctx.getHeaders.putSingle("If-None-Match", etag);
      }

      if (lastModified != null) {
         ctx.getHeaders.putSingle("If-Modified-Since", lastModified);
      }
   }

}
```

I'll show you later how to register these client-side filters, but our request filter must be registered as a singleton and constructed with an instance of a Cache. I'm not going to go into the details of this Cache class, but hopefully you can make an educated guess of how its implemented.

Our ClientCacheRequestFilter.filter() method performs a variety of actions based on the state of the underlying cache. First, it checks the ClientRequestContext to see if we're doing an HTTP GET. If not, it just returns and does nothing. Next, we look up the request's URI in the cache. If there is no entry, again, just return. If there is an entry, we must check to see if it's expired or not. If it isn't, we create a Response object that returns a 200, "OK," status. We populate the Response object with the content and Content-Header stored in the cache entry and abort the invocation by calling ClientRequestContext.abortWith(). Depending on how the application initiated the client invocation, the aborted Response object will either be returned directly to the client application, or unmarshalled into the appropriate Java type. If the cache entry has expired, we perform a conditional GET by setting the If-None-Match and/or If-Modified-Since request headers with values stored in the cache entry.

Now that we've seen the request filter, let's finish this example by implementing the response filter:

```java
public class CacheResponseFilter implements ClientResponseFilter {
    private Cache cache;

    public CacheResponseFilter(Cache cache) {
        this.cache = cache;
    }

    public void filter(ClientRequestContext request,
                        ClientResponseContext response)
            throws IOException {
        if (!request.getMethod().equalsIgnoreCase("GET")) return;

        if (response.getStatus() == 200) {
            cache.cacheResponse(response, request.getUri());
        } else if (response.getStatus() == 304) {
            CacheEntry entry = cache.getEntry(request.getUri());
            entry.updateCacheHeaders(response);
            response.getHeaders().clear();
            response.setStatus(200);
            response.getHeaders().putSingle("Content-Type", entry.getContentType());
            ByteArrayInputStream is = new ByteArrayInputStream(entry.getContent());
            response.setInputStream(is);
        }
    }
}
```

The CacheResponseFilter.filter() method starts off by checking if the invoked request was an HTTP GET. If not, it just returns. If the response status was 200, "OK," then we ask the Cache object to cache the response for the specific request URI. The Cache.cacheResponse() method is responsible for buffering the response and storing relevant response headers and the message body. For brevity's sake, I'm not going to go into the details of this method. If instead the response code is 304, "Not Modified," this means that we have performed a successful conditional GET. We update the cache entry with any ETag or Last-Modified response headers. Also, because the response will have no message body, we must rebuild the response based on the cache entry. We clear all the headers from ClientResponseContext and set the appropriate Content-Type. Finally we override the response's InputStream with the buffer stored in the cache entry.

Deploying Filters and Interceptors

On the server side, filters and interceptors are deployed the same way any other `@Pro vider` is deployed. You either annotate it with `@Provider` and let it be scanned and automatically registered, or you add the filter or interceptor to the `Application` class's classes or singletons list.

On the client side, you register filters and interceptors the same way you would register any other provider. There are a few components in the Client API that implement the `Configurable` interface. This interface has a `register()` method that allows you to pass in your filter or interceptor class or singleton instance. `ClientBuilder`, `Client`, and `WebTarget` all implement the `Configurable` interface. What's interesting here is that you can have different filters and interceptors per `WebTarget`. For example, you may have different security requirements for different HTTP resources. For one `WebTar get` instance, you might register a Basic Auth filter. For another, you might register a token filter.

Ordering Filters and Interceptors

When you have more than one registered filter or interceptor, there may be some sensitivities on the order in which these components are executed. For example, you usually don't want unauthenticated users executing any of your JAX-RS components. So, if you have a custom authentication filter, you probably want that filter to be executed first. Another example is the combination of our GZIP encoding example with a separate `WriterInterceptor` that encrypts the message body. You probably don't want to encrypt a GZIP-encoded representation. Instead you'll want to GZIP-encode an encrypted representation. So ordering is important.

In JAX-RS, filters and interceptors are assigned a numeric priority either through the `@Priority` annotation or via a programmatic interface defined by `Configurable`. The JAX-RS runtime sorts filters and interceptors based on this numeric priority. Smaller numbers are first in the chain:

```
package javax.annotation;

public @interface Priority {
    int value();
}
```

The `@Priority` annotation is actually reused from the injection framework that comes with JDK 7. This annotation would be used as follows:

```
import javax.annotation.Priority;
import javax.ws.rs.Priorities;

@Provider
```

```
@PreMatching
@Priority(Priorities.AUTHENTICATION)
public class BearerTokenFilter implements ContainerRequestFilter {
    ...
}
```

The `@Priority` annotation can take any numeric value you wish. The `Priorities` class specifies some common constants that you can use when applying the `@Priority` annotation:

```
package javax.ws.rs;

public final class Priorities {

    private Priorities() {
        // prevents construction
    }

    /**
     * Security authentication filter/interceptor priority.
     */
    public static final int AUTHENTICATION = 1000;
    /**
     * Security authorization filter/interceptor priority.
     */
    public static final int AUTHORIZATION = 2000;
    /**
     * Header decorator filter/interceptor priority.
     */
    public static final int HEADER_DECORATOR = 3000;
    /**
     * Message encoder or decoder filter/interceptor priority.
     */
    public static final int ENTITY_CODER = 4000;
    /**
     * User-level filter/interceptor priority.
     */
    public static final int USER = 5000;
}
```

If no priority is specified, the default is USER, 5000. There's a few `Configurable.regis ter()` methods that you can use as an alternative to the `@Priority` annotation to manually assign or override the priority for a filter or interceptor. As mentioned before, the client classes `ClientBuilder`, `Client`, `WebTarget`, and `Invocation.Builder` all implement the `Configurable` interface. Here's an example of manually setting an interceptor priority using this inherited `Configurable.register()`:

```
ClientBuilder builder = ClientBuilder.newBuilder();
builder.register(GZipEncoder.class, Priorities.ENTITY_CODER);
```

On the server side, you can inject an instance of Configurable into the constructor of your Application class:

```
import javax.ws.rs.core.Configurable;

@ApplicationPath("/")
public class MyApplication {

    public MyApplication(@Context Configurable configurable) {
        configurable.register(BearerTokenFilter.class, Priorities.AUTHENTICATION);
    }
}
```

Personally, I prefer using the @Priority annotation, as then my filters and interceptors are self-contained. Users can just plug in my components without having to worry about priorities.

Per-JAX-RS Method Bindings

On the server side, you can apply a filter or interceptor on a per-JAX-RS-method basis. This allows you to do some really cool things like adding annotation extensions to your JAX-RS container. There are two ways to accomplish this. One is by registering an implementation of the DynamicFeature interface. The other is through annotation binding. Let's look at DynamicFeature first.

DynamicFeature

```
package javax.ws.rs.container;

public interface DynamicFeature {
    public void configure(ResourceInfo resourceInfo, FeatureContext context);
}

public interface ResourceInfo {

    /**
     * Get the resource method that is the target of a request,
     * or <code>null</code> if this information is not available.
     *
     * @return resource method instance or null
     * @see #getResourceClass()
     */
    Method getResourceMethod();

    /**
     * Get the resource class that is the target of a request,
     * or <code>null</code> if this information is not available.
     *
     * @return resource class instance or null
```

```
 * @see #getResourceMethod()
 */
Class<?> getResourceClass();
}
```

The `DynamicFeature` interface has one callback method, `configure()`. This `config
ure()` method is invoked for each and every deployed JAX-RS method. The `Resour
ceInfo` parameter contains information about the current JAX-RS method being de-
ployed. The `FeatureContext` is an extension of the `Configurable` interface. You'll use
the `register()` methods of this parameter to bind the filters and interceptors you want
to assign to this method.

To illustrate how you'd use `DynamicFeature`, let's expand on the `CacheControlFilter`
response filter we wrote earlier in this chapter. The previous incarnation of this class
would set the same `Cache-Control` header value for each and every HTTP request. Let's
modify this filter and create a custom annotation called `@MaxAge` that will allow you to
set the `max-age` of the `Cache-Control` header per JAX-RS method:

```
package com.commerce.MaxAge;

@Target(ElementType.METHOD)
@Retention(RetentionPolicy.RUNTIME)
public @interface MaxAge {
    int value();
}
```

The modification of the filter looks like this:

```
import javax.ws.rs.container.ContainerResponseFilter;
import javax.ws.rs.container.ContainerRequestContext;
import javax.ws.rs.container.ContainerResponseContext;
import javax.ws.rs.core.CacheControl;

public class CacheControlFilter implements ContainerResponseFilter {
    private int maxAge;

    public CacheControlFilter(int maxAge) {
        this.maxAge = maxAge;
    }

    public void filter(ContainerRequestContext req, ContainerResponseContext res)
        throws IOException
    {
        if (req.getMethod().equals("GET")) {
            CacheControl cc = new CacheControl();
            cc.setMaxAge(this.maxAge);
            res.getHeaders().add("Cache-Control", cc);
        }
    }
}
```

The `CacheControlFilter` has a new constructor that has a max age parameter. We'll use this max age to set the `Cache-Control` header on the response. Notice that we do not annotate `CacheControlFilter` with `@Provider`. Removing `@Provider` will prevent this filter from being picked up on a scan when we deploy our JAX-RS application. Our `DynamicFeature` implementation is going to be responsible for creating and registering this filter:

```java
import javax.ws.rs.container.DynamicFeature;
import javax.ws.rs.container.ResourceInfo;
import javax.ws.rs.core.FeatureContext;

@Provider
public class MaxAgeFeature implements DynamicFeature {

    public void configure(ResourceInfo ri, FeatureContext ctx) {
        MaxAge max = ri.getResourceMethod().getAnnotation(MaxAge.class);
        if (max == null) return;
        CacheControlFilter filter = new CacheControlFilter(max.value());
        ctx.register(filter);
    }
}
```

The `MaxAgeFeature.configure()` method is invoked for every deployed JAX-RS re-source method. The `configure()` method first looks for the `@MaxAge` annotation on the `ResourceInfo`'s method. If it exists, it constructs an instance of the `CacheControlFil`ter, passing in the value of the `@MaxAge` annotation. It then registers this created filter with the `FeatureContext` parameter. This filter is now bound to the JAX-RS resource method represented by the `ResourceInfo` parameter. We've just created a JAX-RS extension!

Name Bindings

The other way to bind a filter or interceptor to a particular JAX-RS method is to use the `@NameBinding` meta-annotation:

```java
package javax.ws.rs;

import java.lang.annotation.Documented;
import java.lang.annotation.ElementType;
import java.lang.annotation.Retention;
import java.lang.annotation.RetentionPolicy;
import java.lang.annotation.Target;

@Target(ElementType.ANNOTATION_TYPE)
@Retention(RetentionPolicy.RUNTIME)
@Documented
public @interface NameBinding {
}
```

You can bind a filter or interceptor to a particular annotation and when that custom annotation is applied, the filter or interceptor will automatically be bound to the annotated JAX-RS method. Let's take our previous `BearerTokenFilter` example and bind to a new custom `@TokenAuthenticated` annotation. The first thing we do is define our new annotation:

```
import javax.ws.rs.NameBinding;

@NameBinding
@Target({ElementType.METHOD, ElementType.TYPE})
@Retention(RetentionPolicy.RUNTIME)
public @interface TokenAuthenticated {}
```

Notice that `@TokenAuthenticated` is annotated with `@NameBinding`. This tells the JAX-RS runtime that this annotation triggers a specific filter or interceptor. Also notice that the `@Target` is set to both methods and classes. To bind the annotation to a specific filter, we'll need to annotate the filter with it:

```
@Provider
@PreMatching
@TokenAuthenticated
public class BearerTokenFilter implements ContainerRequestFilter {
...
}
```

Now, we can use `@TokenAuthenticated` on any method we want and the `BearerToken Filter` will be bound to that annotated method:

```
@Path("/customers")
public class CustomerResource {

    @GET
    @Path("{id}")
    @TokenAuthenticated
    public String getCustomer(@PathParam("id") String id) {...}
}
```

DynamicFeature Versus @NameBinding

To be honest, I'm not a big fan of `@NameBinding` and lobbied for its removal from early specification drafts. For one, any application of `@NameBinding` can be reimplemented as a `DynamicFeature`. Second, using `@NameBinding` can be pretty inefficient depending on your initialization requirements. For example, let's reimplement our `@MaxAge` example as an `@NameBinding`. The filter class would need to change as follows:

```
import javax.ws.rs.container.ContainerResponseFilter;
import javax.ws.rs.container.ContainerRequestContext;
import javax.ws.rs.container.ContainerResponseContext;
import javax.ws.rs.core.CacheControl;
```

```
@MaxAge
@Provider
public class CacheControlFilter implements ContainerResponseFilter {

    @Context ResourceInfo info;

    public void filter(ContainerRequestContext req, ContainerResponseContext res)
        throws IOException
    {
        if (req.getMethod().equals("GET")) {
            MaxAge max = info.getMethod().getAnnotation(MaxAge.class);
            CacheControl cc = new CacheControl();
            cc.setMaxAge(max.value());
            res.getHeaders().add("Cache-Control", cc);
        }
    }
}
```

If we bound CacheControlFilter via a name binding, the filter class would have to inject ResourceInfo, then look up the @MaxAge annotation of the JAX-RS method so it could determine the actual max age value to apply to the Cache-Control header. This is less efficient at runtime than our DynamicFeature implementation. Sure, in this case the overhead probably will not be noticeable, but if you have more complex initialization scenarios the overhead is bound to become a problem.

Exception Processing

So what happens if a filter or interceptor throws an exception? On the server side, the JAX-RS runtime will process exceptions in the same way as if an exception were thrown in a JAX-RS method. It will try to find an ExceptionMapper for the exception and then run it. If an exception is thrown by a ContainerRequestFilter or ReaderIntercep tor and mapped by an ExceptionMapper, then any bound ContainerResponseFil ter must be invoked. The JAX-RS runtime ensures that at most one ExceptionMap per will be invoked in a single request processing cycle. This avoids infinite loops.

On the client side, if the exception thrown is an instance of WebApplicationExcep tion, then the runtime will propagate it back to application code. Otherwise, the exception is wrapped in a javax.ws.rs.client.ProcessingException if it is thrown before the request goes over the wire. The exception is wrapped in a javax.ws.rs.cli ent.ResponseProcessingException when processing a response.

Wrapping Up

In this chapter we learned about client- and server-side filters and interceptors. Filters generally interact with HTTP message headers, while interceptors are exclusive to processing HTTP message bodies. Filters and interceptors are applied to all HTTP requests by default, but you can bind them to individual JAX-RS resource methods by using `DynamicFeature` or `@NameBinding`. Chapter 26 walks you through a bunch of code examples that show most of these component features in action.

CHAPTER 13

Asynchronous JAX-RS

Another interesting new feature introduced in JAX-RS 2.0 is asynchronous request and response processing both on the client and server side. If you are mashing together a lot of data from different websites or you have something like a stock quote application that needs to push events to hundreds or thousands of idle blocking clients, then the JAX-RS 2.0 asynchronous APIs are worth looking into.

AsyncInvoker Client API

The client asynchronous API allows you to spin off a bunch of HTTP requests in the background and then either poll for a response, or register a callback that is invoked when the HTTP response is available. To invoke an HTTP request asynchronously on the client, you interact with the `javax.ws.rs.client.AsyncInvoker` interface or the `submit()` methods on `javax.ws.rs.client.Invocation`. First, let's take a look at polling HTTP requests that are run in the background.

Using Futures

The `AsyncInvoker` interface has a bunch of methods that invoke HTTP requests asynchronously and that return a `java.util.concurrent.Future` instance. You can use the `AsyncInvoker` methods by invoking the `async()` method on the `Invocation.Build er` interface.

```java
package javax.ws.rs.client;

public interface AsyncInvoker {
    Future<Response> get();
    <T> Future<T> get(Class<T> responseType);

    Future<Response> put(Entity<?> entity);
    <T> Future<T> put(Entity<?> entity, Class<T> responseType);
```

```
    Future<Response> post(Entity<?> entity);
    <T> Future<T> post(Entity<?> entity, Class<T> responseType);

    Future<Response> delete(Entity<?> entity);
    <T> Future<T> delete(Entity<?> entity, Class<T> responseType);

    ...
}
```

The Future interface is defined within the java.util.concurrent package that comes
with the JDK. For JAX-RS, it gives us a nice reusable interface for polling HTTP responses in either a blocking or nonblocking manner. If you've used java.util.concur
rent.Executors or @Asynchronous within an EJB container, using the Future interface
should be very familiar to you.

```
package java.util.concurrent;

public interface Future<V> {
    boolean cancel(boolean mayInterruptIfRunning);
    boolean isCancelled();
    boolean isDone();
    V get() throws InterruptedException, ExecutionException;
    V get(long timeout, TimeUnit unit)
        throws InterruptedException, ExecutionException, TimeoutException;
}
```

This is best explained in a full example:

```
Client client = ClientBuilder.newClient();

Future<Response> future1 = client.target("http://example.com/customers/123")
                                 .request()
                                 .async().get();

Future<Order> future2 = client.target("http://foobar.com/orders/456")
                              .request()
                              .async().get(Order.class);

// block until complete
Response res1 = future1.get();
Customer result1 = res.readEntity(Customer.class);

// Wait 5 seconds
try {
   Order result2 = future2.get(5, TimeUnit.SECONDS);
} catch (TimeoutException timeout ) {
   ... handle exception ...
}
```

In this example, two separate requests are executed in parallel. With future1 we want
a full javax.ws.rs.core.Response. After executing both requests, we poll and block

indefinitely on `future1` by calling `Future.get()` until we get a `Response` back from that service.

With `future2`, we instead poll and block for five seconds only. For this second HTTP asynchronous request, we let JAX-RS automatically unmarshal the HTTP response body into an `Order`. `java.util.concurrent.TimeoutException` is thrown if the call takes longer than five seconds. You can also invoke the nonblocking `isDone()` or `is Cancelled()` methods on `Future` to see if the request is finished or cancelled.

Exception handling

Exceptions that can be thrown by `Future.get()` methods are defined by that interface. `java.util.concurrent.TimeoutException` occurs if we are calling `Future.get()` with a timeout. `InterruptedException` happens if the calling thread has been interrupted. `java.util.concurrent.ExecutionException` is a wrapper exception. Any exception thrown by the JAX-RS runtime is caught and wrapped by this exception. Let's expand on the `future2` example to see how this works:

```
// Wait 5 seconds
try {
   Order result2 = future2.get(5, TimeUnit.SECONDS);
} catch (TimeoutException timeout ) {
    System.err.println("request timed out");
} catch (InterruptedException ie) {
    System.err.println("Request was interrupted");
} catch (ExecutionException ee) {
  Throwable cause = ee.getCause();

  if (cause instanceof WebApplicationException) {
    (WebApplicationException)wae = (WebApplicationException)cause;
    wae.close();
  } else if (cause instanceof ResponseProcessingException) {
    ResponseProcessingException rpe = (ResponseProcessingException)cause;
    rpe.close();
  } else if (cause instanceof ProcessingException) {
    // handle processing exception
  } else {
    // unknown
  }
}
```

You can obtain any exception thrown by the JAX-RS runtime when an asynchronous request is executed by calling the `ExecutionException.getCause()` method. The possible wrapped JAX-RS exceptions are the same as the synchronous ones discussed in Chapter 8.

In the example, the call to `future2.get()` unmarshalls the response to an `Order` object. If the response is something other than 200, "OK," then the JAX-RS runtime throws one of the exceptions from the JAX-RS error exception hierarchy (i.e., `NotFoundExcep tion` or `BadRequestException`). If an exception is thrown while you're unmarshalling the response to a `Order`, then `ResponseProcessingException` is thrown.

 You should always make sure that the underlying JAX-RS response is closed. While most JAX-RS containers will have their `Response` objects implement a `finalize()` method, it is not a good idea to rely on the garbage collector to clean up your client connections. If you do not clean up your connections, you may end up with intermittent errors that pop up if the underlying `Client` or operating system has exhausted its limit of allowable open connections.

In fact, if we examine our initial example a bit further, there's a lot of code we have to add to ensure that we are being good citizens and closing any open `Response` objects. Here's what the final piece of code would look like:

```
Client client = ClientBuilder.newClient();

Future<Response> future1 = client.target("http://example.com/service")
                                 .request()
                                 .async().get();
Future<Order> future2 = null;
try {
   future2 = client.target("http://foobar.com/service2")
                   .request()
                   .async().get(Order.class);
} catch (Throwable ignored) {
   ignored.printStackTrace();
}

// block until complete
Response res1 = future1.get();
try {
   Customer result1 = res.readEntity(Customer.class);
} catch (Throwable ignored) {
   ignored.printStackTrace();
} finally {
   res1.close();
}

// if we successfully executed 2nd request
if (future2 != null) {
   // Wait 5 seconds
   try {
      Order result2 = future2.get(5, TimeUnit.SECONDS);
   } catch (TimeoutException timeout ) {
```

```
              System.err.println("request timed out");
        } catch (InterruptedException ie) {
              System.err.println("Request was interrupted");
        } catch (ExecutionException ee) {
              Throwable cause = ee.getCause();

              if (cause instanceof WebApplicationException) {
                 (WebApplicationException)wae = (WebApplicationException)cause;
                 wae.close();
              } else if (cause instanceof ResponseProcessingException) {
                 ResponseProcessingException rpe = (ResponseProcessingException)cause;
                 rpe.close();
              } else if (cause instanceof ProcessingException) {
                 // handle processing exception
              } else {
                 // unknown
              }
        }
   }
}
```

As you can see, there's a few more try/catch blocks we need to add to make sure that the response of each async request is closed.

Using Callbacks

The AsyncInvoker interface has an additional callback invocation style. You can register an object that will be called back when the asynchronous invocation is ready for processing:

```
package javax.ws.rs.client;

public interface AsyncInvoker {
    <T> Future<T> get(InvocationCallback<T> callback);
    <T> Future<T> post(Entity<?> entity, InvocationCallback<T> callback);
    <T> Future<T> put(Entity<?> entity, InvocationCallback<T> callback);
    <T> Future<T> delete(Entity<?> entity, InvocationCallback<T> callback);

    ...
}
```

The InvocationCallback interface is a parameterized generic interface and has two simple methods you have to implement—one for successful responses, the other for failures:

```
package javax.rs.ws.client;

public interface InvocationCallback<RESPONSE> {
    public void completed(RESPONSE response);
    public void failed(Throwable throwable);
}
```

JAX-RS introspects the application class that implements InvocationCallback to determine whether your callback wants a Response object or if you want to unmarshal to a specific type. Let's convert our Future example to use callbacks. First, we'll implement a callback for our initial request:

```java
public class CustomerCallback implements InvocationCallback<Response> {
    public void completed(Response response) {
        if (response.getStatus() == 200) {
            Customer cust = response.readEntity(Customer.class);
        } else {
            System.err.println("Request error: " + response.getStatus());
        }
    }

    public void failed(Throwable throwable) {
        throwable.printStackTrace();
    }
}
```

The CustomerCallback class implements InvocationCallback with a Response generic parameter. This means JAX-RS will call the completed() method and pass in an untouched Response object. If there is a problem sending the request to the server or the JAX-RS runtime is unable to create a Response, the failed() method will be invoked with the appropriate exception. Otherwise, if there is an HTTP response, then completed() will be called.

Next, let's implement a different callback for our second parallel request. This time we want our successful HTTP responses to be converted into Order objects:

```java
public class OrderCallback implements InvocationCallback<Order> {
    public void completed(Order order) {
        System.out.println("We received an order.");
    }

    public void failed(Throwable throwable) {
        if (throwable instanceof WebApplicationException) {
            WebApplicationException wae = (WebApplicationException)throwable;
            System.err.println("Failed with status:
                        " + wae.getResponse().getStatus());
        } else if (throwable instanceof ResponseProcessingException) {
            ResponseProcessingException rpe = (ResponseProcessingException)cause;
            System.err.println("Failed with status:
                        " + rpe.getResponse().getStatus());
        } else {
            throwable.printStackTrace();
        }
    }
}
```

This case is a little bit different than when we implement InvocationCallback with a Response. If there is a successful HTTP response from the server (like 200, "OK"), JAX-RS will attempt to unmarshal the response into an Order object. If there were an HTTP error response, or the JAX-RS runtime failed to unmarshal the response body into an Order object, then the failed() method is invoked with the appropriate exception. Basically, we see the same kind of exceptions thrown by similar synchronous invocations or the Future example we discussed earlier. You do not have to close the underlying Response object; JAX-RS will do this after completed() or failed() is invoked.

Now that our callback classes have been implemented, let's finish our example by invoking on some services:

```
Client client = ClientBuilder.newClient();

Future<Response> future1 = client.target("http://example.com/customers/123")
                                 .request()
                                 .async().get(new CustomerCallback());

Future<Order> future2 = client.target("http://foobar.com/orders/456")
                              .request()
                              .async().get(new OrderCallback());
```

That's all we have to do. Notice that the get() methods return a Future object. You can ignore this Future, or interact with it as we did previously. I suggest that you only use the Future.cancel() and Future.isDone() methods, though, as you may have concurrency issues with InvocationCallback.

Futures Versus Callbacks

Given that we have two different ways to do asynchronous client invocations, which style should you use? Futures or callbacks? In general, use futures if you need to *join* a set of requests you've invoked asynchronously. By *join*, I mean you need to know when each of the requests has finished and you need to perform another task after *all* the asynchronous requests are complete. For example, maybe you are gathering information from a bunch of different web services to build a larger aggregated document (a mashup).

Use callbacks when each invocation is its own distinct unit and you do not have to do any coordination or mashing up.

Server Asynchronous Response Processing

For a typical HTTP server, when a request comes in, one thread is dedicated to the processing of that request and its HTTP response to the client. This is fine for the vast majority of HTTP traffic both on the Internet and on your company's internal networks.

Most HTTP requests are short-lived, so a few hundred threads can easily handle a few thousand concurrent users and have relatively decent response times.

The nature of HTTP traffic started to change somewhat as JavaScript clients started to become more prevalent. One problem that popped up often was the need for the server to push events to the client. A typical example is a stock quote application where you need to update a string of clients with the latest stock price. These clients would make an HTTP GET or POST request and just block indefinitely until the server was ready to send back a response. This resulted in a large amount of open, long-running requests that were doing nothing other than idling. Not only were there a lot of open, idle sockets, but there were also a lot of dedicated threads doing nothing at all. Most HTTP servers were designed for short-lived requests with the assumption that one thread could process requests from multiple concurrent users. When you have a very large number of threads, you start to consume a lot of operating system resources. Each thread consumes memory, and context switching between threads starts to get quite expensive when the OS has to deal with a large number of threads. It became really hard to scale these types of server-push applications since the Servlet API, and by association JAX-RS, was a "one thread per connection" model.

In 2009, the Servlet 3.0 specification introduced asynchronous HTTP. With the Servlet 3.0 API, you can suspend the current server-side request and have a separate thread, other than the calling thread, handle sending back a response to the client. For a server-push app, you could then have a small handful of threads manage sending responses back to polling clients and avoid all the overhead of the "one thread per connection" model. JAX-RS 2.0 introduced a similar API that we'll discuss in this section.

 Server-side async response processing is only meant for a specific small subset of applications. Asynchronous doesn't necessarily mean automatic scalability. For the typical web app, using server asynchronous response processing will only complicate your code and make it harder to maintain. It may even hurt performance.

AsyncResponse API

To use server-side async response processing, you interact with the `AsyncResponse` interface:

```
package javax.ws.rs.container;

public interface AsyncResponse {
    boolean resume(Object response);
    boolean resume(Throwable response);

    ...
}
```

You get access to an `AsyncResponse` instance by injecting it into a JAX-RS method using the `@Suspended` annotation:

```
import javax.ws.rs.container.AsyncResponse;
import javax.ws.rs.container.Suspended;

@Path("/orders")
public class OrderResource {

    @POST
    @Consumes("application/json")
    public void submit(final Order order,
                        final @Suspended AsyncResponse response) {
    }
}
```

Here we have our very familiar `OrderResource`. Order submission has been turned into an asynchronous operation. When you inject an instance of `AsyncResponse` using the `@Suspended` annotation, the HTTP request becomes suspended from the current thread of execution. In this particular example, the `OrderResource.submit()` method will never send back a response to the client. The client will just time out with an error condition. Let's expand on this example:

```
import javax.ws.rs.container.AsyncResponse;
import javax.ws.rs.container.Suspended;

@Path("/orders")
public class OrderResource {

    @POST
    @Consumes("application/json")
    @Produces("application/json")
    public void submit(final Order order,
                        final @Suspended AsyncResponse response) {
        new Thread() {
            public void run() {
                OrderConfirmation confirmation = orderProcessor.process(order);
                response.resume(order);
            }
        }.start();
    }
}
```

In the previous example, the client would just time out. Now, the `OrderResource.sub` `mit()` method spawns a new thread to handle order submission. This background thread processes the `Order` to obtain an `OrderConfirmation`. It then sends a response back to the client by calling the `AsyncResponse.resume()` method, passing in the `Or` `derConfirmation` instance. Invoking `resume()` in this manner means that it is a successful response. So, a status code of 200 is sent back to the client. Also, because we're passing a Java object, the `resume()` method will marshal this object and send it within

the HTTP response body. The media type used is determined by the @Produces annotation placed on the original JAX-RS method. If the @Produces annotation has more
than one value, then the request's Accept header is examined to pick the returned media
type. Basically, this is the same algorithm a regular JAX-RS method uses to determine
the media type.

Alternatively, you can pass resume() a Response object to send the client a more specific
response:

```
import javax.ws.rs.container.AsyncResponse;
import javax.ws.rs.container.Suspended;

@Path("/orders")
public class OrderResource {

    @POST
    @Consumes("application/json")
    public void submit(final Order order,
                       final @Suspended AsyncResponse response) {
       new Thread() {
          public void run() {
             OrderConfirmation confirmation = orderProcessor.process(order);
             Response res= Response.ok(confirmation,
                                       MediaType.APPLICATION_XML_TYPE)
                                    .build();
             res.resume(response);
          }
       }.start();
    }
}
```

In this example, we've manually created a Response. We set the entity to the OrderCon
firmation and the content type to XML.

Exception Handling

In Chapter 7, we discussed what happens when a JAX-RS method throws an exception.
When you invoke AsyncResponse.resume(Object), the response filter and interceptor
chains (see Chapter 12) are invoked, and then finally the MessageBodyWriter. If an
exception is thrown by any one of these components, then the exception is handled in
the same way as its synchronous counterpart with one caveat. Unhandled exceptions
are not propagated, but instead the server will return a 500, "Internal Server Error," back
to the client.

Finally, the previous example is pretty simple, but what if it were possible for orderPro
cessor.process() to throw an exception? We can handle this exception by using the
AsyncResponse.resume(Throwable) method:

```java
import javax.ws.rs.container.AsyncResponse;
import javax.ws.rs.container.Suspended;

@Path("/orders")
public class OrderResource {

   @POST
   @Consumes("application/json")
   public void submit(final Order order,
                      final @Suspended AsyncResponse response) {
      new Thread() {
         public void run() {
            OrderConfirmation confirmation = null;
            try {
               confirmation = orderProcessor.process(order);
            } catch (Exception ex) {
               response.resume(ex);
               return;
            }
            Response response = Response.ok(confirmation,
                                    MediaType.APPLICATION_XML_TYPE)
                                 .build();
            response.resume(response);
         }
      }.start();
   }
}
```

Invoking `AsyncResponse.resume(Throwable)` is like throwing an exception from a regular synchronous JAX-RS method. Standard JAX-RS exception handling is performed on the passed-in `Throwable`. If a matching `ExceptionMapper` exists for the passed-in `Throwable`, it will be used. Otherwise, the server will send back a 500 status code.

Cancel

There's a few other convenience methods on `AsyncResponse` we haven't covered yet:

```java
package javax.ws.rs.container;

public interface AsyncResponse {
   boolean cancel();
   boolean cancel(int retryAfter);
   boolean cancel(Date retryAfter);
   ...
}
```

Each of the `cancel()` methods is really a precanned call to `resume()`:

```java
// cancel()
response.resume(Response.status(503).build());
```

```
// cancel(int)
response.resume(Response.status(503)
                        .header(HttpHeaders.RETRY_AFTER, 100)
                        .build());
// cancel(Date)
response.resume(Response.status(503)
                        .header(HttpHeaders.RETRY_AFTER, date)
                        .build());
```

Internally, a Response object is built with a 503 status code. For cancel() methods that accept input, the parameter is used to initialize a Retry-After HTTP response header.

Status Methods

There's a few status methods on AsyncResponse that specify the state of the response:

```
public interface AsyncResponse {
    boolean isSuspended();
    boolean isCancelled();
    boolean isDone();

    ...
}
```

The AsyncResponse.isCancelled() method can be called to see if a AsyncResponse has been cancelled. isSuspended() specifies whether or not the response can have resume() or cancel() invoked. The isDone() method tells you if the response is finished.

Timeouts

If an AsyncResponse is not resumed or cancelled, it will eventually time out. The default timeout is container-specific. A timeout results in a 503, "Service Unavailable," response code sent back to the client. You can explicitly set the timeout by invoking the setTimeout() method:

```
response.setTimeout(5, TimeUnit.SECONDS);
```

You can also register a callback that is triggered when a timeout occurs by implementing the TimeoutHandler interface. For example:

```
response.setTimeoutHandler(
    new TimeoutHandler {
        public void handleTimeout(AsyncResponse response) {
            response.resume(Response.serverError().build());
        }
    }
);
```

Here, instead of sending the default 503 response code to the client on a timeout, the example registers a `TimeoutHandler` that sends a 500 response code instead.

Callbacks

The `AsyncResponse` interface also allows you to register callback objects for other types of events:

```
package javax.ws.rs.container;

public interface CompletionCallback {
        public void onComplete(Throwable throwable);
}
```

`CompletionCallback.onComplete()` is called after the response has been sent to the client. The `Throwable` is set to any unmapped exception thrown internally when processing a `resume()`. Otherwise, it is `null`.

```
package javax.ws.rs.container;

public interface ConnectionCallback {
        public void onDisconnect(AsyncResponse response);
}
```

The JAX-RS container does not require implementation of the `ConnectionCallback`. It allows you to be notified if the socket connection is disconnected while processing the response.

You enable callbacks by invoking the `AsyncResponse.register()` methods. You can pass one or more classes that will be instantiated by the JAX-RS container, and you can pass one or more instances:

```
response.register(MyCompletionCallback.class);
response.register(new MyConnectionCallback());
```

Callbacks are generally used to receive notification of error conditions caused after invoking `resume()`. You may have resources to clean up or even transactions to roll back or undo as a result of an asynchronous failure.

Use Cases for AsyncResponse

The examples used in the previous section were really contrived to make it simple to explain the behavior of the asynchronous APIs. As I mentioned before, there is a specific set of use cases for async response processing. Let's go over it.

Server-side push

With server-side push, the server is sending events back to the client. A typical example is stock quotes. The client wants to be notified when a new quote is available. It does a long-poll GET request until the quote is ready.

```
Client client = ClientBuilder.newClient();
final WebTarget target = client.target("http://quote.com/quote/RHT");
target.request().async().get(new InvocationCallback<String> {

    public void completed(String quote) {
        System.out.println("RHT: " + quote);
        target.request().async().get(this);
    }

    public void failed(Throwable t) {}
}
```

The preceding continuously polls for a quote using InvocationCallback. On the server side, we want our JAX-RS resource classes to use suspended requests so that we can have one thread that writes quotes back to polling clients. With one writer thread, we can scale this quote service to thousands and thousands of clients, as we're not beholden to a "one thread per request" model. Here's what the JAX-RS resource class might look like:

```
@Path("quote/RHT")
public class RHTQuoteResource {

    protected List<AsyncResponse> responses;

    @GET
    @Produces("text/plain")
    public void getQuote(@Suspended AsyncResponse response) {
        synchronized (responses) {
            responses.put(response);
        }
    }
}
```

The example code is overly simplified, but the idea is that there is a List of AsyncResponse objects that are waiting for the latest stock quote for Red Hat. This List would be shared by a background thread that would send a response back to all waiting clients when a new quote for Red Hat became available.

```
Executor executor = Executors.newSingleThreadExecutor();
final List<AsyncResponse> responses = ...;
final Ticker rhtTicker = nyse.getTicker("RHT");
executor.execute(new Runnable() {

    public void run() {
        while (true) {
            String quote = ticker.await();
```

```
            synchronized (responses) {
                for (AsyncResponse response : responses) response.resume(quote);
            }
        }
    }
});
```

So, here we're starting a background thread that runs continuously using the Execu
tors class from the `java.util.concurrent` package that comes with the JDK. This
thread blocks until a quote for Red Hat is available. Then it loops over every awaiting
AsyncResponse to send the quote back to each client. Some of the implementation is
missing here, but hopefully you get the idea.

Publish and subscribe

Another great use case for AsyncResponse is publish and subscribe applications, an
example being a chat service. Here's what the server code might look like:

```
@Path("chat")
public class ChatResource {
    protected List<AsyncResponse> responses = new ArrayList<AsyncResponse>();

    @GET
    @Produces("text/plain")
    public synchronized void receive(@Suspended AsyncResponse response) {
        responses.add(response);
    }

    @POST
    @Consume("text/plain")
    public synchronized void send(String message) {
        for (AsyncResponse response : responses) {
            response.resume(message);
        }
    }
}
```

This is a really poor chat implementation, as messages could be lost for clients that are
repolling, but hopefully it illustrates how you might create such an application. In
Chapter 27, we'll implement a more robust and complete chat service.

With protocols like WebSocket[1] and Server Sent Events (SSE)[2] being supported in most browsers, pure HTTP server push and pub-sub are fast becoming legacy. So, if you're only going to have browser clients for this kind of app, you're probably better off using WebSockets or SSE.

Priority scheduling

Sometimes there are certain services that are highly CPU-intensive. If you have too many of these types of requests running, you can completely starve users who are making simple, fast requests. To resolve this issue, you can queue up these expensive requests in a separate thread pool that guarantees that only a few of these expensive operations will happen concurrently:

```java
@Path("orders")
public class OrderResource {

    Executor executor;

    public OrderResource {
        executor = Executors.newSingleThreadExecutor();
    }

    @POST
    @Path("year_to_date_report")
    @Produces("application/json")
    public void ytdReport(final @FormParam("product") String product,
                          @AsyncResponse response) {

        executor.execute( new Runnable() {
            public void run() {
                Report report = generateYTDReportFor(product);
                response.resume(report);
            }
        }

    }


    protected Report generateYTDReportFor(String product) {
        ...
    }
}
```

Here we're back to our familiar `OrderResource` again. We have a `ytdReport()` method that calculates buying patterns for a specific product for the year to date. We want to

---

1. For more information, see *http://www.websocket.org*.

2. For more information, see *http://www.w3.org/TR/2011/WD-eventsource-20110208*.

allow only one of these requests to execute at a time, as the calculation is extremely expensive. We set up a single-threaded `java.util.concurrent.Executor` in the `Order Resource` constructor. The `ytdReport()` method queues up a `Runnable` in this `Executor` that generates the report and sends it back to the client. If the `Executor` is currently busy generating a report, the request is queued up and executed after that report is finished.

Wrapping Up

In this chapter, we discussed how you can use JAX-RS asynchronously both on the client and server side. On the client, you can execute one or more requests in the background and either poll for their response, or receive a callback. On the server, we saw that you can suspend requests so that a different thread can handle response processing. This is a great way to scale specific kinds of applications. Chapter 27 walks you through a bunch of code examples that show most of these features in action.

CHAPTER 14

Deployment and Integration

Throughout this book, I have focused on teaching you the basics of JAX-RS and REST with simple examples that have very few moving parts. In the real world, though, your JAX-RS services are going to interact with databases and a variety of server-side component models. They will need to be secure and sometimes transactional. Chapter 3 was a very simple example of deploying JAX-RS within a Java EE environment. In this chapter, we'll look into more deployment details of JAX-RS and how it integrates with Java EE and other component models.

Deployment

JAX-RS applications are deployed within a standalone servlet container, like Apache Tomcat, Jetty, JBossWeb, or the servlet container of your favorite application server, like JBoss, Wildfly, Weblogic, Websphere, or Glassfish. Think of a servlet container as a web server. It understands the HTTP protocol and provides a low-level component model (the servlet API) for receiving HTTP requests.

Servlet-based applications are organized in deployment units called Web ARchives (WAR). A WAR is a JAR-based packaging format that contains the Java classes and libraries used by the deployment as well as static content like images and HTML files that the web server will publish. Here's what the structure of a WAR file looks like:

```
<any static content>
WEB-INF/
        web.xml
        classes/
        lib/
```

Any files outside and above the *WEB-INF/* directory of the archive are published and available directly through HTTP. This is where you would put static HTML files and images that you want to expose to the outside world. The *WEB-INF/* directory has two subdirectories. Within the *classes/* directory, you can put any Java classes you want. They must be in a Java package structure. The *lib/* directory can contain any application or third-party libraries that will be used by the deployment. The *WEB-INF/* directory also contains a *web.xml* deployment descriptor file. This file defines the configuration of the WAR and how the servlet container should initialize it.

You will need to define a *web.xml* file for your JAX-RS deployments. How JAX-RS is deployed within a servlet container varies between JAX-RS-aware (like within Java EE application servers or standalone Servlet 3.x containers like Tomcat) and older JAX-RS–unaware servlet containers. Let's dive into these details.

The Application Class

Before looking at what we have to do to configure a *web.xml* file, we need to learn about the `javax.ws.rs.core.Application` class. The `Application` class is the only portable way of telling JAX-RS which web services (`@Path` annotated classes) as well as which filters, interceptors, `MessageBodyReaders`, `MessageBodyWriters`, and `ContextResolv ers` (providers) you want deployed. I first introduced you to the `Application` class back in Chapter 3:

```
package javax.ws.rs.core;

import java.util.Collections;
import java.util.Set;

public abstract class Application {
    private static final Set<Object> emptySet =
                                        Collections.emptySet();

    public abstract Set<Class<?>> getClasses();


    public Set<Object> getSingletons() {
        return emptySet;
    }

}
```

The `Application` class is very simple. All it does is list classes and objects that JAX-RS is supposed to deploy. The `getClasses()` method returns a list of JAX-RS web service and provider classes. JAX-RS web service classes follow the *per-request* model mentioned in Chapter 3. Provider classes are instantiated by the JAX-RS container and registered once per application.

The `getSingletons()` method returns a list of preallocated JAX-RS web services and providers. You, as the application programmer, are responsible for creating these objects. The JAX-RS runtime will iterate through the list of objects and register them internally. When these objects are registered, JAX-RS will also inject values for @Context annotated fields and setter methods.

Let's look at a simple example of an Application class:

```
package com.restfully.shop.services;

import javax.ws.rs.core.Application;

public class ShoppingApplication extends Application {

    public ShoppingApplication() {}

    public Set<Class<?>> getClasses() {
        HashSet<Class<?>> set = new HashSet<Class<?>>();
        set.add(CustomerResource.class);
        set.add(OrderResource.class);
        set.add(ProduceResource.class);
        return set;
    }

    public Set<Object> getSingletons() {

        JsonWriter json = new JsonWriter();
        CreditCardResource service = new CreditCardResource();

        HashSet<Object> set = new HashSet();
        set.add(json);
        set.add(service);
        return set;
    }
}
```

Here, we have a ShoppingApplication class that extends the Application class. The getClasses() method allocates a HashSet, populates it with @Path annotated classes, and returns the set. The getSingletons() method allocates a MessageBodyWriter class named JsonWriter and an @Path annotated class CreditCardResource. It then creates a HashSet and adds these instances to it. This set is returned by the method.

Deployment Within a JAX-RS-Aware Container

Java EE stands for Java Enterprise Edition. It is the umbrella specification of JAX-RS and defines a complete enterprise platform that includes services like a servlet container, EJB, transaction manager (JTA), messaging (JMS), connection pooling (JCA), database persistence (JPA), web framework (JSF), and a multitude of other services. Application servers that are certified under Java EE 6 are required to have built-in support for JAX-RS 1.1. Java EE 7 containers are required to have built-in support for JAX-RS 2.0.

For standalone Servlet 3.x containers like Tomcat and Jetty, most JAX-RS implementations can seamlessly integrate JAX-RS just as easily as with Java EE. They do this through the Servlet 3.0 `ServletContainerInitializer` SPI, which we will not cover here. The only difference between standalone servlet deployments and Java EE is that your WAR deployments will also need to include the libraries of your JAX-RS implementation.

Deploying a JAX-RS application is very easy in a JAX-RS-aware servlet container. You still need at least an empty *web.xml* file:

```
<?xml version="1.0" encoding="UTF-8"?>
<web-app xmlns="http://java.sun.com/xml/ns/javaee"
    xmlns:xsi="http://www.w3.org/2001/XMLSchema-instance"
    xsi:schemaLocation="http://java.sun.com/xml/ns/javaee
    http://java.sun.com/xml/ns/javaee/web-app_3_0.xsd"
    version="3.0">
</web-app>
```

If you have at least one `Application` class implementation annotated with `@Applica tionPath`, the JAX-RS–aware container will automatically deploy that `Application`. For example:

```
package com.restfully.shop.services;

import javax.ws.rs.core.Application;
import javax.ws.rs.ApplicationPath;

@ApplicationPath("/root")
public class ShoppingApplication extends Application {

    public ShoppingApplication() {}

    public Set<Class<?>> getClasses() {
        HashSet<Class<?>> set = new HashSet<Class<?>>();
        set.add(CustomerResource.class);
        set.add(OrderResource.class);
        set.add(ProduceResource.class);
        return set;
    }

    public Set<Object> getSingletons() {

        JsonWriter json = new JsonWriter();
        CreditCardResource service = new CreditCardResource();

        HashSet<Object> set = new HashSet();
        set.add(json);
        set.add(service);
        return set;
    }
}
```

The @ApplicationPath annotation here will set up a base path to whatever the WAR's context root is, with root appended.

You can fully leverage the servlet class scanning abilities if you have both getClass es() and getSingletons() return an empty set. For example:

```
package com.restfully.shop.services;

import javax.ws.rs.core.Application;
import javax.ws.rs.ApplicationPath;

@ApplicationPath("/root")
public class ShoppingApplication extends Application {
    // complete
}
```

When scanning, the application server will look within *WEB-INF/classes* and any JAR file within the *WEB-INF/lib* directory. It will add any class annotated with @Path or @Provider to the list of things that need to be deployed and registered with the JAX-RS runtime. You can also deploy as many Application classes as you want in one WAR. The scanner will also ignore any Application classes not annotated with @Applica tionPath.

You can also override the @ApplicationPath annotation via a simple servlet mapping within *web.xml*:

```
<?xml version="1.0" encoding="UTF-8"?>
<web-app xmlns="http://java.sun.com/xml/ns/javaee"
      xmlns:xsi="http://www.w3.org/2001/XMLSchema-instance"
      xsi:schemaLocation="http://java.sun.com/xml/ns/javaee
                          http://java.sun.com/xml/ns/javaee/web-app_3_0.xsd"
      version="3.0">

    <servlet-mapping>
        <servlet-name>com.rest.ShoppingApplication</servlet-name>
        <url-pattern>/*</url-pattern>
    </servlet-mapping>

</web-app>
```

The servlet-name is the fully qualified class name of your Application class. With this configuration, you can also omit the @ApplicationPath annotation entirely.

Deployment Within a JAX-RS-Unaware Container

If you are running in 2.x or older Servlet containers, you'll have to manually configure your *web.xml* file to load your JAX-RS implementation's proprietary servlet class. For example:

```
<?xml version="1.0"?>
<web-app>
    <servlet>
        <servlet-name>JAXRS</servlet-name>
        <servlet-class>
            org.jboss.resteasy.plugins.server.servlet.HttpServletDispatcher
        </servlet-class>
        <init-param>
            <param-name>
                javax.ws.rs.Application
            </param-name>
            <param-value>
                com.restfully.shop.services.ShoppingApplication
            </param-value>
        </init-param>
    </servlet>

    <servlet-mapping>
        <servlet-name>JAXRS</servlet-name>
        <url-pattern>/*</url-pattern>
    </servlet-mapping>
</web-app>
```

Here, we've registered and initialized the RESTEasy JAX-RS implementation with the `ShoppingApplication` class we created earlier in this chapter. The `<servlet-mapping>` element specifies the base URI path for the JAX-RS runtime. The `/*` `<url-pattern>` specifies that all incoming requests should be routed through our JAX-RS implementation.

Configuration

All the examples in this book so far have been simple and pretty self-contained. Your RESTful web services will probably need to sit in front of a database and interact with other local and remote services. Your services will also need configuration settings that are described outside of code. I don't want to get into too much detail, but the servlet and Java EE specifications provide annotations and XML configurations that allow you to get access to various Java EE services and configuration information. Let's look at how JAX-RS can take advantage of these features.

Basic Configuration

Any JAX-RS implementation, whether it sits within a JAX-RS-aware or Java EE container, must support the @Context injection of the `javax.servlet.ServletContext` and `javax.servlet.ServletConfig` interfaces. Through these interfaces, you can get access to configuration information expressed in the WAR's *web.xml* deployment descriptor. Let's take this *web.xml* file, for example:

```
<?xml version="1.0"?>
<web-app>
  <context-param>
    <param-name>max-customers-size</param-name>
    <param-value>10</param-value>
  </context-param>
</web-app>
```

In this *web.xml* file, we want to define a default maximum dataset size for a JAX-RS–based customer database that returns a collection of customers through XML. We do this by defining a `<context-param>` named `max-customers-size` and set the value to 10. We can get access to this value within our JAX-RS service by injecting a reference to `ServletContext` with the `@Context` annotation. For example:

```
@Path("/customers")
public class CustomerResource {

    protected int defaultPageSize = 5;

    @Context
    public void setServletContext(ServletContext context) {
        String size = context.getInitParameter("max-customers-size");
        if (size != null) {
            defaultPageSize = Integer.parseInt(size);
        }
    }

    @GET
    @Produces("application/xml")
    public String getCustomerList() {
        ... use defaultPageSize to create
                and return list of XML customers...
    }
}
```

Here, we use the `@Context` annotation on the `setServletContext()` method of our `CustomerResource` class. When an instance of `CustomerResource` gets instantiated, the `setServletContext()` method is called with access to a `javax.servlet.ServletContext`. From this, we can obtain the value of `max-customers-size` that we defined in our *web.xml* and save it in the member variable `defaultPageSize` for later use.

Another way you might want to do this is to use your `javax.ws.rs.core.Application` class as a factory for your JAX-RS services. You could define or pull in configuration information through this class and use it to construct your JAX-RS service. Let's first rewrite our `CustomerResource` class to illustrate this technique:

```
@Path("/customers")
public class CustomerResource {

    protected int defaultPageSize = 5;
```

```
        public void setDefaultPageSize(int size) {
            defaultPageSize = size;
        }

        @GET
        @Produces("application/xml")
        public String getCustomerList() {
            ... use defaultPageSize to create and return list of XML customers...
        }
    }
```

We first remove all references to the ServletContext injection we did in our previous
incarnation of the CustomerResource class. We replace it with a setter method, setDe
faultPageSize(), which initializes the defaultPageSize member variable. This is a
better design for our CustomerResource class because we've abstracted away how it
obtains configuration information. This gives the class more flexibility as it evolves over
time.

We then inject the ServletContext into our Application class and extract the needed
information to initialize our services:

```
import javax.ws.rs.core.Application;
import javax.naming.InitialContext;

@ApplicationPath("/")
public class ShoppingApplication extends Application {

    public ShoppingApplication() {}

    public Set<Class<?>> getClasses() {
        return Collections.emptySet();
    }

    @Context
    ServletContext servletContext

    public Set<Object> getSingletons() {
        int pageSize = 0;

        try {
            Integer size =
                (Integer)servletContext.getInitParameter(
            pageSize = size.getValue();
        } catch (Exception ex) {
            ... handle example ...
        }
        CustomerResource custService = new CustomerResource();
        custService.setDefaultPageSize(pageSize);

        HashSet<Object> set = new HashSet();
```

```
        set.add(custService);
        return set;
    }
}
```

EJB Integration

EJBs are Java EE components that help you write business logic more easily. They support integration with security, transactions, and persistence. Further explanation of EJB is beyond the scope of this book. I suggest reading the book that I co-wrote with Andrew Rubinger, *Enterprise JavaBeans 3.1* (O'Reilly), if you want more information. Java EE requires that EJB containers support integration with JAX-RS. You are allowed to use JAX-RS annotations on local interfaces or no-interface beans of stateless session or singleton beans. No other integration with other bean types is supported.

If you are using the full-scanning deployment mechanism I mentioned before, you can just implement your services and put the classes of your EJBs directly within the WAR, and JAX-RS will find them automatically. Otherwise, you have to return the bean class of each JAX-RS EJB from your `Application.getClasses()` method. For example, let's say we have this EJB bean class:

```
@Stateless
@Path("/customers")
public class CustomerResourceBean implements CustomerResource {
...
}
```

If you are manually registering your resources via your `Application` class, you must register the bean class of the EJB via the `Application.getClasses()` method. For example:

```
package com.restfully.shop.services;

import javax.ws.rs.core.Application;
import javax.ws.rs.ApplicationPath;

@ApplicationPath("/root")
public class ShoppingApplication extends Application {

    public Set<Class<?>> getClasses() {
        HashSet<Class<?>> set = new HashSet<Class<?>>();
        set.add(CustomerResourceBean.class);
        return set;
    }
}
```

Spring Integration

Spring is an open source framework similar to EJB. Like EJB, it provides a great abstraction for transactions, persistence, and security. Further explanation of Spring is beyond the scope of this book. If you want more information on it, check out *Spring: A Developer's Notebook* by Bruce A. Tate and Justin Gehtland (O'Reilly). Most JAX-RS implementations have their own proprietary support for Spring and allow you to write Spring beans that are JAX-RS web services. If portability is not an issue for you, I suggest that you use the integration with Spring provided by your JAX-RS implementation.

There is a simple, portable way to integrate with Spring that we can talk about in this chapter. What you can do is write an `Application` class that loads your Spring XML files and then registers your Spring beans with JAX-RS through the `getSingletons()` method. First, let's define a Spring bean that represents a customer database. It will pretty much look like the `CustomerResource` bean described in "EJB Integration" on page 211:

```
@Path("/customers")
public interface CustomerResource {

    @GET
    @Produces("application/xml")
    public String getCustomers();

    @GET
    @Produces("application/xml")
    @Path("{id}")
    public String getCustomer(@PathParam("id") int id);
}
```

In this example, we first create an interface for our `CustomerResource` that is annotated with JAX-RS annotations:

```
public class CustomerResourceBean implements CustomerResource {

    public String getCustomers() {...}
    public String getCustomer(int id) {...}
}
```

Our Spring bean class, `CustomerResourceBean`, simply implements the `CustomerRe source` interface. Although you can opt to not define an interface and use JAX-RS annotations directly on the bean class, I highly suggest that you use an interface. Interfaces work better in Spring when you use features like Spring transactions.

Now that we have a bean class, we should declare it within a Spring XML file called *spring-beans.xml* (or whatever you want to name the file):

```
<beans xmlns="http://www.springframework.org/schema/beans"
    <bean id="custService"
          class="com.shopping.restful.services.CustomerResourceBean"/>
</beans>
```

Place this *spring-beans.xml* file within your WAR's *WEB-INF/classes* directory or within a JAR within the *WEB-INF/lib* directory. For this example, we'll put it in the *WEB-INF/ classes* directory. We will find this file through a class loader resource lookup later on when we write our `Application` class.

Next we write our *web.xml* file:

```
<web-app>
    <context-param>
        <param-name>spring-beans-file</param-name>
        <param-value>META-INF/applicationContext.xml</param-value>
    </context-param>
</web-app>
```

In our *web.xml* file, we define a `<context-param>` that contains the classpath location of our Spring XML file. We use a `<context-param>` so that we can change this value in the future if needed. We then need to wire everything together in our `Application` class:

```
@ApplicationPath("/")
public class ShoppingApplication extends Application
{
    protected ApplicationContext springContext;

    @Context
    protected ServletContext servletContext;

    public Set<Object> getSingletons()
    {
        try
        {
            InitialContext ctx = new InitialContext();
            String xmlFile = (String)servletContext.getInitParameter
                            ("spring-beans-file");
            springContext = new ClassPathXmlApplicationContext(xmlFile);
        }
        catch (Exception ex)
        {
            throw new RuntimeException(ex);
        }
        HashSet<Object> set = new HashSet();
        set.add(springContext.getBean("customer"));
        return set;
    }

}
```

In this `Application` class, we look up the classpath location of the Spring XML file that we defined in the `<context-param>` of our *web.xml* deployment descriptor. We then load this XML file through Spring's `ClassPathXmlApplicationContext`. This will also create the beans defined in this file. From the Spring `ApplicationContext`, we look up the bean instance for our `CustomerResource` using the `ApplicationContext.get Bean()` method. We then create a `HashSet` and add the `CustomerResource` bean to it and return it to be registered with the JAX-RS runtime.

Wrapping Up

In this chapter, you learned how deployment works within Java EE and standalone Servlet 3.x containers as well as in environments that are JAX-RS aware. We also looked at some portable ways to configure your JAX-RS applications. Finally, you saw how you can portably integrate with EJB and Spring. Chapter 28 will allow you to test-drive some of the concepts presented in this chapter. It will walk you through the deployment of a full application that integrates with EJB, Spring, and Java Persistence (JPA).

CHAPTER 15

Securing JAX-RS

Many RESTful web services will want secure access to the data and functionality they provide. This is especially true for services that will be performing updates. They will want to prevent sniffers on the network from reading their messages. They may also want to fine-tune which users are allowed to interact with a specific service and disallow certain actions for specific users. The Web and the umbrella specification for JAX-RS, Java EE, provide a core set of security services and protocols that you can leverage from within your RESTful web services. These include:

Authentication

Authentication is about validating the identity of a client that is trying to access your services. It usually involves checking to see if the client has provided an existing user with valid credentials, such as a password. The Web has a few standardized protocols you can use for authentication. Java EE, specifically your servlet container, has facilities to understand and configure these Internet security authentication protocols.

Authorization

Once a client is authenticated, it will want to interact with your RESTful web service. Authorization is about deciding whether or not a certain user is allowed to access and invoke on a specific URI. For example, you may want to allow write access (PUT/POST/DELETE operations) for one set of users and disallow it for others. Authorization is not part of any Internet protocol and is really the domain of your servlet container and Java EE.

Encryption

When a client is interacting with a RESTful web service, it is possible for hostile individuals to intercept network packets and read requests and responses if your HTTP connection is not secure. Sensitive data should be protected with crypto-graphic services like SSL. The Web defines the HTTPS protocol to leverage SSL and encryption.

JAX-RS has a small programmatic API for interacting with servlet and Java EE security, but enabling security in a JAX-RS environment is usually an exercise in configuration and applying annotation metadata.

Beyond Java EE, servlet, and JAX-RS security configuration and APIs, there's a few areas these standards don't cover. One area is digital signatures and encryption of the HTTP message body. Your representations may be passing through untrusted intermediaries and signing or encrypting the message body may add some extra protection for your data. There's also advanced authentication protocols like OAuth, which allow you to make invocations on services on behalf of other users.

This chapter first focuses on the various web protocols used for authentication in a standard, vanilla Java EE, and servlet environment. You'll learn how to configure your JAX-RS applications to use standard authentication, authorization, and encryption. Next you'll learn about various formats you can use to digitally sign or encrypt message bodies. Finally, we'll talk about the OAuth protocol and how you can use it within your applications.

Authentication

When you want to enforce authentication for your RESTful web services, the first thing you have to do is decide which authentication protocol you want to use. Internet protocols for authentication vary in their complexity and their perceived reliability. In Java land, most servlet containers support the protocols of Basic Authentication, Digest Authentication, and authentication using X.509 certificates. Let's look into how each of these protocols works.

Basic Authentication

Basic Authentication is the simplest protocol available for performing authentication over HTTP. It involves sending a Base 64–encoded username and password within a request header to the server. The server checks to see if the username exists within its system and verifies the sent password. To understand the details of this protocol, let's look at an example.

Say an unauthorized client tries to access one of our secure RESTful web services:

```
GET /customers/333 HTTP/1.1
```

Since the request does not contain any authentication information, the server would reply with an HTTP response of:

```
HTTP/1.1 401 Unauthorized
WWW-Authenticate: Basic realm="CustomerDB Realm"
```

The 401 response tells the client that it is not authorized to access the URI it tried to invoke on. The WWW-Authenticate header specifies which authentication protocol the client should use. In this case, `Basic` means Basic Authentication should be used. The `realm` attribute identifies a collection of secured resources on a website. The client can use the realm information to match against a username and password that is required for this specific URI.

To perform authentication, the client must send a request with the `Authorization` header set to a Base 64–encoded string of our username and a colon character, followed by the password. If our username is bburke and our password geheim, the Base 64–encoded string of bburke:geheim will be YmJ1cmtlOmdlaGVpbQ==. Put all this together, and our authenticated GET request would look like this:

```
GET /customers/333 HTTP/1.1
Authorization: Basic YmJ1cmtlOmdlaGVpbQ==
```

The client needs to send this `Authorization` header with each and every request it makes to the server.

The problem with this approach is that if this request is intercepted by a hostile entity on the network, the hacker can easily obtain the username and password and use it to invoke its own requests. Using an encrypted HTTP connection, HTTPS, solves this problem. With an encrypted connection, a rogue programmer on the network will be unable to decode the transmission and get at the `Authorization` header. Still, security-paranoid network administrators are very squeamish about sending passwords over the network, even if they are encrypted within SSL packets.

Digest Authentication

Although not used much anymore, Digest Authentication was invented so that clients would not have to send clear-text passwords over HTTP. It involves exchanging a set of secure MD5 hashes of the username, password, operation, URI, and optionally the hash of the message body itself. The protocol starts off with the client invoking an insecure request on the server:

```
GET /customers/333 HTTP/1.1
```

Since the request does not contain any authentication information, the server replies with an HTTP response of:

```
HTTP/1.1 401 Unauthorized
WWW-Authenticate: Digest realm="CustomerDB Realm",
                         qop="auth,auth-int",
                         nonce="12dcde223152321ab99cd",
                         opaque="aa9321534253bcd00121"
```

Like before, a 401 error code is returned along with a `WWW-Authenticate` header. The `nonce` and `opaqu` attributes are special server-generated keys that will be used to build the subsequent authenticated request.

Like Basic Authentication, the client uses the `Authorization` header, but with digest-specific attributes. Here's a request example:

```
GET /customers/333 HTTP/1.1
Authorization: Digest username="bburke",
                      realm="CustomerDB Realm",
                      nonce="12dcde223152321ab99cd",
                      uri="/customers/333",
                      qop="auth",
                      nc=00000001,
                      cnonce="43fea",
                      response="11132fffdeab993421",
                      opaque="aa9321534253bcd00121"
```

The `nonce` and `opaque` attributes are a copy of the values sent with the earlier `WWW-Authenticate` header. The `uri` attribute is the base URI you are invoking on. The `nc` attribute is a request counter that should be incremented by the client with each request. This prevents hostile clients from replaying a request. The `cnonce` attribute is a unique key generated by the client and can be anything the client wants. The `response` attribute is where all the meat is. It is a hash value generated with the following pseudocode:

```
H1 = md5("username:realm:password")
H2 = md5("httpmethod:uri")
response = md5(H1 + ":nonce:nc:cnonce:qop:" + H2)
```

If our username is `bburke` and our password `geheim`, the algorithm will resolve to this pseudocode:

```
H1 = md5("bburke:CustomerDB Realm:geheim")
H2 = md5("GET:/customers/333")
response = md5(H1 + ":12dcde223152321ab99cd:00000001:43fea:auth:" + H2)
```

When the server receives this request, it builds its own version of the response hash using its stored, secret values of the username and password. If the hashes match, the user and its credentials are valid.

One advantage of this approach is that the password is never used directly by the protocol. For example, the server doesn't even need to store clear-text passwords. It can instead initialize its authorization store with prehashed values. Also, since request hashes are built with a `nonce` value, the server can expire these nonce values over time. This, combined with a request counter, can greatly reduce replay attacks.

The disadvantage to this approach is that unless you use HTTPS, you are still vulnerable to man-in-the-middle attacks, where the middleman can tell a client to use Basic Authentication to obtain a password.

Client Certificate Authentication

When you buy things or trade stocks on the Internet, you use the HTTPS protocol to obtain a secure connection with the server. HTTPS isn't only an encryption mechanism—it can also be used for authentication. When you first interact with a secure website, your browser receives a digitally signed certificate from the server that identifies it. Your browser verifies this certificate with a central authority like VeriSign. This is how you guarantee the identity of the server you are interacting with and make sure you're not dealing with some man-in-the-middle security breach.

HTTPS can also perform two-way authentication. In addition to the client receiving a signed digital certificate representing the server, the server can receive a certificate that represents and identifies the client. When a client initially connects to a server, it exchanges its certificate and the server matches it against its internal store. Once this link is established, there is no further need for user authentication, since the certificate has already positively identified the user.

Client Certificate Authentication is perhaps the most secure way to perform authentication on the Web. The only disadvantage of this approach is the managing of the certificates themselves. The server must create a unique certificate for each client that wants to connect to the service. From the browser/human perspective, this can be a pain, as the user has to do some extra configuration to interact with the server.

Authorization

While authentication is about establishing and verifying user identity, authorization is about permissions. Is my user allowed to perform the operation it is invoking? None of the standards-based Internet authorization protocols discussed so far deals with authorization. The server and application know the permissions for each user and do not need to share this information over a communication protocol. This is why authorization is the domain of the server and application.

JAX-RS relies on the servlet and Java EE specifications to define how authorization works. Authorization is performed in Java EE by associating one or more roles with a given user and then assigning permissions based on that role. While an example of a user might be "Bill" or "Monica," roles are used to identify a group of users—for instance, "adminstrator," "manager," or "employee." You do not assign access control on a per-user basis, but rather on a per-role basis.

Authentication and Authorization in JAX-RS

To enable authentication, you need to modify the *WEB-INF/web.xml* deployment descriptor of the WAR file your JAX-RS application is deployed in. You enable authorization through XML or by applying annotations to your JAX-RS resource classes. To see how all this is put together, let's do a simple example. We have a customer database that allows us to create new customers by posting an XML document to the JAX-RS resource located by the @Path("/customers") annotation. This service is deployed by a scanned Application class annotated with @ApplicationPath("/services") so the full URI is /services/customers. We want to secure our customer service so that only administrators are allowed to create new customers. Let's look at a full XML-based implementation of this example:

```xml
<?xml version="1.0"?>
<web-app>
    <security-constraint>
        <web-resource-collection>
            <web-resource-name>customer creation</web-resource-name>
            <url-pattern>/services/customers</url-pattern>
            <http-method>POST</http-method>
        </web-resource-collection>
        <auth-constraint>
            <role-name>admin</role-name>
        </auth-constraint>
    </security-constraint>

    <login-config>
        <auth-method>BASIC</auth-method>
        <realm-name>jaxrs</realm-name>
    </login-config>

    <security-role>
        <role-name>admin</role-name>
    </security-role>

</web-app>
```

The <login-config> element defines how we want our HTTP requests to be authenticated for our entire deployment. The <auth-method> subelement can be BASIC, DIGEST, or CLIENT_CERT. These values correspond to Basic, Digest, and Client Certificate Authentication, respectively.

The <login-config> element doesn't turn on authentication. By default, any client can access any URL provided by your web application with no constraints. To enforce authentication, you must specify a URL pattern you want to secure. In our example, we use the <url-pattern> element to specify that we want to secure the /services/customers URL. The <http-method> element says that we only want to secure POST requests to this URL. If we leave out the <http-method> element, all HTTP methods are secured. In our example, we only want to secure POST requests, so we must define the <http-method> element.

Next, we have to specify which roles are allowed to POST to /services/customers. In the *web.xml* file example, we define an <auth-constraint> element within a

`<security-constraint>`. This element has one or more `<role-name>` elements that define which roles are allowed to access the defined constraint. In our example, applying this XML only gives the `admin` role permission to access the `/services/customers` URL.

If you set a `<role-name>` of * instead, any user would be able to access the constrained URL. Authentication with a valid user would still be required, though. In other words, a `<role-name>` of * means anybody who is able to log in can access the resource.

Finally, there's an additional bit of syntactic sugar we need to specify in *web.xml*. For every `<role-name>` we use in our `<auth-constraints>` declarations, we must define a corresponding `<security-role>` in the deployment descriptor.

There is a minor limitation when you're declaring `<security-constraints>` for JAX-RS resources. The `<url-pattern>` element does not have as rich an expression syntax as JAX-RS `@Path` annotation values. In fact, it is extremely limited. It supports only simple wildcard matches via the * character. No regular expressions are supported. For example:

- /*
- /foo/*
- *.txt

The wildcard pattern can only be used at the end of a URL pattern or to match file extensions. When used at the end of a URL pattern, the wildcard matches every character in the incoming URL. For example, `/foo/*` would match any URL that starts with `/foo`. To match file extensions, you use the format `*.<suffix>`. For example, the `*.txt` pattern matches any URL that ends with `.txt`. No other uses of the wildcard character are permitted in URL patterns. For example, here are some illegal expressions:

- /foo/*/bar
- /foo/*.txt

Enforcing Encryption

By default, the servlet specification will not require access over HTTPS to any user constraints you declare in your *web.xml* file. If you want to enforce HTTPS access for these constraints, you can specify a `<user-data-constraint>` within your `<security-constraint>` definitions. Let's modify our previous example to enforce HTTPS:

```
<web-app>
...

    <security-constraint>
        <web-resource-collection>
```

```
      <web-resource-name>customer creation</web-resource-name>
      <url-pattern>/services/customers</url-pattern>
      <http-method>POST</http-method>
    </web-resource-collection>
    <auth-constraint>
      <role-name>admin</role-name>
    </auth-constraint>
    <user-data-constraint>
      <transport-guarantee>CONFIDENTIAL</transport-guarantee>
    </user-data-constraint>
  </security-constraint>
  ...
</web-app>
```

All you have to do is declare a `<transport-guarantee>` element within a `<user-data-constraint>` that has a value of CONFIDENTIAL. If a user tries to access the URL pattern with HTTP, she will be redirected to an HTTPS-based URL.

Authorization Annotations

Java EE defines a common set of annotations that can define authorization metadata. The JAX-RS specification suggests, but does not require, vendor implementations to support these annotations in a non–Java EE 6 environment. These annotations live in the `javax.annotation.security` package and are `@RolesAllowed`, `@DenyAll`, `@PermitAll`, and `@RunAs`.

The `@RolesAllowed` annotation defines the roles permitted to execute a specific operation. When placed on a JAX-RS annotated class, it defines the default access control list for all HTTP operations defined in the JAX-RS class. If placed on a JAX-RS method, the constraint applies only to the method that is annotated.

The `@PermitAll` annotation specifies that any authenticated user is permitted to invoke your operation. As with `@RolesAllowed`, you can use this annotation on the class to define the default for the entire class or you can use it on a per-method basis. Let's look at an example:

```
@Path("/customers")
@RolesAllowed({"ADMIN", "CUSTOMER"})
public class CustomerResource {

    @GET
    @Path("{id}")
    @Produces("application/xml")
    public Customer getCustomer(@PathParam("id") int id) {...}

    @RolesAllowed("ADMIN")
    @POST
    @Consumes("application/xml")
    public void createCustomer(Customer cust) {...}
```

```
    @PermitAll
    @GET
    @Produces("application/xml")
    public Customer[] getCustomers() {}
}
```

Our CustomerResource class is annotated with @RolesAllowed to specify that, by default, only ADMIN and CUSTOMER users can execute HTTP operations and paths defined in that class. The getCustomer() method is not annotated with any security annotations, so it inherits this default behavior. The createCustomer() method is annotated with @RolesAllowed to override the default behavior. For this method, we only want to allow ADMIN access. The getCustomers() method is annotated with @PermitAll. This overrides the default behavior so that any authenticated user can access that URI and operation.

In practice, I don't like to specify security metadata using annotations. Security generally does not affect the behavior of the business logic being executed and falls more under the domain of configuration. Administrators may want to add or remove role constraints periodically. You don't want to have to recompile your whole application when they want to make a simple change. So, if I can avoid it, I usually use *web.xml* to define my authorization metadata.

There are some advantages to using annotations, though. For one, it is a workaround for doing fine-grained constraints that are just not possible in *web.xml* because of the limited expression capabilities of <url-pattern>. Also, because you can apply constraints per method using these annotations, you can fine-tune authorization per media type. For example:

```
@Path("/customers")
public class CustomerService {

    @GET
    @Produces("application/xml")
    @RolesAllowed("XML-USERS")
    public Customer getXmlCustomers() {}


    @GET
    @Produces("application/json")
    @RolesAllowed("JSON-USERS")
    public Customer getJsonCustomers() {}
}
```

Here we only allow XML-USERS to obtain application/xml content and JSON-USERS to obtain application/json content. This might be useful for limiting users in getting data formats that are expensive to create.

Programmatic Security

The security features defined in this chapter have so far focused on declarative security metadata, or metadata that is statically defined before an application even runs. JAX-RS also has a small programmatic API for gathering security information about a secured request. Specifically, the `javax.ws.rs.core.SecurityContext` interface has a method for determining the identity of the user making the secured HTTP invocation. It also has a method that allows you to check whether or not the current user belongs to a certain role:

```
public interface SecurityContext {

    public Principal getUserPrincipal();
    public boolean isUserInRole(String role);
    public boolean isSecure();
    public String getAuthenticationScheme();
}
```

The `getUserPrincipal()` method returns a standard Java Standard Edition (SE) `javax.security.Principal` security interface. A `Principal` object represents the individual user who is currently invoking the HTTP request. The `isUserInRole()` method allows you to determine whether the current calling user belongs to a certain role. The `isSecure()` method returns true if the current request is a secure connection. The `getAuthenticationScheme()` tells you which authentication mechanism was used to secure the request. `BASIC`, `DIGEST`, `CLIENT_CERT`, and `FORM` are typical values returned by this method. You get access to a `SecurityContext` instance by injecting it into a field, setter method, or resource method parameter using the `@Context` annotation.

Let's examine this security interface with an example. Let's say we want to have a security log of all access to a customer database by users who are not administrators. Here is how it might look:

```
@Path("/customers")
public class CustomerService {

    @GET
    @Produces("application/xml")
    public Customer[] getCustomers(@Context SecurityContext sec) {

        if (sec.isSecure() && !sec.isUserInRole("ADMIN")) {
            logger.log(sec.getUserPrincipal() +
                        " accessed customer database.");
        }
        ...
    }
}
```

In this example, we inject the `SecurityContext` as a parameter to our `getCustomer()` JAX-RS resource method. We use the method `SecurityContext.isSecure()` to determine whether or not this is an authenticated request. We then use the method `SecurityContext.isUserInRole()` to find out if the caller is an `ADMIN` or not. Finally, we print out to our audit log.

With the introduction of the filter API in JAX-RS 2.0, you can implement the `SecurityContext` interface and override the current request's `SecurityContext` via the `ContainerRequestContext.setSecurityContext()` method. What's interesting about this is that you can implement your own custom security protocols. Here's an example:

```
import javax.ws.rs.container.ContainerRequestContext;
import javax.ws.rs.container.ContainerRequestFilter;
import javax.ws.rs.container.PreMatching;
import javax.ws.rs.core.SecurityContext;
import javax.ws.rs.core.HttpHeaders;

@PreMatching
public class CustomAuth implements ContainerRequestFilter {
    protected MyCustomerProtocolHandler customProtocol = ...;

    public void filter(ContainerRequestContext requestContext) throws IOException
    {
        String authHeader = request.getHeaderString(HttpHeaders.AUTHORIZATION);
        SecurityContext newSecurityContext = customProtocol.validate(authHeader);
        requestContext.setSecurityContext(authHeader);
    }

}
```

This filter leaves out a ton of detail, but hopefully you get the idea. It extracts the `Authorization` header from the request and passes it to the `customProtocol` service that you have written. This returns an implementation of `SecurityContext`. You override the default `SecurityContext` with this variable.

Client Security

The JAX-RS 2.0 specification didn't do much to define a common client security API. What's weird is that while it has a stardard API for rarely used protocols like two-way SSL with client certificates, it doesn't define one for simple protocols like Basic or Digest Authentication. Instead, you have to rely on the vendor implementation of JAX-RS to provide these security features. For example, the RESTEasy framework provides a `ClientRequestFilter` you can use to enable Basic Authentication:

```
import org.jboss.resteasy.client.jaxrs.BasicAuthentication;

Client client = ClientBuilder.newClient();
client.register(new BasicAuthentication("username", "password"));
```

You construct the BasicAuthentication filter with the username and password you want to authenticate with. That's it. Other JAX-RS implementations might have other mechanisms for doing this.

JAX-RS 2.0 does have an API for enabling two-way SSL with client certificates. The ClientBuilder class allows you to specify a java.security.KeyStore that contains the client certificate you want to use to authenticate:

```
abstract class ClientBuilder {
    public ClientBuilder keyStore(final KeyStore keyStore, final String password)
}
```

Alternatively, it has methods to create your own SSLContext, but creating one is quite complicated and beyond the scope of this book.

Verifying the Server

HTTPS isn't only about encrypting your network connection, it is also about establishing trust. One aspect of this on the client side is verifying that the server you are talking to is the actual server you want to talk to and not some middleman on the network that is spoofing it. With most secure Internet servers, you do not have to worry about establishing trust because the server's certificates are signed by a trusted authority like VeriSign, and your JAX-RS client implementation will know how to verify certificates signed by these authorities.

In some cases, though, especially in test environments, you may be dealing with servers whose certificates are self-signed or signed by an unknown authority. In this case, you must obtain a truststore that contains the server certificates you trust and register them with the Client API. The ClientBuilder has a method for this:

```
abstract class ClientBuilder {
    public abstract ClientBuilder trustStore(final KeyStore trustStore);
}
```

How you initialize and populate the KeyStore is beyond the scope of this book.

OAuth 2.0

OAuth 2.0 is an authentication protocol that allows an entity to gain access to a user's data in a secure manner without having to know the user's credentials.[1] A typical example is a news site like cnn.com. You're reading an interesting political editorial and want to voice your opinion on the article in its comment section. To do this, though, you have to tell CNN who you are and what your email address is. It gives you the option of logging in via your Google or Facebook account. You are forwarded to Google and

---

1. For more information, see the OAuth 2.0 Authorization Framework (*http://tools.ietf.org/html/rfc6749*).

---

log in there. You grant CNN permission to ask Google who you are and what your email address is, and then you are forwarded back to cnn.com so that you can enter in your comment. Through this interaction CNN is granted an access token, which it then uses to obtain information about you via a separate HTTP request.

Here's how it works:

1. The CNN website redirects your browser to Google's login page. This redirect sets a special cnn.com session cookie that contains a randomly generated value. The redirect URL contains `client_id`, `state`, and `redirect_uri`. The `client_id` is the Google username CNN has registered with Google.com. The `state` parameter is the same value that was set in the session cookie. The `redirect_uri` is a URL you want Google to redirect the browser back to after authentication. A possible redirect URL in this scenario thus would be `http://googleapis.com/oauth?client_id=cnn&state=23423423123412352314&redirect_uri=http%3A%2F%2Fcnn.com`.

2. You enter your username and password on Google's login page. You then are asked if you will grant CNN access to your personal information.

3. If you say yes, Google generates an access code and remembers the `client_id` and `redirect_uri` that was sent in the original browser redirect.

4. Google redirects back to CNN.com using the `redirect_uri` sent by CNN's initial redirect. The redirect URL contains the original `state` parameter you forwarded along with a `code` parameter that contains the access code: `http://cnn.com/state=23423423123412352314&code=0002222`.

5. With this redirection, CNN will also get the value of the special cookie that it set in step 1. It checks the value of this cookie with the `state` query parameter to see if they match. It does this check to make sure that it initiated the request and not some rogue site.

6. The CNN server then extracts the `code` query parameter from the redirect URL. In a separate authenticated HTTP request to Google, it posts this access code. Google.com authenticates that CNN is sending the request and looks up the access code that was sent. If everything matches up, it sends back an access token in the HTTP response.

7. CNN can now make HTTP requests to other Google services to obtain information it wants. It does this by passing the token in an `Authorization` header with a value of `Bearer` plus the access token. For example:

```
GET /contacts?user=billburke
Host: contacts.google.com
Authorization: Bearer 2a23452342361223423441bc234123612341234123412adf
```

In reality, sites like Google, Facebook, and Twitter don't use this protocol exactly. They all put their own spin on it and all have a little bit different way of implementing this protocol. The same is true of OAuth libraries. While the core of what they do will follow the protocol, there will be many custom attributes to each library. This is because the OAuth specification is more a set of detailed guidelines rather than a specific protocol set in stone. It leaves out details like how a user or OAuth client authenticates or what additional parameters must be sent. So using OAuth may take a bunch of integration work on your part.

There are many different Java frameworks out there that can help you turn your applications into OAuth providers or help you integrate with servers that support OAuth authentication. This is where I make my own personal plug. In 2013, I started a new project at Red Hat called Keycloak. It is a complete end-to-end solution for OAuth and SSO. It can also act as a social broker with social media sites like Google and Facebook to make leveraging social media easier. Please check us out at *http://www.keycloak.org*.

Signing and Encrypting Message Bodies

Sometimes you have RESTful clients or services that may have to send or receive HTTP messages from unknown or untrusted intermediaries. A great example of an intermediary is Twitter. You post tweets to Twitter through the Twitter REST API, and one or more people can receive these tweets via Twitter. What if a tweet receiver wanted to verify that the tweet originator is who he says he is? Or what if you wanted to post encrypted tweets through Twitter that only trusted receivers could decode and read? This interaction is different from HTTPS in that HTTPS is a trusted SSL socket connection between one client and one server. For the Twitter example, we're sending a representation that is retransmitted via a totally different HTTP request involving different clients and servers. Digitally signing or encrypting the representation gives you the protection you need in this retransmission scenario.

Digital Signatures

Java developers are intimately familiar with the HashMap class. The way maps work is that a semi-unique hash code is generated for the key you are storing in the map. The key's hash code is used as an array index to quickly look up a value in the map. Under the covers, a digital signature is simply an encrypted hash code of the piece of data you are transmitting.

While a shared secret can be used to generate and verify a digital signature, the best approach is to use an asymmetric key pair: in other words, a private and public key. The signer creates the digital signature of the message using its private key. It then publishes its public key to the world. The receiver of the message uses the public key to verify the signature. If you use the right hash and encryption algorithms, it is virtually impossible to derive the private key of the sender or fake the signatures. I'm going to go over two methods you can use to leverage digital signatures in your RESTful web services.

DKIM/DOSETA

DomainKeys Identified Mail (DKIM)[2].] is a digital signature protocol that was designed for email. Work is also being done to apply this header to protocols other than email (e.g., HTTP) through the DOSETA[3] specifications. DKIM is simply a request or response header that contains a digital signature of one or more headers of the message and the content. What's nice about DKIM is that its header is self-contained and not part of the transmitted representation. So if the receiver of an HTTP message doesn't care about digital signatures, it can just ignore the header.

The format of a DKIM header is a semicolon-delimited list of name/value pairs. Here's an example:

```
DKIM-Signature: v=1;
                a=rsa-sha256;
                d=example.com;
                s=burke;
                c=simple/simple;
                h=Content-Type;
                x=0023423111111;
                bh=2342322111;
                b=M232234=
```

While it's not *that* important to know the structure of the header, here's an explanation of each parameter:

v

 Protocol version. Always 1.

a

 Algorithm used to hash and sign the message. RSA signing and SHA256 hashing is the only supported algorithm at the moment by RESTEasy.

d

 Domain of the signer. This is used to identify the signer as well as discover the public key to use to verify the signature.

s

 Selector of the domain. Also used to identify the signer and discover the public key.

---

2. For more information, see *http://dkim.org*

3. For more information, see the DomainKeys Security Tagging (*http://bit.ly/17ZnESs*).

c

Canonical algorithm. Only simple/simple is supported at the moment. Basically, this allows you to transform the message body before calculating the hash.

h

Semicolon-delimited list of headers that are included in the signature calculation.

x

When the signature expires. This is a numeric long value of the time in seconds since epoch. Allows the signer to control when a signed message's signature expires.

t

Timestamp of signature. Numeric long value of the time in seconds since epoch. Allows the verifier to control when a signature expires.

bh

Base 64–encoded hash of the message body.

b

Base 64–encoded signature.

What's nice about DKIM is that you can include individual headers within your digital signature of the message. Usually Content-Type is included.

To verify a signature, you need a public key. DKIM uses DNS text records to discover a public key. To find a public key, the verifier concatenates the selector (s parameter) with the domain (d parameter):

```
<selector>._domainKey.<domain>
```

It then takes that string and does a DNS request to retrieve a TXT record under that entry. In our previous example, burke._domainKey.example.com would be used as the lookup string.

This is a very interesting way to publish public keys. For one, it becomes very easy for verifiers to find public keys, as there's no real central store that is needed. Second, DNS is an infrastructure IT knows how to deploy. Third, signature verifiers can choose which domains they allow requests from. If you do not want to be dependent on DNS, most DKIM frameworks allow you to define your own mechanisms for discovering public keys.

Right now, support for DKIM in the Java world is quite limited. The RESTEasy framework does have an API, though, if you're interested in using it.

JOSE JWS

JOSE JSON Web Signature is a self-contained signature format that contains both the message you want to sign as well as the digital signature of the message.[4] The format is completely text-based and very compact. It consists of three Base 64–encoded strings delimited by a . character. The three encoded strings in the JOSE JWS format are a JSON header describing the message, the actual message that is being transmitted, and finally the digital signature of the message. The media type for JOSE JWS is `applica tion/jose+json`. Here's what a full HTTP response containing JWS might look like:

```
HTTP/1.1 200 OK
Content-Type: application/jose+json


eyJhbGciOiJSUzI1NiJ9
.
eyJpc3MiOiJqb2UiLA0KICJleHAiOjEzMDA4MTkzODAsDQogImh0dHA6Ly9leGFt
cGxlLmNvbS9pc19yb290Ijp0cnVlfQ
.
cC4hiUPoj9Eetdgtv3hF80EGrhuB__dzERat0XF9g2VtQgr9PJbu3XOiZj5RZmh7
AAuHIm4Bh-0Qc_lF5YKt_O8W2Fp5jujGbds9uJdbF9CUAr7t1dnZcAcQjbKBYNX4
BAynRFdiuB--f_nZLgrnbyTyWzO75vRK5h6xBArLIARNPvkSjtQBMHlb1L07Qe7K
0GarZRmB_eSN9383LcOLn6_dO--xi12jzDwusC-eOkHWEsqtFZESc6BfI7noOPqv
hJ1phCnvWh6IeYI2w9QOYEUipUTI8np6LbgGY9Fs98rqVt5AXLIhWkWywlVmtVrB
p0igcN_IoypGlUPQGe77Rw
```

Let's break down how an encoded JWS is created. The first encoded part of the format is a JSON header document that describes the message. Minimally, it has an `alg` value that describes the algorithm used to sign the message. It also often has a `cty` header that describes the `Content-Type` of the message signed. For example:

```
{
    "alg" : "RS256",
    "cty" : "application/xml"
}
```

The second encoded part of the JWS format is the actual content you are sending. It can be anything you want, like a simple text mesage, a JSON or XML document, or even an image or audio file; really, it can be any set of bytes or formats you want to transmit.

Finally, the third encoded part of the JWS format is the encoded digital signature of the content. The algorithm used to create this signature should match what was described in the header part of the JWS message.

What I like about JOSE JWS is that it is HTTP-header-friendly. Since it is a simple ASCII string, you can include it within HTTP header values. This allows you to send JSON or even binary values within an HTTP header quite easily.

---

4. For more information, see the JSON Web Signature (*http://bit.ly/HJ1g5F*).

Encrypting Representations

While you can rely on HTTPS to encrypt your HTTP requests and responses, I noted earlier that you may have some scenarios where you want to encrypt the HTTP message body of your requests and responses. Specifically, consider scenarios where you are sending messages to a public or untrusted intermediary. While there are a few standard ways to encrypt your representations, my favorite is JOSE JSON Web Encryption.[5]

JWE is a compact text format. It consists of five Base 64–encoded strings delimited by a . character. The first encoded string is a JSON header describing what is being transmitted. The second encoded string is an encrypted key used to encrypt the message. The third is the initialization vector used to encrypt the first block of bytes. The fourth is the actual encrypted messsage. And finally, the fifth is some extra metadata used to validate the message. The media type for JOSE JWE is `application/jose+json`. So here's what a full an HTTP response containing JWE might look like:

```
HTTP/1.1 200 OK
Content-Type: application/jose+json

eyJhbGciOiJSU0ExXzUiLCJlbmMiOiJBMTI4Q0JDLUhTMjU2In0.
UGhIOguC7IuEvf_NPVaXsGMoLOmwvc1GyqlIKOK1nN94nHPoltGRhWhw7Zx0-kFm
1NJn8LE9XShH59_i8J0PH5ZZyNfGy2xGdULU7sHNF6Gp2vPLgNZ__deLKxGHZ7Pc
HALUzoOegEI-8E66jX2E4zyJKx-YxzZIItRzC5hlRirb6Y5Cl_p-ko3YvkkysZIF
NPccxRU7qve1WYPxqbb2Yw8kZqa2rMWI5ng8OtvzlV7elprCbuPhcCdZ6XDP0_F8
rkXds2vE4X-ncOIM8hAYHHi29NX0mcKiRaD0-D-ljQTP-cFPgwCp6X-nZZd9OHBv
-B3oWh2TbqmScqXMR4gp_A.
AxY8DCtDaGlsbGljb3RoZQ.
KDlTtXchhZTGufMYmOYGS4HffxPSUrfmqCHXaI9wOGY.
9hH0vgRfYgPnAHOd8stkvw
```

Like JSON Web Signatures, the encoded header for JWE is a simple JSON document that describes the message. Minimally, it has an `alg` value that describes the algorithm used to encrypt the message and a `enc` value that describes the encryption method. It often has a `cty` header that describes the `Content-Type` of the message signed. For example:

```
{
    "alg":"RSA1_5",
    "enc":"A128CBC-HS256",
    "cty" : "application/xml"
}
```

The algorithms you can use for encryption come in two flavors. You can use a shared secret (i.e., a password) to encrypt the data, or you can use an asymmetric key pair (i.e., a public and private key).

---

5. For more information, see the JSON Web Encryption (*http://tools.ietf.org/html/draft-ietf-jose-json-web-encryption-14*).

As for the other encoded parts of the JWE format, these are really specific to the algorithm you are using and something I'm not going to go over.

As with JWS, the reason I like JWE is that it is HTTP-header-friendly. If you want to encrypt an HTTP header value, JWE works quite nicely.

Wrapping Up

In this chapter, we discussed a few of the authentication protocols used on the Internet —specifically, Basic, Digest, and Client Certificate Authentication. You learned how to configure your JAX-RS applications to be secure using the metadata provided by the servlet and Java EE specifications. You also learned about OAuth as well as digital signatures and encryption of HTTP messages. Chapter 29 contains some code you can use to test-drive many of the concepts in this chapter.

CHAPTER 16

Alternative Java Clients

While JAX-RS 2.0 added client support, there are other Java clients you can use to interact with web services if you do not have JAX-RS 2.0 available in your environment.

java.net.URL

Like most programming languages, Java has a built-in HTTP client library. It's nothing fancy, but it's good enough to perform most of the basic functions you need. The API is built around two classes, `java.net.URL` and `java.net.HttpURLConnection`. The URL class is just a Java representation of a URL. Here are some of the pertinent constructors and methods:

```
public class URL {

    public URL(java.lang.String s)
            throws java.net.MalformedURLException {}

    public java.net.URLConnection
            openConnection() throws java.io.IOException {}
    ...
}
```

From a URL, you can create an `HttpURLConnection` that allows you to invoke specific requests. Here's an example of doing a simple GET request:

```
URL url = new URL("http://example.com/customers/1");
connection = (HttpURLConnection) url.openConnection();
connection.setRequestMethod("GET");
connection.setRequestProperty("Accept", "application/xml");

if (connection.getResponseCode() != 200) {
  throw new RuntimeException("Operation failed: "
                            + connection.getResponseCode());
}
```

```
System.out.println("Content-Type: " + connection.getContentType());

BufferedReader reader = new BufferedReader(new
            InputStreamReader(connection.getInputStream()));

String line = reader.readLine();
while (line != null) {
   System.out.println(line);
   line = reader.readLine();
}
connection.disconnect();
```

In this example, we instantiate a URL instance and then open a connection using the
URL.openConnection() method. This method returns a generic URLConnection type,
so we need to typecast it to an HttpURLConnection. Once we have a connection, we set
the HTTP method we are invoking by calling HttpURLConnection.setMethod(). We
want XML from the server, so we call the setRequestProperty() method to set the
Accept header. We get the response code and Content-Type by calling getResponse
Code() and getContentType(), respectively. The getInputStream() method allows us
to read the content sent from the server using the Java streaming API. We finish up by
calling disconnect().

Sending content to the server via a PUT or POST is a little different. Here's an example
of that:

```
URL url = new URL("http://example.com/customers");
HttpURLConnection connection = (HttpURLConnection) url.openConnection();
connection.setDoOutput(true);
connection.setInstanceFollowRedirects(false);
connection.setRequestMethod("POST");
connection.setRequestProperty("Content-Type", "application/xml");
OutputStream os = connection.getOutputStream();
os.write("<customer id='333'/>".getBytes());
os.flush();
if (connection.getResponseCode() != HttpURLConnection.HTTP_CREATED) {
   throw new RuntimeException("Failed to create customer");
}
System.out.println("Location: " + connection.getHeaderField("Location"));
connection.disconnect();
```

In this example, we create a customer by using POST. We're expecting a response of 201,
"Created," as well as a Location header in the response that points to the URL of our
newly created customer. We need to call HttpURLConnection.setDoOutput(true). This
allows us to write a body for the request. By default, HttpURLConnection will automatically follow redirects. We want to look at our Location header, so we call setInstan
ceFollowRedirects(false) to disable this feature. We then call setRequestMe
thod() to tell the connection we're making a POST request. The setRequestProper
ty() method is called to set the Content-Type of our request. We then get a java.io.Out

putStream to write out the data and the Location response header by calling getHea
derField(). Finally, we call disconnect() to clean up our connection.

Caching

By default, HttpURLConnection will cache results based on the caching response headers
discussed in Chapter 11. You must invoke HttpURLConnection.setUseCaches(false)
to turn off this feature.

Authentication

The HttpURLConnection class supports Basic, Digest, and Client Certificate Authentication. Basic and Digest Authentication use the java.net.Authenticator API. Here's
an example:

```
Authenticator.setDefault(new Authenticator() {
    protected PasswordAuthentication getPasswordAuthentication() {
        return new PasswordAuthentication ("username, "password".toCharArray());
    }
});
```

The setDefault() method is a static method of Authenticator. You pass in an Authen
ticator instance that overrides the class's getPasswordAuthentication() method.
You return a java.net.PasswordAuthentication object that encapsulates the username and password to access your server. When you do HttpURLConnection invocations, authentication will automatically be set up for you using either Basic or Digest,
depending on what the server requires.

The weirdest part of the API is that it is driven by the static method setDefault(). The
problem with this is that your Authenticator is set VM-wide. So, doing authenticated
requests in multiple threads to different servers is a bit problematic with the basic example just shown. You can address this by using java.lang.ThreadLocal variables to
store username and passwords:

```
public class MultiThreadedAuthenticator extends Authenticator {

    private static ThreadLocal<String> username = new ThreadLocal<String>();
    private static ThreadLocal<String> password = new ThreadLocal<String>();

    public static void setThreadUsername(String user) {
        username.set(user);
    }

    public static void setThreadPassword(String pwd) {
        password.set(pwd);
    }

    protected PasswordAuthentication getPasswordAuthentication() {
```

```
        return new PasswordAuthentication (username.get(),
                                    password.get().toCharArray());
    }
}
```

The ThreadLocal class is a standard class that comes with the JDK. When you call set()
on it, the value will be stored and associated with the calling thread. Each thread can
have its own value. ThreadLocal.get() returns the thread's current stored value. So,
using this class would look like this:

```
Authenticator.setDefault(new MultiThreadedAuthenticator());

MultiThreadedAuthenticator.setThreadUsername("bill");
MultiThreadedAuthenticator.setThreadPassword("geheim");
```

Client Certificate Authentication

Client Certificate Authentication is a little different. First, you must generate a client
certificate using the keytool command-line utility that comes with the JDK:

```
$ <JAVA_HOME>/bin/keytool -genkey -alias client-alias -keyalg RSA
-keypass changeit -storepass changeit -keystore keystore.jks
```

Next, you must export the certificate into a file so it can be imported into a truststore:

```
$ <JAVA_HOME>/bin/keytool -export -alias client-alias
-storepass changeit -file client.cer -keystore keystore.jks
```

Finally, you create a truststore and import the created client certificate:

```
$ <JAVA_HOME>\bin\keytool -import -v -trustcacerts
-alias client-alias -file client.cer
-keystore cacerts.jks
-keypass changeit -storepass changeit
```

Now that you have a truststore, use it to create a javax.net.ssl.SSLSocketFactory
within your client code:

```
import javax.net.ssl.SSLContext;
import javax.net.ssl.KeyManagerFactory;
import javax.net.ssl.SSLSocketFactory;
import java.security.SecureRandom;
import java.security.KeyStore;
import java.io.FileInputStream;
import java.io.InputStream;
import java.io.File;

public class MyClient {

    public static SSLSocketFactory
            getFactory( File pKeyFile, String pKeyPassword )
                                            throws Exception {
        KeyManagerFactory keyManagerFactory =
                        KeyManagerFactory.getInstance("SunX509");
```

```
KeyStore keyStore = KeyStore.getInstance("PKCS12");

InputStream keyInput = new FileInputStream(pKeyFile);
keyStore.load(keyInput, pKeyPassword.toCharArray());
keyInput.close();

keyManagerFactory.init(keyStore, pKeyPassword.toCharArray());

SSLContext context = SSLContext.getInstance("TLS");
context.init(keyManagerFactory.getKeyManagers(), null
            , new SecureRandom());

return context.getSocketFactory();
}
```

This code loads the truststore into memory and creates an SSLSocketFactory. The factory can then be registered with a java.net.ssl.HttpsURLConnection:

```
public static void main(String args[]) throws Exception {
    URL url = new URL("https://someurl");
    HttpsURLConnection con = (HttpsURLConnection) url.openConnection();
    con.setSSLSocketFactory(getFactory(new File("cacerts.jks"),
                            "changeit"));
}
}
```

You may then make invocations to the URL, and the client certificate will be used for authentication.

Advantages and Disadvantages

The biggest advantage of using the java.net package as a RESTful client is that it is built in to the JDK. You don't need to download and install a different client framework.

There are a few disadvantages to the java.net API. First, it is not JAX-RS–aware. You will have to do your own stream processing and will not be able to take advantage of any of the MessageBodyReaders and MessageBodyWriters that come with your JAX-RS implementation.

Second, the framework does not do preemptive authentication for Basic or Digest Authentication. This means that HttpURLConnection will first try to invoke a request without any authentication headers set. If the server requires authentication, the initial request will fail with a 401, "Unauthorized," response code. The HttpURLConnection implementation then looks at the WWW-Authenticate header to see whether Basic or Digest Authentication should be used and retries the request. This can have an impact on the performance of your system because each authenticated request will actually be two requests between the client and server.

Third, the framework can't do something as simple as form parameters. All you have to work with are `java.io.OutputStream` and `java.io.InputStream` to perform your input and output.

Finally, the framework only allows you to invoke the HTTP methods GET, POST, DELETE, PUT, TRACE, OPTIONS, and HEAD. If you try to invoke any HTTP method other than those, an exception is thrown and your invocation will abort. In general, this is not that important unless you want to invoke newer HTTP methods like those defined in the WebDAV specification.

Apache HttpClient

The Apache foundation has written a nice, extensible, HTTP client library called HttpClient.[1] It is currently on version 4.x as of the writing of this book. Although it is not JAX-RS–aware, it does have facilities for preemptive authentication and APIs for dealing with a few different media types like forms and multipart. Some of its other features are a full interceptor model, automatic cookie handling between requests, and pluggable authentication. Let's look at a simple example:

```
import org.apache.http.*;
import org.apache.http.client.*;

public class MyClient {

    public static void main(String[] args) throws Exception {

        DefaultHttpClient client = new DefaultHttpClient();
        HttpGet get = new HttpGet("http://example.com/customers/1");
        get.addHeader("accept", "application/xml");

        HttpResponse response = client.execute(get);
        if (response.getStatusLine().getStatusCode() != 200) {
            throw new RuntimeException("Operation failed: " +
                    response.getStatusLine().getStatusCode());
        }

        System.out.println("Content-Type: " +
            response.getEntity().getContentType().getValue());

        BufferedReader reader = new BufferedReader(new
                InputStreamReader(response.getEntity()
                                        .getInputStream()));

        String line = reader.readLine();
        while (line != null) {
            System.out.println(line);
```

---

1. For more information, see *http://hc.apache.org*.

```
        line = reader.readLine();
    }
    client.getConnectionManager().shutdown();
    }
}
```

In Apache HttpClient 4.x, the org.apache.http.impl.client.DefaultHttpClient class is responsible for managing HTTP connections. It handles the default authentication settings, and pools and manages persistent HTTP connections (keepalive) and any other default configuration settings. It is also responsible for executing requests. The org.apache.http.client.methods.HttpGet class is used to build an actual HTTP GET request. You initialize it with a URL and set any request headers you want using the HttpGet.addHeader() method. There are similar classes in this package for doing POST, PUT, and DELETE invocations. Once you have built your request, you execute it by calling DefaultHttpClient.execute(), passing in the request you built. This returns an org.apache.http.HttpResponse object. To get the response code from this object, execute HttpResponse.getStatusLine().getStatusCode(). The HttpRes ponse.getEntity() method returns an org.apache.http.HttpEntity object, which represents the message body of the response. From it, you can get the Content-Type by executing HttpEntity.getContentType() as well as a java.io.InputStream so you can read the response. When you are done invoking requests, you clean up your connections by calling HttpClient.getConnectionManager().shutdown().

To push data to the server via a POST or PUT operation, you need to encapsulate your data within an instance of the org.apache.http.HttpEntity interface. The framework has some simple prebuilt ones for sending strings, forms, byte arrays, and input streams. Let's look at sending some XML.

In this example, we want to create a customer in a RESTful customer database. The API works by POSTing an XML representation of the new customer to a specific URI. A successful response is 201, "Created." Also, a Location response header is returned that points to the newly created customer:

```
import org.apache.http.*;
import org.apache.http.client.*;
import org.apache.impl.client.*;

public class MyClient {

  public static void main(String[] args) throws Exception {

      DefaultHttpClient client = new DefaultHttpClient();
      HttpPost post = new HttpPost("http://example.com/customers");
      StringEntity entity = new StringEntity("<customer id='333'/>");
      entity.setContentType("application/xml");
      post.setEntity(entity);
      HttpClientParams.setRedirection(post.getParams(), false);
      HttpResponse response = client.execute(post);
```

```
        if (response.getStatusLine().getStatusCode() != 201) {
            throw new RuntimeException("Operation failed: " +
                        response.getStatusLine().getStatusCode());
        }

        String location = response.getLastHeader("Location")
                                .getValue();

        System.out.println("Object created at: " + location);
        System.out.println("Content-Type: " +
            response.getEntity().getContentType().getValue());

        BufferedReader reader = new BufferedReader(new
            InputStreamReader(response.getEntity().getContent()));

        String line = reader.readLine();
        while (line != null) {
            System.out.println(line);
            line = reader.readLine();
        }
        client.getConnectionManager().shutdown();
    }
}
```

We create an `org.apache.http.entity.StringEntity` to encapsulate the XML we want to send across the wire. We set its `Content-Type` by calling `StringEntity.set ContentType()`. We add the entity to the request by calling `HttpPost.setEntity()`. Since we are expecting a redirection header with our response and we do not want to be automatically redirected, we must configure the request to not do automatic redirects. We do this by calling `HttpClientParams.setRedirection()`. We execute the request the same way we did with our GET example. We get the `Location` header by calling `HttpResponse.getLastHeader()`.

Authentication

The Apache HttpClient 4.x supports Basic, Digest, and Client Certificate Authentication. Basic and Digest Authentication are done through the `DefaultHttpClient.get CredentialsProvider().setCredentials()` method. Here's an example:

```
DefaultHttpClient client = new DefaultHttpClient();
client.getCredentialsProvider().setCredentials(
    new AuthScope("example.com", 443),
    new UsernamePasswordCredentials("bill", "geheim"));
);
```

The `org.apache.http.auth.AuthScope` class defines the server and port that you want to associate with a username and password. The `org.apache.http.auth.Username PasswordCredentials` class encapsulates the username and password into an object.

You can call `setCredentials()` for every domain you need to communicate with securely.

Apache HttpClient, by default, does not do preemptive authentication for the Basic and Digest protocols, but does support it. Since the code to do this is a bit verbose, we won't cover it in this book.

Client Certificate authentication

Apache HttpClient also supports Client Certificate Authentication. As with `HttpsURL Connection`, you have to load in a `KeyStore` that contains your client certificates. The section "java.net.URL" on page 235 describes how to do this. You initialize an `org.apache.http.conn.ssl.SSLSocketFactory` with a loaded `KeyStore` and associate it with the `DefaultHttpClient`. Here is an example of doing this:

```
import java.io.File;
import java.io.FileInputStream;
import java.security.KeyStore;

import org.apache.http.*;
import org.apache.http.HttpResponse;
import org.apache.http.client.methods.*;
import org.apache.http.conn.scheme.*;
import org.apache.http.conn.ssl.*;
import org.apache.http.impl.client.DefaultHttpClient;

public class MyClient {

    public final static void main(String[] args) throws Exception {
        DefaultHttpClient client = new DefaultHttpClient();

        KeyStore trustStore  = KeyStore.getInstance(
                                    KeyStore.getDefaultType());
        FileInputStream instream = new FileInputStream(
                                    new File("my.keystore"));
        try {
            trustStore.load(instream, "changeit".toCharArray());
        } finally {
            instream.close();
        }

        SSLSocketFactory socketFactory =
                                    new SSLSocketFactory(trustStore);
        Scheme scheme = new Scheme("https", socketFactory, 443);
        client.getConnectionManager()
                .getSchemeRegistry().register(scheme);

        HttpGet httpget = new HttpGet("https://localhost/");

        ... proceed with the invocation ...
```

```
        }
    }
```

Advantages and Disadvantages

Apache HttpClient is a more complete solution and is better designed than `java.net.HttpURLConnection`. Although you have to download it separately from the JDK, I highly recommend you take a look at it. It has none of the disadvantages of `HttpURLConnection`, except that it is not JAX-RS–aware. Many JAX-RS implementations, including RESTEasy, allow you to use Apache HttpClient as the underlying HTTP client engine, so you can get the best of both worlds.

RESTEasy Client Proxies

The RESTEasy Client Proxy Framework is a different way of writing RESTful Java clients. The idea of the framework is to reuse the JAX-RS annotations on the client side. When you write JAX-RS services, you are using the specification's annotations to turn an HTTP invocation into a Java method call. The RESTEasy Client Proxy Framework flips this around to instead use the annotations to turn a method call into an HTTP request.

You start off by writing a Java interface with methods annotated with JAX-RS annotations. For example, let's define a RESTful client interface to the customer service application we have talked about over and over again throughout this book:

```
@Path("/customers")
public interface CustomerResource {

    @GET
    @Produces("application/xml")
    @Path("{id}")
    public Customer getCustomer(@PathParam("id") int id);

    @POST
    @Consumes("application/xml")
    public Response createCustomer(Customer customer);

    @PUT
    @Consumes("application/xml")
    @Path("{id}")
    public void updateCustomer(@PathParam("id") int id, Customer cust);
}
```

This interface looks exactly like the interface a JAX-RS service might implement. Through RESTEasy, we can turn this interface into a Java object that can invoke HTTP requests. To do this, we use the `org.jboss.resteasy.client.jaxrs.ResteasyWebTar get` interface:

```
Client client = ClientFactory.newClient();
WebTarget target = client.target("http://example.com/base/uri");
ResteasyWebTarget target = (ResteasyWebTarget)target;

CustomerResource customerProxy = target.proxy(CustomerResource.class);
```

If you are using RESTEasy as your JAX-RS implementation, all you have to do is typecast an instance of `WebTarget` to `ResteasyWebTarget`. You can then invoke the `Resteasy WebTarget.proxy()` method. This method returns an instance of the `CustomerRe source` interface that you can invoke on. Here's the proxy in use:

```
// Create a customer
Customer newCust = new Customer();
newCust.setName("bill");
Response response = customerProxy.createCustomer(newCust);

// Get a customer
Customer cust = customerProxy.getCustomer(333);

// Update a customer
cust.setName("burke");
customerProxy.updateCustomer(333, cust);
```

When you invoke one of the methods of the returned `CustomerResource` proxy, it converts the Java method call into an HTTP request to the server using the metadata defined in the annotations applied to the `CustomerResource` interface. For example, the `get Customer()` invocation in the example code knows that it must do a GET request on the *http://example.com/customers/333* URI, because it has introspected the values of the `@Path`, `@GET`, and `@PathParam` annotations on the method. It knows that it should be getting back XML from the `@Produces` annotation. It also knows that it should unmarshal it using a JAXB `MessageBodyReader`, because the `getCustomer()` method returns a JAXB annotated class.

Advantages and Disadvantages

A nice side effect of writing Java clients with this proxy framework is that you can use the Java interface for Java clients and JAX-RS services. With one Java interface, you also have a nice, clear way of documenting how to interact with your RESTful Java service. As you can see from the example code, it also cuts down on a lot of boilerplate code. The disadvantage, of course, is that this framework, while open source, is proprietary.

Wrapping Up

In this chapter, you learned three alternative ways to write RESTful clients in Java using the JDK's `java.net.HttpURLConnection` class, Apache HttpClient, and the RESTEasy Client Proxy Framework. All three have their merits as alternatives to the JAX-RS 2.0 Client API.

PART II

JAX-RS Workbook

CHAPTER 17

Workbook Introduction

Reading a book on a new technology gives you a nice foundation to build on, but you cannot truly understand and appreciate a new technology until you see it in action. The following workbook chapters were designed to be a companion to the main chapters of this book. Their goal is to provide step-by-step instructions for installing, configuring, and running various JAX-RS examples found throughout this book with the RESTEasy framework.

This chapter focuses on downloading and installing RESTEasy and the workbook examples. Following this, each workbook chapter corresponds to a specific chapter in the book. For example, if you are reading Chapter 3 on writing your first JAX-RS service, use Chapter 18 of the workbook to develop and run the examples shown in that chapter with RESTEasy.

This workbook is based on the production release of RESTEasy JAX-RS 3.0.5. I picked RESTEasy as the JAX-RS framework for the workbook for no other reason than I am the project lead for it and I know it backward and forward. That said, I took great care to ensure that you can easily port the examples to other JAX-RS implementations.

Installing RESTEasy and the Examples

The workbook examples are embedded within the RESTEasy distribution so that as future versions of RESTEasy are released, the workbook examples will be updated along with that release. (I discovered that having a separate download for the workbook examples causes various problems—users can get confused about which package to download, and the examples can get out of sync with specific software versions.)

You can download the distribution by following the download links at *http://jboss.org/ resteasy*.

Download the latest RESTEasy JAX-RS distribution (for example, *resteasy-jaxrs-3.0.5.Final.zip*). Figure 17-1 shows the directory structure of the distribution.

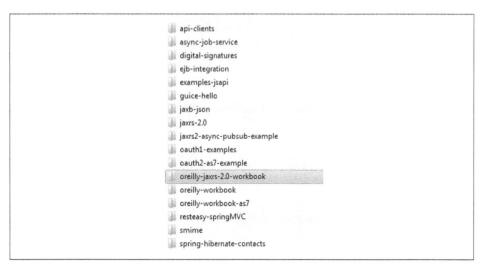

Figure 17-1. RESTEasy directory structure

Table 17-1 describes the purpose of the various directories.

Table 17-1. RESTEasy directories

Directory	Description
docs/javadocs	Generated Javadocs for both the JAX-RS APIs and RESTEasy
docs/userguide	Reference guide for RESTEasy in both HTML and PDF format
examples	Top-level directory containing all RESTEasy examples
examples/oreilly-jaxrs-2.0-workbook	Contains workbook example code for each workbook chapter
lib	All the RESTEasy JARs and the third-party libraries they depend on
embedded-lib	Optional JAR files used when you are running RESTEasy in embedded mode
resteasy-jaxrs.war	Sample RESTEasy servlet deployment

Don't get confused by the other *examples/oreilly-workbook* directories. These are examples from the previous revision of this book.

For Apache Maven users, RESTEasy also has a Maven repository at *http://bit.ly/HCHZm6*.

The `groupId` for all RESTEasy artifacts is `org.jboss.resteasy`. You can view all available artifacts at *http://bit.ly/1esCSDp*.

Example Requirements and Structure

The RESTEasy distribution does not have all the software you need to run the examples. You will also need the following components:

- JDK 7.0 or later. You will, of course, need Java installed on your computer.
- Maven 3.0.4. Maven is the build system used to compile and run the examples. Later versions of Maven may work, but it is recommended that you use 3.0.4. You can download Maven from *http://maven.apache.org*.

Code Directory Structure

The EXAMPLE code is organized as a set of directories, one for each exercise (see Figure 17-2). You'll find the server source code for each example in the *src/main/java* directory. The servlet configuration for each example lives in the *src/main/webapp/WEB-INF* directory. The client code that runs the example is in *src/test/java*.

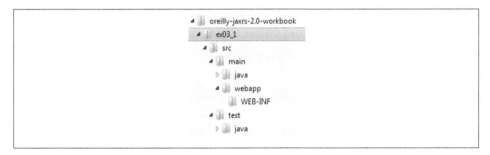

Figure 17-2. Code directory structure

To build and run the exercises, you'll use the Maven build tool. A product object model (POM) is provided in the *pom.xml* file at the top-level directory of each example. It contains the Maven configuration needed to compile, build, and run the specific example.

Environment Setup

For Maven to work correctly, you will have to make sure the Maven scripts are in your path. Depending on your platform, you'll have to execute commands like these:

- Windows:

```
C:\> set PATH=\maven\bin;%PATH%
```

- Unix:

```
$ export PATH=/home/username/maven/bin:$PATH
```

In each chapter, you'll find detailed instructions on how to build, deploy, and run the exercise using Maven.

CHAPTER 18

Examples for Chapter 3

Chapter 3 walked you through a very basic example of creating a JAX-RS service and a JAX-RS client that invokes on it. This service was a simple in-memory customer database. It was modeled as a singleton JAX-RS resource class and exchanged simple XML documents.

This chapter takes the code from Chapter 3 and shows you how to run it using the downloadable workbook example code. I'll walk you through how the code is structured on disk as well as how the examples use the Maven build system to compile, build, and run it.

Build and Run the Example Program

Perform the following steps:

1. Open a command prompt or shell terminal and change to the *ex03_1* directory of the workbook example code.

2. Make sure your PATH is set up to include both the JDK and Maven, as described in Chapter 17.

3. Perform the build by typing `mvn install`. Maven uses *pom.xml* to figure out how to compile, build, and run the example code.

Before we examine the build file for this example, you might want to take a quick look at the Maven utility at its Apache website (*http://maven.apache.org*).

Maven is a build-by-convention tool. It expects that your source code be laid out in a certain directory structure. From this standard directory structure, it knows how to automatically find, compile, and package your main class files. It also knows where your test code is and will compile and run it.

Every exercise in this book will follow the directory structure shown in Figure 18-1. Table 18-1 describes the purpose of the various directories.

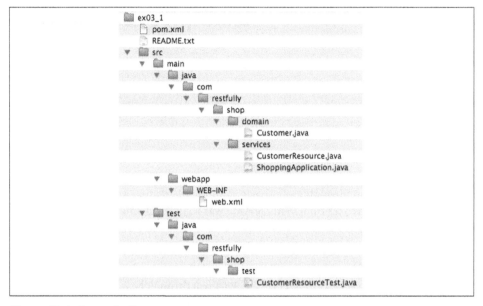

Figure 18-1. Example directory structure

Table 18-1. Directory structure description

Directory	Description
src	Top-level directory that contains all source and configuration files.
src/main	Contains all Java source code and configuration files that are used to create your package. In this case, we're creating a WAR file.
src/main/java	Contains server-side Java source code.
src/main/webapp	Contains servlet configuration files, specifically *web.xml*.
src/test/java	Contains Java source code that will be used to run tests on the packaged archive. This code will not be included within our WAR file.

Deconstructing pom.xml

The *pom.xml* file provided for each workbook exercise gives the Maven utility information about how to compile and deploy your Java programs. In our case, Maven will use the information within the *pom.xml* file to compile the code within *src/main/java*, create a WAR file using the *web.xml* file within *src/main/webapp*, deploy the WAR file automatically using the Jetty-embedded servlet container, and finally, run any test code that is within the *src/test/java* directory.

Here's a breakdown of what is contained within *pom.xml*:

```xml
<project xmlns="http://maven.apache.org/POM/4.0.0"
         xmlns:xsi="http://www.w3.org/2001/XMLSchema-instance"
         xsi:schemaLocation="http://maven.apache.org/
                    POM/4.0.0 http://maven.apache.org/maven-v4_0_0.xsd">
    <parent>
        <groupId>com.oreilly.rest.workbook</groupId>
        <artifactId>jaxrs-2.0-workbook-pom</artifactId>
        <version>1.0</version>
        <relativePath>../pom.xml</relativePath>
    </parent>
    <modelVersion>4.0.0</modelVersion>
```

In this initial part of the *pom.xml* file, we're inheriting from a parent Maven module. This parent module defines the default configuration for Maven plug-ins as well as the location of remote Maven repositories to use to download library dependencies.

```xml
<groupId>com.oreilly.rest.workbook</groupId>
<artifactId>jaxrs-2.0-workbook-ex03_1</artifactId>
```

`artifactId` is the name of the project. It is also used for the name of the WAR file that is created by the build unless you override it with the `finalName` element in the build section of the POM. This artifact belongs to a family of packages defined by the element `groupId`.

```xml
<version>2.0</version>
```

The `version` element identifies the version of the project we are creating. Generally, this version text is appended to the `artifactId` when Maven creates the WAR file, but you'll see later that we have overridden this with the `finalName` element.

```xml
<packaging>war</packaging>
```

The `packaging` element tells Maven that this project is building a WAR file. Other values for packaging could be `jar`, if we were creating a JAR, or `ear` for a Java EE enterprise archive.

```xml
<dependencies>
    <dependency>
        <groupId>org.jboss.resteasy</groupId>
        <artifactId>resteasy-jaxrs</artifactId>
        <version>3.0.5.Final</version>
    </dependency>
    <dependency>
        <groupId>org.jboss.resteasy</groupId>
        <artifactId>resteasy-client</artifactId>
        <version>3.0.5.Final</version>
    </dependency>
    <dependency>
        <groupId>org.jboss.resteasy</groupId>
        <artifactId>async-http-servlet-3.0</artifactId>
```

```
            <version>3.0.5.Final</version>
        </dependency>
        <dependency>
            <groupId>org.jboss.resteasy</groupId>
            <artifactId>jaxrs-api</artifactId>
            <version>3.0.5.Final</version>
        </dependency>
        <dependency>
            <groupId>org.jboss.resteasy</groupId>
            <artifactId>resteasy-servlet-initializer</artifactId>
            <version>3.0.5.Final</version>
        </dependency>
        <dependency>
            <groupId>junit</groupId>
            <artifactId>junit</artifactId>
            <version>4.1</version>
            <scope>test</scope>
        </dependency>
    </dependencies>
```

The dependencies element lists all library dependencies our ex03_1 project needs to
compile and run. We are dependent on the RESTEasy project, as this is the JAX-RS
implementation we are using. We are also dependent on the JUnit library for running
the test code in our project. Prior to building, Maven will search for these libraries within
the remote repositories listed in the parent POM. It will then download these libraries
to your machine along with each of the transitive dependencies that these libraries have.
What do I mean by *transitive dependencies*? Well, for example, RESTEasy depends on
a multitude of third-party libraries like the servlet and JAXB APIs. The repository in
which RESTEasy resides contains metadata about RESTEasy's dependencies. Maven
will discover these extra dependencies when it tries to download the RESTEasy JAR.

Unless you define a scope element, each dependency and its transitive dependencies
will be included in your WAR's *WEB-INF/lib* directory when it is built. Take a look
specifically at the junit dependency:

```
        <dependency>
            <groupId>junit</groupId>
            <artifactId>junit</artifactId>
            <version>4.1</version>
            <scope>test</scope>
        </dependency>
```

The junit dependency has a scope of test. This means that this library is only used to
run the tests and therefore does not need to be included within the WAR. If you were
building this WAR file to be deployed on the JBoss or Wildfly application servers, you
would not want to include all of these RESTEasy dependencies within the WAR file.
This is because these application servers already come with JAX-RS preinstalled. In this
case, you would define a scope of provided for each of the other dependencies listed
in this file. For example:

```
<dependency>
    <groupId>org.jboss.resteasy</groupId>
    <artifactId>resteasy-jaxrs</artifactId>
    <version>3.0.5.Final</version>
    <scope>provided</scope>
</dependency>
```

The `provided` scope tells Maven that this is a dependency that is needed to compile your code, but that the environment in which you will deploy this WAR already includes the dependency.

OK, now that we've got that covered. Let's look at the rest of our *pom.xml* file:

```
<build>
    <finalName>ex03_1</finalName>
```

The `build` element contains configuration information related to how Maven should build our project. The first item we have under this section is the `finalName` element. This element overrides the default file naming conventions of Maven. Here we're stating that we want our WAR file to be named *ex03_1.war*.

Next we have the `plugins` element. This section defines the configuration for the Maven plug-ins that will be used to build the project:

```
<plugins>
    <plugin>
        <groupId>org.apache.maven.plugins</groupId>
        <artifactId>maven-compiler-plugin</artifactId>
        <configuration>
            <source>1.6</source>
            <target>1.6</target>
        </configuration>
    </plugin>
```

The first `plugin` listed is the compiler plug-in, which is used to configure the Java compiler. Here, the plug-in is configured to compile our source code into the Java 6 bytecode format:

```
<plugin>
    <groupId>org.apache.maven.plugins</groupId>
    <artifactId>maven-surefire-plugin</artifactId>
    <configuration>
        <skip>true</skip>
    </configuration>
    <executions>
        <execution>
            <id>surefire-it</id>
            <phase>integration-test</phase>
            <goals>
                <goal>test</goal>
            </goals>
            <configuration>
```

```
                    <skip>false</skip>
                </configuration>
            </execution>
        </executions>
    </plugin>
```

The next plug-in we need to configure is surefire-it. This plug-in controls how our test execution works. By default, Maven will compile the source code under *src/main/java* and *src/test/java* and then try to run the tests under *src/test/java*. If the tests succeed, it packages the *.class* files into a WAR or JAR file. In our case, though, we want to create a WAR file and deploy it to the Jetty-embedded servlet container *before* we run our test code. The surefire-it configuration listed tells Maven not to run the test code until the WAR file has been built and deployed to Jetty:

```
<plugin>
    <groupId>org.mortbay.jetty</groupId>
    <artifactId>jetty-maven-plugin</artifactId>
    <version>8.1.11.v20130520</version>
    <configuration>
        <webApp>
            <contextPath>/</contextPath>
        </webApp>
        <scanIntervalSeconds>10</scanIntervalSeconds>
        <stopKey>foo</stopKey>
        <stopPort>9999</stopPort>
    </configuration>
    <executions>
        <execution>
            <id>start-jetty</id>
            <phase>pre-integration-test</phase>
            <goals>
                <goal>run</goal>
            </goals>
            <configuration>
                <scanIntervalSeconds>0</scanIntervalSeconds>
                <daemon>true</daemon>
            </configuration>
        </execution>
        <execution>
            <id>stop-jetty</id>
            <phase>post-integration-test</phase>
            <goals>
                <goal>stop</goal>
            </goals>
        </execution>
    </executions>
</plugin>
```

The final plug-in is the Jetty plug-in, which is responsible for running the Jetty-embedded servlet container. After the WAR file is built, the Jetty container will boot up an HTTP server under port 8080. The WAR file is then deployed into Jetty.

I don't really need to explain the specifics of the entire Jetty plug-in configuration. The interesting bits that you might want to tweak are the port (8080) and the stopPort (9999). You may have to change these if there is a service on your computer already using these network ports.

Running the Build

To run the build, simply type **mvn install** at the command prompt from the *ex03_1* directory. The output will look something like this:

```
[INFO] Scanning for projects...
[INFO]
[INFO] ------------------------------------------------------------------------
[INFO] Building ex03_1 2.0
[INFO] ------------------------------------------------------------------------
[INFO]
Downloading: http://download.java.net/maven/1
                /org.jboss.resteasy/poms/resteasy-jaxrs-3.0.5.Final.pom
...
```

You'll see Maven downloading a bunch of files from the repositories. This may take a while the first time you run the build script, as Maven needs to pull down a huge number of dependencies:

```
[INFO] Compiling 3 source files to C:\resteasy\p1b-repo\master\jaxrs
                \examples\oreilly-jaxrs-2.0-workbook
                \ex03_1\target\classes
[INFO]
[INFO]
[INFO] Compiling 1 source file to C:\resteasy\p1b-repo\master\jaxrs
                \examples\oreilly-jaxrs-2.0-workbook
                \ex03_1\target\test-classes
```

Next, you'll see Maven compiling your main and test source code:

```
[INFO] Tests are skipped.
[INFO]
[INFO] Packaging webapp
[INFO] Assembling webapp [jaxrs-2.0-workbook-ex03_1] in
                [C:\resteasy\p1b-repo\master\jaxrs
                \examples\oreilly-jaxrs-2.0-workbook
                \ex03_1\target\ex03_1]
[INFO] Processing war project
[INFO] Copying webapp resources [C:\resteasy\p1b-repo
                \master\jaxrs
                \examples\oreilly-jaxrs-2.0-workbook
                \ex03_1\src\main\webapp]
[INFO] Webapp assembled in [172 msecs]
[INFO] Building war: C:\resteasy\p1b-repo\master\jaxrs
                \examples
                \oreilly-jaxrs-2.0-workbook
                \ex03_1\target\ex03_1.war
```

Then you'll see that the WAR file is built:

```
[INFO] Started Jetty Server
[INFO]
[INFO] Surefire report directory: C:\resteasy\p1b-repo
                              \master\jaxrs\examples
                    \oreilly-jaxrs-2.0-workbook\
                    ex03_1\target\surefire-reports


[source,java]
-------------------------------------------------------
 T E S T S
-------------------------------------------------------
Running com.restfully.shop.test.CustomerResourceTest
*** Create a new Customer ***
Created customer 1
Location: http://localhost:8080/services/customers/1
*** GET Created Customer **
<customer id="1">
   <first-name>Bill</first-name>
   <last-name>Burke</last-name>
   <street>256 Clarendon Street</street>
   <city>Boston</city>
   <state>MA</state>
   <zip>02115</zip>
   <country>USA</country>
</customer>

**** After Update ***
<customer id="1">
   <first-name>William</first-name>
   <last-name>Burke</last-name>
   <street>256 Clarendon Street</street>
   <city>Boston</city>
   <state>MA</state>
   <zip>02115</zip>
   <country>USA</country>
</customer>

Tests run: 1, Failures: 0, Errors: 0, Skipped: 0, Time elapsed: 0.487 sec

Results :

Tests run: 1, Failures: 0, Errors: 0, Skipped: 0
```

Finally, Maven will start Jetty, deploy the WAR file created, and run the test code under
src/test/java:

```
[INFO]
[INFO]
[INFO] ------------------------------------------------------------------------
[INFO] BUILD SUCCESS
[INFO] ------------------------------------------------------------------------
```

```
[INFO] Total time: 4.462s
[INFO] Finished at: Mon Aug 26 12:44:11 EDT 2013
[INFO] Final Memory: 23M/618M
[INFO] ------------------------------------------------------------------------
```

The output of the build should end with BUILD SUCCESS.

Examining the Source Code

The server-side source code is exactly as posted in Chapter 3. The guts of the client code are the same as in Chapter 3, but the client code is structured as a JUnit class. JUnit is an open source Java library for defining unit tests. Maven automatically knows how to find JUnit-enabled test code and run it with the build. It scans the classes within the *src/test/java* directory, looking for classes that have methods annotated with @org.ju nit.Test. This example has only one: com.restfully.shop.test.CustomerResour ceTest. Let's go over the code for it that is different from the book:

src/test/java/com/restfully/shop/test/CustomerResourceTest.java

```java
package com.restfully.shop.test;

import org.junit.Test;

import javax.ws.rs.client.Client;
import javax.ws.rs.client.ClientBuilder;
import javax.ws.rs.client.Entity;
import javax.ws.rs.core.Response;


/**
 * @author <a href="mailto:bill@burkecentral.com">Bill Burke</a>
 * @version $Revision: 1 $
 */
public class CustomerResourceTest
{
    @Test
    public void testCustomerResource() throws Exception {
```

Our test class has only one method: testCustomerResource(). It is annotated with @Test. This tells Maven that this method is a JUnit test. The code for this method is exactly the same as the client code in Chapter 3. When you run the build, Maven will execute the code within this method to run the example.

That's it! The rest of the examples in this book have the same Maven structure as *ex03_1* and are tested using JUnit.

CHAPTER 19

Examples for Chapter 4

Chapter 4 discussed three things. First, it mentioned how the @javax.ws.rs.HttpMe thod annotation works and how to define and bind Java methods to new HTTP methods. Next, it talked about the intricacies of the @Path annotation, and explained how you can use complex regular expressions to define your application's published URIs. Finally, the chapter went over the concept of subresource locators.

This chapter walks you through three different example programs that you can build and run to illustrate the concepts in Chapter 4. The first example uses @HttpMethod to define a new HTTP method called PATCH. The second example expands on the customer service database example from Chapter 18 by adding some funky regular expression mappings with @Path. The third example implements the subresource locator example shown in "Full Dynamic Dispatching" on page 52 in Chapter 4.

Example ex04_1: HTTP Method Extension

This example shows you how your JAX-RS services can consume HTTP methods other than the common standard ones defined in HTTP 1.1. Specifically, the example implements the PATCH method. The PATCH method was originally mentioned in an earlier draft version of the HTTP 1.1 specification:[1]

> The PATCH method is similar to PUT except that the entity contains a list of differences between the original version of the resource identified by the Request-URI and the desired content of the resource after the PATCH action has been applied.

The idea of PATCH is that instead of transmitting the entire representation of a resource to update it, you only have to provide a partial representation in your update request.

---

1. For more information, see *http://www.ietf.org/rfc/rfc2068.txt*.

PUT requires that you transmit the entire representation, so the original plan was to include PATCH for scenarios where sending everything is not optimal.

Build and Run the Example Program

Perform the following steps:

1. Open a command prompt or shell terminal and change to the *ex04_1* directory of the workbook example code.
2. Make sure your PATH is set up to include both the JDK and Maven, as described in Chapter 17.
3. Perform the build and run the example by typing `mvn install`.

The Server Code

Using PATCH within JAX-RS is very simple. The source code under the *ex04_1* directory contains a simple annotation that implements PATCH:

src/main/java/org/ieft/annotations/PATCH.java

```
package org.ieft.annotations;

import javax.ws.rs.HttpMethod;
import java.lang.annotation.*;

@Target({ElementType.METHOD})
@Retention(RetentionPolicy.RUNTIME)
@HttpMethod("PATCH")
public @interface PATCH
{
}
```

As described in Chapter 4, all you need to do to use a custom HTTP method is annotate an annotation class with `@javax.ws.rs.HttpMethod`. This `@HttpMethod` declaration must contain the value of the new HTTP method you are defining.

To illustrate the use of our new `@PATCH` annotation, I expanded a little bit on the example code discussed in Chapter 18. A simple JAX-RS method is added to the `CustomerRe` source class that can handle PATCH requests:

src/main/java/com/restfully/shop/services/CustomerResource.java

```
package com.restfully.shop.services;

@Path("/customers")
public class CustomerResource {
...
```

```
    @PATCH
    @Path("{id}")
    @Consumes("application/xml")
    public void patchCustomer(@PathParam("id") int id, InputStream is)
    {
        updateCustomer(id, is);
    }
...
}
```

The @PATCH annotation is used on the patchCustomer() method. The implementation of this method simply delegates to the original updateCustomer() method.

The Client Code

The client code for *ex04_1* is pretty straightforward and similar to *ex03_1*. Let's look at some initial minor changes we've made:

src/test/java/com/restfully/shop/test/PatchTest.java

```
package com.restfully.shop.test;

import org.junit.AfterClass;
import org.junit.BeforeClass;
import org.junit.Test;

import javax.ws.rs.client.Client;
import javax.ws.rs.client.ClientBuilder;
import javax.ws.rs.client.Entity;
import javax.ws.rs.core.Response;


/**
 * @author <a href="mailto:bill@burkecentral.com">Bill Burke</a>
 * @version $Revision: 1 $
 */
public class PatchTest
{
    private static Client client;

    @BeforeClass
    public static void initClient()
    {
        client = ClientBuilder.newClient();
    }

    @AfterClass
    public static void closeClient()
    {
        client.close();
    }
```

First, we initialize our Client object within a JUNit @BeforeClass block. Any static method you annotate with @BeforeClass in JUnit will be executed once before all @Test methods are executed. So, in the initClient() method we initialize an instance of Client. Static methods annotated with @AfterClass are executed once after all @Test methods have run. The closeClient() method cleans up our Client object by invoking close() after all tests have run. This is a nice way of putting repetitive initialization and cleanup code that is needed for each test in one place.

The rest of the class is pretty straightforward and similar to *ex03_1*. I'll highlight only the interesting parts:

```
String patchCustomer = "<customer>"
        + "<first-name>William</first-name>"
        + "</customer>";
response = client.target(location)
                .request().method("PATCH", Entity.xml(patchCustomer));
if (response.getStatus() != 204)
    throw new RuntimeException("Failed to update");
response.close();
```

To make a PATCH HTTP invocation, we use the `javax.ws.rs.client.SyncInvoker.method()` method. The parameters to this method are a string denoting the HTTP method you want to invoke and the entity you want to pass as the message body. Simple as that.

Example ex04_2: @Path with Expressions

For this section, I'll illustrate the use of an @Path annotation with regular expressions. The example is a direct copy of the code in *ex03_1* with a few minor modifications.

Build and Run the Example Program

Perform the following steps:

1. Open a command prompt or shell terminal and change to the *ex04_2* directory of the workbook example code.

2. Make sure your PATH is set up to include both the JDK and Maven, as described in Chapter 17.

3. Perform the build and run the example by typing `mvn install`.

The Server Code

The CustomerResource class copied from the *ex03_1* example is pretty much the same in *ex04_2*, except that a few of the @Path expressions have been modified. I also added an extra method that allows you to reference customers by their first and last names within the URL path:

```
@Path("/customers")
public class CustomerResource {
...

    @GET
    @Path("{id : \\d+}")
    @Produces("application/xml")
    public StreamingOutput getCustomer(@PathParam("id") int id)
    {
        ...
    }

    @PUT
    @Path("{id : \\d+}")
    @Consumes("application/xml")
    public void updateCustomer(@PathParam("id") int id, InputStream is)
    {
        ...
    }
```

The @Path expression for getCustomer() and updateCustomer() was changed a little bit to use a Java regular expression for the URI matching. The expression dictates that the id segment of the URI can only be a string of digits. So, /customers/333 is a legal URI, but /customers/a32ab would result in a 404, "Not Found," response code being returned to the client:

```
@GET
@Path("{first : [a-zA-Z]+}-{last:[a-zA-Z]+}")
@Produces("application/xml")
public StreamingOutput getCustomerFirstLast(
                            @PathParam("first") String first,
                            @PathParam("last") String last)
{
    ...
}
```

To show a more complex regular expression, I added the getCustomerFirstLast() method to the resource class. This method provides a URI pointing to a specific customer, using the customer's first and last names instead of a numeric ID. This @Path expression matches a string of the first name and last name separated by a hyphen character. A legal URI is /customers/Bill-Burke. The name can only have letters within it, so /customers/Bill7-Burke would result in a 404, "Not Found," being returned to the client.

The Client Code

The client code is in *src/test/java/com/restfully/shop/test/ClientResourceTest.java*. It is really not much different than the code in example *ex03_1*, other than the fact that it additionally invokes the URI represented by the `getCustomerFirstLast()` method. If you've examined the code from Chapter 18, you can probably understand what is going on in this client example, so I won't elaborate further.

Example ex04_3: Subresource Locators

The *ex04_3* example implements the subresource locator example shown in "Full Dynamic Dispatching" on page 52 in Chapter 4.

Build and Run the Example Program

Perform the following steps:

1. Open a command prompt or shell terminal and change to the *ex04_3* directory of the workbook example code.

2. Make sure your PATH is set up to include both the JDK and Maven, as described in Chapter 17.

3. Perform the build and run the example by typing `mvn install`.

The Server Code

There's really not much to go over that wasn't explained in Chapter 4.

The Client Code

The client code lives in *src/test/java/com/restfully/shop/test/CustomerResourceTest.java*:

```
public class CustomerResourceTest
{
    @Test
    public void testCustomerResource() throws Exception {
        ...
    }

    @Test
    public void testFirstLastCustomerResource() throws Exception {
        ...
    }
}
```

The code contains two methods: `testCustomerResource()` and `testFirstLastCustomerResource()`.

The `testCustomerResource()` method first performs a POST to `/customers/europe-db` to create a customer using the `CustomerResource` subresource. It then retrieves the created customer using GET `/customers/europe-db/1`.

The `testFirstLastCustomerResource()` method performs a POST to `/customers/northamerica-db` to create a customer using the `FirstLastCustomerResource` subresource. It then uses GET `/customers/northamerica-db/Bill-Burke` to retrieve the created customer.

CHAPTER 20

Examples for Chapter 5

Chapter 5 showed you how to use JAX-RS annotations to inject specific information about an HTTP request into your Java methods and fields. This chapter implements most of the injection scenarios introduced in Chapter 5 so that you can see these things in action.

Example ex05_1: Injecting URI Information

This example illustrates the injection annotations that are focused on pulling in information from the incoming request URI. Specifically, it shows how to use `@PathParam`, `@MatrixParam`, and `@QueryParam`. Parallel examples are also shown using `javax.ws.rs.core.UriInfo` to obtain the same data.

The Server Code

The first thing you should look at on the server side is `CarResource`. This class pulls the various examples in Chapter 5 together to illustrate using `@MatrixParam` and `@PathParam` with the `javax.ws.rs.core.PathSegment` class:

src/main/java/com/restfully/shop/services/CarResource.java

```
@Path("/cars")
public class CarResource
{
    public static enum Color
    {
        red,
        white,
        blue,
        black
    }
```

```
@GET
@Path("/matrix/{make}/{model}/{year}")
@Produces("text/plain")
public String getFromMatrixParam(
                        @PathParam("make") String make,
                        @PathParam("model") PathSegment car,
                        @MatrixParam("color") Color color,
                        @PathParam("year") String year)
{
   return "A " + color + " " + year + " "
              + make + " " + car.getPath();
}
```

The getFromMatrixParam() method uses the @MatrixParam annotation to inject the matrix parameter color. An example of a URI it could process is /cars/matrix/mercedes/e55;color=black/2006. Notice that it automatically converts the matrix parameter into the Java enum Color:

```
@GET
@Path("/segment/{make}/{model}/{year}")
@Produces("text/plain")
public String getFromPathSegment(@PathParam("make") String make,
                             @PathParam("model") PathSegment car,
                             @PathParam("year") String year)
{
   String carColor = car.getMatrixParameters().getFirst("color");
   return "A " + carColor + " " + year + " "
                     + make + " " + car.getPath();
}
```

The getFromPathSegment() method also illustrates how to extract matrix parameter information. Instead of using @MatrixParam, it uses an injected PathSegment instance representing the model path parameter to obtain the matrix parameter information:

```
@GET
@Path("/segments/{make}/{model : .+}/year/{year}")
@Produces("text/plain")
public String getFromMultipleSegments(
                        @PathParam("make") String make,
                        @PathParam("model") List<PathSegment> car,
                        @PathParam("year") String year)
{
   String output = "A " + year + " " + make;
   for (PathSegment segment : car)
   {
      output += " " + segment.getPath();
   }
   return output;
}
```

The getFromMultipleSegments() method illustrates how a path parameter can match multiple segments of a URI. An example of a URI that it could process is /cars/

segments/mercedes/e55/amg/year/2006. In this case, e55/amg would match the mod el path parameter. The example injects the model parameter into a list of PathSeg ment instances:

```
@GET
@Path("/uriinfo/{make}/{model}/{year}")
@Produces("text/plain")
public String getFromUriInfo(@Context UriInfo info)
{
    String make = info.getPathParameters().getFirst("make");
    String year = info.getPathParameters().getFirst("year");
    PathSegment model = info.getPathSegments().get(3);
    String color = model.getMatrixParameters().getFirst("color");

    return "A " + color + " " + year + " "
                 + make + " " + model.getPath();
}
```

The final method, getFromUriInfo(), shows how you can obtain the same information using the UriInfo interface. As you can see, the matrix parameter information is extracted from PathSegment instances.

The next piece of code you should look at on the server is CustomerResource. This class shows how @QueryParam and @DefaultValue can work together to obtain information about the request URI's query parameters. An example using UriInfo is also shown so that you can see how this can be done without injection annotations:

src/main/java/com/restfully/shop/services/CustomerResource.java

```
@Path("/customers")
public class CustomerResource {
...

    @GET
    @Produces("application/xml")
    public StreamingOutput getCustomers(
                final @QueryParam("start") int start,
                final @QueryParam("size") @DefaultValue("2") int size)
    {
        ...
    }
```

The getCustomers() method returns a set of customers from the customer database. The start parameter defines the start index and the size parameter specifies how many customers you want returned. The @DefaultValue annotation is used for the case in which a client does not use the query parameters to index into the customer list.

The next implementation of getCustomers() uses UriInfo instead of injection parameters:

```
@GET
@Produces("application/xml")
@Path("uriinfo")
public StreamingOutput getCustomers(@Context UriInfo info)
{
   int start = 0;
   int size = 2;
   if (info.getQueryParameters().containsKey("start"))
   {
      start = Integer.valueOf(
                     info.getQueryParameters().getFirst("start"));
   }
   if (info.getQueryParameters().containsKey("size"))
   {
      size = Integer.valueOf(
                     info.getQueryParameters().getFirst("size"));
   }
   return getCustomers(start, size);
}
```

As you can see, the code to access query parameter data programmatically is a bit more verbose than using injection annotations.

The Client Code

The client code for this example lives in the file *src/test/java/com/restfully/shop/test/ InjectionTest.java*. The code is quite boring, so I won't get into too much detail.

The `testCarResource()` method invokes these requests on the server to test the `Car Resource` class:

```
GET http://localhost:8080/services/cars/matrix/mercedes/e55;color=black/2006
GET http://localhost:8080/services/cars/segment/mercedes/e55;color=black/2006
GET http://localhost:8080/services/cars/segments/mercedes/e55/amg/year/2006
GET http://localhost:8080/services/cars/uriinfo/mercedes/e55;color=black/2006
```

The `testCustomerResource()` method invokes these requests on the server to test the `CustomerResource` class:

```
GET http://localhost:8080/services/customers
GET http://localhost:8080/services/customers?start=1&size=3
GET http://localhost:8080/services/customers/uriinfo?start=2&size=2
```

The request without query parameters shows `@DefaultValue` in action. It is worth noting how query parameters are handled in the client code. Let's look at `testCustomer Resource()` a little bit:

```
list = client.target("http://localhost:8080/services/customers/uriinfo")
            .queryParam("start", "2")
            .queryParam("size", "2")
            .request().get(String.class);
```

The `javax.ws.rs.client.WebTarget.queryParam()` method is used to fill out the query parameters for the invocation. This is a nice convenience method to use, especially if your values might have characters that need to be encoded.

Build and Run the Example Program

Perform the following steps:

1. Open a command prompt or shell terminal and change to the *ex05_1* directory of the workbook example code.
2. Make sure your PATH is set up to include both the JDK and Maven, as described in Chapter 17.
3. Perform the build and run the example by typing `mvn install`.

Example ex05_2: Forms and Cookies

The *ex05_2* exercise includes examples of injecting form data, cookies, and HTTP headers using the `@FormParam`, `@CookieParam`, and `@HeaderParam` annotations. This example is a bit different than former examples, as there is no client code. Instead, to see these annotations in action, you will use a browser as your client.

The Server Code

The example starts off with an HTML form defined in *src/main/webapp/index.html*:

```html
<html>
<body>

<form action="/rest/customers" method="post">
    First Name: <input type="text" name="firstname"/><br/>
    Last Name: <input type="text" name="lastname"/><br/>
    <INPUT type="submit" value="Send">
</form>

</body>
</html>
```

It is a simple form for creating a customer using our familiar `CustomerResource` service:

src/main/java/com/restfully/shop/CustomerResource.java

```java
@Path("/customers")
public class CustomerResource {
...
    @POST
    @Produces("text/html")
    public Response createCustomer(
```

```
                          @FormParam("firstname") String first,
                          @FormParam("lastname") String last)
      {
```

The HTML form posts data to the createCustomer() method of CustomerResource when users click the Send button:

```
      Customer customer = new Customer();
      customer.setId(idCounter.incrementAndGet());
      customer.setFirstName(first);
      customer.setLastName(last);
      customerDB.put(customer.getId(), customer);
      System.out.println("Created customer " + customer.getId());
      String output = "Created customer <a href=\"customers/" +
              customer.getId() + "\">" + customer.getId()
              + "</a>";
      String lastVisit = DateFormat.getDateTimeInstance(
            DateFormat.SHORT, DateFormat.LONG).format(new Date());
      return Response.created(URI.create("/customers/"
                                      + customer.getId()))
            .entity(output)
            .cookie(new NewCookie("last-visit", lastVisit))
            .build();

      }
```

The createCustomer() method does a couple things. First, it uses the form data injected with @FormParam to create a Customer object and insert it into an in-memory map. It then builds an HTML response that shows text linking to the new customer. Finally, it sets a cookie on the client by calling the ResponseBuilder.cookie() method. This cookie, named last-visit, holds the current time and date. This cookie will be used so that on subsequent requests, the server knows the last time the client accessed the website:

```
      @GET
      @Path("{id}")
      @Produces("text/plain")
      public Response getCustomer(
                          @PathParam("id") int id,
                          @HeaderParam("User-Agent") String userAgent,
                          @CookieParam("last-visit") String date)
      {
```

The getCustomer() method retrieves a Customer object from the in-memory map referenced by the id path parameter. The @HeaderParam annotation injects the value of the User-Agent header. This is a standard HTTP 1.1 header that denotes the type of client that made the request (Safari, Firefox, Internet Explorer, etc.). The @CookieParam annotation injects the value of the last-visit cookie that the client should be passing along with each request:

```
    final Customer customer = customerDB.get(id);
    if (customer == null) {
        throw new WebApplicationException(Response.Status.NOT_FOUND);
    }
    String output = "User-Agent: " + userAgent + "\r\n";
    output += "Last visit: " + date + "\r\n\r\n";
    output += "Customer: " + customer.getFirstName() + " "
                    + customer.getLastName();
    String lastVisit = DateFormat.getDateTimeInstance(
            DateFormat.SHORT, DateFormat.LONG).format(new Date());
    return Response.ok(output)
            .cookie(new NewCookie("last-visit", lastVisit))
            .build();
}
```

The implementation of this method is very simple. It outputs the User-Agent header and last-visit cookie as plain text (text/plain). It also resets the last-visit cookie to the current time and date.

Build and Run the Example Program

Perform the following steps:

1. Open a command prompt or shell terminal and change to the *ex05_2* directory of the workbook example code.

2. Make sure your PATH is set up to include both the JDK and Maven, as described in Chapter 17.

3. Perform the build and run the example by typing mvn jetty:run. This command is a bit different than our previous examples. This script builds the WAR file, but it also starts up the Jetty servlet container.

You test-drive *ex05_2* by using your browser. The first step is to go to *http://localhost: 8080*, as shown in Figure 20-1.

When you click Send, you will see the screen shown in Figure 20-2.

Clicking the customer link will show you a plain-text representation of the customer, as shown in Figure 20-3.

If you refresh this page, you will see the timestamp of the "last visit" string increment each time as the CustomerResource updates the last-visit cookie.

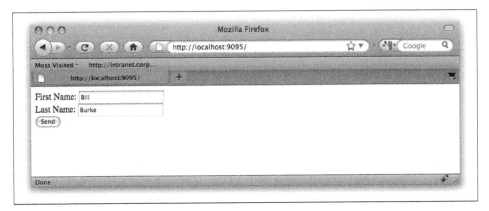

Figure 20-1. Customer creation form

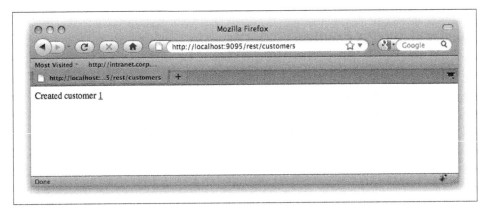

Figure 20-2. Creation response

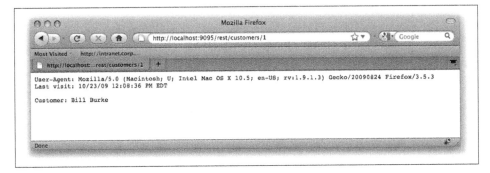

Figure 20-3. Customer output

CHAPTER 21

Examples for Chapter 6

In Chapter 3, you saw a quick overview on how to write a simple JAX-RS service. You might have noticed that we needed a lot of code to process incoming and outgoing XML data. In Chapter 6, you learned that all this handcoded marshalling code is unnecessary. JAX-RS has a number of built-in content handlers that can do the processing for you. You also learned that if these prepackaged providers do not meet your requirements, you can write your own content handler.

There are two examples in this chapter. The first rewrites the *ex03_1* example to use JAXB instead of handcoded XML marshalling. The second example implements a custom content handler that can send serialized Java objects over HTTP.

Example ex06_1: Using JAXB

This example shows how easy it is to use JAXB and JAX-RS to exchange XML documents over HTTP. The com.restfully.shop.domain.Customer class is the first interesting piece of the example.

src/main/java/com/restfully/shop/domain/Customer.java

```java
@XmlRootElement(name="customer")
public class Customer {
    private int id;
    private String firstName;
    private String lastName;
    private String street;
    private String city;
    private String state;
    private String zip;
    private String country;

    @XmlAttribute
    public int getId() {
```

```
        return id;
    }

    public void setId(int id) {
        this.id = id;
    }

    @XmlElement(name="first-name")
    public String getFirstName() {
        return firstName;
    }

    public void setFirstName(String firstName) {
        this.firstName = firstName;
    }

    @XmlElement(name="last-name")
    public String getLastName() {
        return lastName;
    }

    public void setLastName(String lastName) {
        this.lastName = lastName;
    }

    @XmlElement
    public String getStreet() {
        return street;
    }
    ...
}
```

The JAXB annotations provide a mapping between the Customer class and XML.

You don't need to write a lot of code to implement the JAX-RS service because JAX-RS already knows how to handle JAXB annotated classes:

src/main/java/com/restfully/shop/services/CustomerResource.java

```
@Path("/customers")
public class CustomerResource {
    private Map<Integer, Customer> customerDB =
                        new ConcurrentHashMap<Integer, Customer>();
    private AtomicInteger idCounter = new AtomicInteger();

    public CustomerResource() {
    }

    @POST
    @Consumes("application/xml")
    public Response createCustomer(Customer customer) {
        customer.setId(idCounter.incrementAndGet());
        customerDB.put(customer.getId(), customer);
```

```
      System.out.println("Created customer " + customer.getId());
      return Response.created(URI.create("/customers/" +
                                  customer.getId())).build();

   }

   @GET
   @Path("{id}")
   @Produces("application/xml")
   public Customer getCustomer(@PathParam("id") int id) {
      Customer customer = customerDB.get(id);
      if (customer == null) {
         throw new WebApplicationException(Response.Status.NOT_FOUND);
      }
      return customer;
   }

   @PUT
   @Path("{id}")
   @Consumes("application/xml")
   public void updateCustomer(@PathParam("id") int id,
                                        Customer update) {
      Customer current = customerDB.get(id);
      if (current == null)
         throw new WebApplicationException(Response.Status.NOT_FOUND);

      current.setFirstName(update.getFirstName());
      current.setLastName(update.getLastName());
      current.setStreet(update.getStreet());
      current.setState(update.getState());
      current.setZip(update.getZip());
      current.setCountry(update.getCountry());
   }
}
```

If you compare this with the `CustomerResource` class in *ex03_1*, you'll see that the code in this example is much more compact. There is no handcoded marshalling code, and our methods are dealing with `Customer` objects directly instead of raw strings.

The Client Code

The client code can also now take advantage of automatic JAXB marshalling. All JAX-RS 2.0 client implementations must support JAXB as a mechanism to transmit XML on the client side. Let's take a look at how the client code has changed from *ex03_1*:

```
   @Test
   public void testCustomerResource() throws Exception
   {
      System.out.println("*** Create a new Customer ***");
      Customer newCustomer = new Customer();
      newCustomer.setFirstName("Bill");
```

```
newCustomer.setLastName("Burke");
newCustomer.setStreet("256 Clarendon Street");
newCustomer.setCity("Boston");
newCustomer.setState("MA");
newCustomer.setZip("02115");
newCustomer.setCountry("USA");
```

We start off by allocating and initializing a `Customer` object with the values of the new customer we want to create.

```
Response response =
        client.target("http://localhost:8080/services/customers")
                .request().post(Entity.xml(newCustomer));
if (response.getStatus() != 201)
    throw new RuntimeException("Failed to create");
```

The code for posting the new customer looks exactly the same as *ex03_1* except that instead of initializing a `javax.ws.rs.client.Entity` with an XML string, we are using the `Customer` object. The JAX-RS client will automatically marshal this object into an XML string and send it across the wire.

Changes to pom.xml

JBoss RESTEasy is broken up into a bunch of smaller JARs so that you can pick and choose which features of RESTEasy to use. Because of this, the core RESTEasy JAR file does not have the JAXB content handlers. Therefore, we need to add a new dependency to our *pom.xml* file:

```
<dependency>
    <groupId>org.jboss.resteasy</groupId>
    <artifactId>resteasy-jaxb-provider</artifactId>
    <version>1.2</version>
</dependency>
```

Adding this dependency will add the JAXB provider to your project. It will also pull in any third-party dependency RESTEasy needs to process XML. If you are deploying on a Java EE application server like Wildfly or JBoss, you will not need this dependency; JAXB support is preinstalled.

Build and Run the Example Program

Perform the following steps:

1. Open a command prompt or shell terminal and change to the *ex06_1* directory of the workbook example code.

2. Make sure your PATH is set up to include both the JDK and Maven, as described in Chapter 17.

---

3. Perform the build and run the example by typing `mvn install`.

Example ex06_2: Creating a Content Handler

For this example, we're going to create something entirely new. The Chapter 6 example of a content handler is a reimplementation of JAXB support. It is suitable for that chapter because it illustrates both the writing of a `MessageBodyReader` and a `MessageBodyWrit er` and demonstrates how the `ContextResolver` is used. For *ex06_2*, though, we're going to keep things simple.

In *ex06_2*, we're going to rewrite *ex06_1* to exchange Java objects between the client and server instead of XML. Java objects, you ask? Isn't this REST? Well, there's no reason a Java object can't be a valid representation of a resource! If you're exchanging Java objects, you can still realize a lot of the advantages of REST and HTTP. You still can do content negotiation (described in Chapter 9) and HTTP caching (described in Chapter 11).

The Content Handler Code

For our Java object content handler, we're going to write one class that is both a `MessageBodyReader` and a `MessageBodyWriter`:

src/main/java/com/restfully/shop/services/JavaMarshaller.java

```
@Provider
@Produces("application/example-java")
@Consumes("application/x-java-serialized-object")
public class JavaMarshaller
                implements MessageBodyReader, MessageBodyWriter
{
```

The `JavaMarshaller` class is annotated with `@Provider`, `@Produces`, and `@Consumes`, as required by the specification. The media type used by the example to represent a Java object is `application/example-java`:[1]

```
public boolean isReadable(Class type, Type genericType,
Annotation[] annotations, MediaType mediaType)
{
    return Serializable.class.isAssignableFrom(type);
}

public boolean isWriteable(Class type, Type genericType,
                Annotation[] annotations, MediaType mediaType)
{
```

---

1. The media type `application/x-java-serialized-object` should actually be used, but as of the second revision of this book, RESTEasy now has this type built in.

```
        return Serializable.class.isAssignableFrom(type);
    }
```

For the isReadable() and isWriteable() methods, we just check to see if our Java type implements the java.io.Serializable interface:

```
public Object readFrom(Class type, Type genericType,
                    Annotation[] annotations, MediaType mediaType,
                        MultivaluedMap httpHeaders,
                            InputStream is)
                    throws IOException, WebApplicationException
{
    ObjectInputStream ois = new ObjectInputStream(is);
    try
    {
        return ois.readObject();
    }
    catch (ClassNotFoundException e)
    {
        throw new RuntimeException(e);
    }
}
```

The readFrom() method uses basic Java serialization to read a Java object from the HTTP input stream:

```
public long getSize(Object o, Class type,
                    Type genericType, Annotation[] annotations,
                        MediaType mediaType)
{
    return -1;
}
```

The getSize() method returns –1. It is impossible to figure out the exact length of our marshalled Java object without serializing it into a byte buffer and counting the number of bytes. We're better off letting the servlet container figure this out for us. The get Size() method has actually been deprecated in JAX-RS 2.0.

```
public void writeTo(Object o, Class type,
                        Type genericType, Annotation[] annotations,
                            MediaType mediaType,
                                MultivaluedMap httpHeaders, OutputStream os)
                            throws IOException, WebApplicationException
{
    ObjectOutputStream oos = new ObjectOutputStream(os);
    oos.writeObject(o);
}
```

Like the readFrom() method, basic Java serialization is used to marshal our Java object into the HTTP response body.

The Resource Class

The CustomerResource class doesn't change much from *ex06_2*:

src/main/java/com/restfully/shop/services/CustomerResource.java

```java
@Path("/customers")
public class CustomerResource
{
...

@POST
   @Consumes("application/example-java")
   public Response createCustomer(Customer customer)
   {
      customer.setId(idCounter.incrementAndGet());
      customerDB.put(customer.getId(), customer);
      System.out.println("Created customer " + customer.getId());
      return Response.created(URI.create("/customers/"
                               + customer.getId())).build();

   }
...
}
```

The code is actually exactly the same as that used in *ex06_1*, except that the @Pro
duces and @Consumes annotations use the application/example-java media type.

The Application Class

The ShoppingApplication class needs to change a tiny bit from the previous examples:

src/main/java/com/restfully/shop/services/ShoppingApplication.java

```java
public class ShoppingApplication extends Application {
    private Set<Object> singletons = new HashSet<Object>();
    private Set<Class<?>> classes = new HashSet<Class<?>>();

    public ShoppingApplication() {
        singletons.add(new CustomerResource());
        classes.add(JavaMarshaller.class);
    }

    @Override
    public Set<Class<?>> getClasses() {
        return classes;
    }

    @Override
    public Set<Object> getSingletons() {
        return singletons;
```

```
    }
  }
```

For our `Application` class, we need to register the `JavaMarshaller` class. If we don't, the JAX-RS runtime won't know how to handle the `application/example-java` media type.

The Client Code

The client code isn't much different from *ex06_1*. We just need to modify the `jav ax.ws.rs.client.Entity` construction to use the `application/example-java` media type. For example, here's what customer creation looks like:

src/test/java/com/restfully/shop/test/CustomerResourceTest.java

```
    public class CustomerResourceTest
    {
      @Test
      public void testCustomerResource() throws Exception
      {
...
        Response response = client.target
               ("http://localhost:8080/services/customers")
               .request().post(Entity.entity
                             (newCustomer, "application/example-java"));
```

The static `Entity.entity()` method is called, passing in the plain `Customer` Java object along with our custom media type.

Build and Run the Example Program

Perform the following steps:

1. Open a command prompt or shell terminal and change to the *ex06_2* directory of the workbook example code.

2. Make sure your PATH is set up to include both the JDK and Maven, as described in Chapter 17.

3. Perform the build and run the example by typing `mvn install`.

CHAPTER 22

Examples for Chapter 7

In Chapter 7, you learned how to create complex responses using the Response and ResponseBuilder classes. You also learned how to map thrown exceptions to a Response using a javax.ws.rs.ext.ExceptionMapper. Since most of our examples use a Re sponse object in one way or another, this chapter focuses only on writing an ExceptionMapper.

Example ex07_1: ExceptionMapper

This example is a slight modification from *ex06_1* to show you how you can use Excep tionMappers. Let's take a look at the CustomerResource class to see what is different:

src/main/java/com/restfully/shop/services/CustomerResource.java

```
@Path("/customers")
public class CustomerResource {
...
   @GET
   @Path("{id}")
   @Produces("application/xml")
   public Customer getCustomer(@PathParam("id") int id)
   {
      Customer customer = customerDB.get(id);
      if (customer == null)
      {
         throw new CustomerNotFoundException("Could not find customer "
                                 + id);
      }
      return customer;
   }

   @PUT
   @Path("{id}")
   @Consumes("application/xml")
```

```
public void updateCustomer(@PathParam("id") int id,
                           Customer update)
{
    Customer current = customerDB.get(id);
    if (current == null)
      throw new CustomerNotFoundException("Could not find customer " + id);

    current.setFirstName(update.getFirstName());
    current.setLastName(update.getLastName());
    current.setStreet(update.getStreet());
    current.setState(update.getState());
    current.setZip(update.getZip());
    current.setCountry(update.getCountry());
  }
}
```

In *ex06_1*, our `getCustomer()` and `updateCustomer()` methods threw a `javax.ws.rs.WebApplicationException`. We've replaced this exception with our own custom class, `CustomerNotFoundException`:

src/main/java/com/restfully/shop/services/CustomerNotFoundException.java

```
public class CustomerNotFoundException extends RuntimeException
{
    public NotFoundException(String s)
    {
       super(s);
    }
}
```

There's nothing really special about this exception class other than it inherits from `java.lang.RuntimeException`. What we are going to do, though, is map this thrown exception to a `Response` object using an `ExceptionMapper`:

src/main/java/com/restfully/shop/services/CustomerNotFoundExceptionMapper.java

```
@Provider
public class NotFoundExceptionMapper
                      implements ExceptionMapper<CustomerNotFoundException>
{
    public Response toResponse(NotFoundException exception)
    {
      return Response.status(Response.Status.NOT_FOUND)
                     .entity(exception.getMessage())
                     .type("text/plain").build();
    }
}
```

When a client makes a GET request to a customer URL that does not exist, the `Custom erResource.getCustomer()` method throws a `CustomerNotFoundException`. This exception is caught by the JAX-RS runtime, and the `NotFoundExceptionMapper.toRes ponse()` method is called. This method creates a `Response` object that returns a 404 status code and a plain-text error message.

The last thing we have to do is modify our `Application` class to register the `Exception Mapper`:

src/main/java/com/restfully/shop/services/ShoppingApplication.java

```java
public class ShoppingApplication extends Application {
    private Set<Object> singletons = new HashSet<Object>();
    private Set<Class<?>> classes = new HashSet<Class<?>>();

    public ShoppingApplication()
    {
        singletons.add(new CustomerResource());
        classes.add(CustomerNotFoundExceptionMapper.class);
    }

    @Override
    public Set<Class<?>> getClasses()
    {
        return classes;
    }

    @Override
    public Set<Object> getSingletons()
    {
        return singletons;
    }
}
```

The Client Code

The client code for this example is very simple. We make a GET request to a customer resource that doesn't exist:

src/test/java/com/restfully/shop/test/CustomerResourceTest.java

```java
package com.restfully.shop.test;

import javax.ws.rs.NotFoundException;

...

    @Test
    public void testCustomerResource() throws Exception
    {
        try
```

```
    {
        Customer customer = client.target
                                 ("http://localhost:8080/services/customers/1")
                                 .request().get(Customer.class);
        System.out.println("Should never get here!");
    }
    catch (NotFoundException e)
    {
        System.out.println("Caught error!");
        String error = e.getResponse().readEntity(String.class);
        System.out.println(error);
    }
}
```

When this client code runs, the server will throw a CustomerNotFoundException, which is converted into a 404 response back to the client. The client code handles the error as discussed in "Exception Handling" on page 122 and throws a javax.ws.rs.NotFoun dException, which is handled in the catch block. The error message is extracted from the HTTP error response and displayed to the console.

Build and Run the Example Program

Perform the following steps:

1. Open a command prompt or shell terminal and change to the *ex07_1* directory of the workbook example code.

2. Make sure your PATH is set up to include both the JDK and Maven, as described in Chapter 17.

3. Perform the build and run the example by typing **mvn install**.

CHAPTER 23

Examples for Chapter 9

In Chapter 9, you learned that clients can use HTTP Content Negotiation to request different data formats from the same URL using the Accept header. You also learned that JAX-RS takes the Accept header into account when deciding how to dispatch an HTTP request to a Java method. In this chapter, you'll see two different examples that show how JAX-RS and HTTP conneg can work together.

Example ex09_1: Conneg with JAX-RS

This example is a slight modification from *ex06_1* and shows two different concepts. First, the same JAX-RS resource method can process two different media types. Chapter 9 gives the example of a method that returns a JAXB annotated class instance that can be returned as either JSON or XML. We've implemented this in *ex09_1* by slightly changing the CustomerResource.getCustomer() method:

src/main/java/com/restfully/shop/services/CustomerResource.java

```
@Path("/customers")
public class CustomerResource {
...
    @GET
    @Path("{id}")
    @Produces({"application/xml", "application/json"})
    public Customer getCustomer(@PathParam("id") int id)
    {
        ...
    }
```

The JAXB provider that comes with RESTEasy can convert JAXB objects to JSON or XML. In this example, we have added the media type application/json to getCusto mer()'s @Produces annotation. The JAX-RS runtime will process the Accept header and pick the appropriate media type of the response for getCustomer(). If the Accept header is application/xml, XML will be produced. If the Accept header is JSON, the Customer object will be outputted as JSON.

The second concept being highlighted here is that you can use the @Produces annotation to dispatch to different Java methods. To illustrate this, we've added the getCustomerString() method, which processes the same URL as getCustomer() but for a different media type:

```java
@GET
@Path("{id}")
@Produces("text/plain")
public Customer getCustomerString(@PathParam("id") int id)
{
    return getCustomer(id).toString();
}
```

The Client Code

The client code for this example executes various HTTP GET requests to retrieve different representations of a Customer. Each request sets the Accept header a little differently so that it can obtain a different representation. For example:

src/test/java/com/restfully/shop/test/CustomerResourceTest.java

```java
public class CustomerResourceTest
{
    @Test
    public void testCustomerResource() throws Exception
    {
        ... initialization code ...

        System.out.println("*** GET XML Created Customer **");
        String xml = client.target(location).request()
                                .accept(MediaType.APPLICATION_XML_TYPE)
                                .get(String.class);
        System.out.println(xml);

        System.out.println("*** GET JSON Created Customer **");
        String json = client.target(location).request()
                    .accept(MediaType.APPLICATION_JSON_TYPE)
                    .get(String.class);
        System.out.println(json);
    }
}
```

The SyncInvoker.accept() method is used to initialize the Accept header. The client extracts a String from the HTTP response so it can show you the request XML or JSON.

Build and Run the Example Program

Perform the following steps:

1. Open a command prompt or shell terminal and change to the *ex09_1* directory of the workbook example code.
2. Make sure your PATH is set up to include both the JDK and Maven, as described in Chapter 17.
3. Perform the build and run the example by typing `mvn install`.

Example ex09_2: Conneg via URL Patterns

Chapter 9 discussed how some clients, particularly browsers, are unable to use the `Accept` header to request different formats from the same URL. To solve this problem, many JAX-RS implementations allow you to map a filename suffix (*.html*, *.xml*, *.txt*) to a particular media type. RESTEasy has this capability. We're going to illustrate this using your browser as a client along with a slightly modified version of *ex09_1*.

The Server Code

A few minor things have changed on the server side. First, we add `getCustomerHtml()` method to our `CustomerResource` class:

```
@GET
@Path("{id}")
@Produces("text/html")
public String getCustomerHtml(@PathParam("id") int id)
{
    return "<h1>Customer As HTML</h1><pre>"
                + getCustomer(id).toString() + "</pre>";
}
```

Since you're going to be interacting with this service through your browser, it might be nice if the example outputs HTML in addition to text, XML, and JSON.

The only other change to the server side is in the configuration for RESTEasy:

src/main/webapp/WEB-INF/web.xml

```
<web-app>

    <context-param>
        <param-name>resteasy.media.type.mappings</param-name>
        <param-value>
                html : text/html,
                txt : text/plain,
                xml : application/xml
```

```
        </param-value>
    </context-param>
  ...
  </web-app>
```

The `resteasy.media.type.mappings` content parameter is added to define a mapping between various file suffixes and the media types they map to. A comma separates each entry. The suffix string makes up the first half of the entry and the colon character delimits the suffix from the media type it maps to. Here, we've defined mappings between *.html* and `text/html`, *.txt* and `text/plain`, and *.xml* and `application/xml`.

Build and Run the Example Program

Perform the following steps:

1. Open a command prompt or shell terminal and change to the *ex09_2* directory of the workbook example code.

2. Make sure your PATH is set up to include both the JDK and Maven, as described in Chapter 17.

3. Perform the build and run the example by typing **mvn jetty:run**.

The `jetty:run` target will run the servlet container so that you can make browser invocations on it. Now, open up your browser and visit *http://localhost:8080/customers/1*.

Doing so will show you which default media type your browser requests. Each browser may be different. For me, Firefox 3.x prefers HTML, and Safari prefers XML.

Next, browse each of the following URLs: *http://localhost:8080/customers/1.html*, *http://localhost:8080/customers/1.txt*, and *http://localhost:8080/customers/1.xml*. You should see a different representation for each.

CHAPTER 24

Examples for Chapter 10

In Chapter 10, you learned about many of the concepts of HATEOAS and how to use JAX-RS to add these principles to your RESTful web services. In this chapter, you'll look through two different examples. The first shows you how to introduce Atom links into your XML documents. The second uses Link headers to publish state transitions within a RESTful web service application.

Example ex10_1: Atom Links

This example is a slight modification of the *ex06_1* example introduced in Chapter 21. It expands the CustomerResource RESTful web service so that a client can fetch subsets of the customer database. If a client does a GET /customers request in our RESTful application, it will receive a subset list of customers in XML. Two Atom links are embedded in this document that allow you to view the next or previous sets of customer data. Example output would be:

```
<customers>
    <customer id="3">
      ...
    </customer>
    <customer id="4">
      ...
    </customer>
    <link rel="next"
        href="http://example.com/customers?start=5&size=2"
        type="application/xml"/>
    <link rel="previous"
        href="http://example.com/customers?start=1&size=2"
        type="application/xml"/>
</customers>
```

The next and previous links are URLs pointing to the same /customers URL, but they contain URI query parameters indexing into the customer database.

The Server Code

The first bit of code is a JAXB class that maps to the <customers> element. It must be capable of holding an arbitrary number of Customer instances as well as the Atom links for our next and previous link relationships. We can use the javax.ws.rs.core.Link class with its JAXB adapter to represent these links:

src/main/java/com/restfully/shop/domain/Customers.java

```java
import javax.ws.rs.core.Link;
...

@XmlRootElement(name = "customers")
public class Customers
{
    protected Collection<Customer> customers;
    protected List<Link> links;

    @XmlElementRef
    public Collection<Customer> getCustomers()
    {
        return customers;
    }

    public void setCustomers(Collection<Customer> customers)
    {
        this.customers = customers;
    }

    @XmlElement(name="link")
    @XmlJavaTypeAdapter(Link.JaxbAdapter.class)
    public List<Link> getLinks()
    {
        return links;
    }

    public void setLinks(List<Link> links)
    {
        this.links = links;
    }

    @XmlTransient
    public URI getNext()
    {
        if (links == null) return null;
        for (Link link : links)
        {
            if ("next".equals(link.getRel())) return link.getUri();
        }
        return null;
    }
```

```
@XmlTransient
public URI getPrevious()
{
    if (links == null) return null;
    for (Link link : links)
    {
        if ("previous".equals(link.getRel())) return link.getUri();
    }
    return null;
}

}
```

There is no nice way to define a map in JAXB, so all the Atom links are stuffed within a collection property in `Customers`. The convenience methods `getPrevious()` and `getNext()` iterate through this collection to find the next and previous Atom links embedded within the document if they exist.

The final difference from the *ex06_1* example is the implementation of GET /custom ers handling:

src/main/java/com/restfully/shop/services/CustomerResource.java

```
@Path("/customers")
public class CustomerResource
{
    @GET
    @Produces("application/xml")
    @Formatted
    public Customers getCustomers(@QueryParam("start") int start,
                    @QueryParam("size") @DefaultValue("2") int size,
                    @Context UriInfo uriInfo)
    {
```

The `@org.jboss.resteasy.annotations.providers.jaxb.Formatted` annotation is a RESTEasy-specific plug-in that formats the XML output returned to the client to include indentations and new lines so that the text is easier to read.

The query parameters for the `getCustomers()` method, `start` and `size`, are optional. They represent an index into the customer database and how many customers you want returned by the invocation. The `@DefaultValue` annotation is used to define a default page size of 2.

The `UriInfo` instance injected with `@Context` is used to build the URLs that define next and previous link relationships.

```
UriBuilder builder = uriInfo.getAbsolutePathBuilder();
builder.queryParam("start", "{start}");
builder.queryParam("size", "{size}");
```

Here, the code defines a URI template by using the UriBuilder passed back from UriInfo.getAbsolutePathBuilder(). The start and size query parameters are added to the template. Their values are populated using template parameters later on when the actual links are built.

```
ArrayList<Customer> list = new ArrayList<Customer>();
ArrayList<Link> links = new ArrayList<Link>();
synchronized (customerDB)
{
   int i = 0;
   for (Customer customer : customerDB.values())
   {
      if (i >= start && i < start + size)
                              list.add(customer);
      i++;
   }
}
```

The code then gathers up the Customer instances that will be returned to the client based on the start and size parameters. All this code is done within a synchronized block to protect against concurrent access on the customerDB map.

```
// next link
if (start + size < customerDB.size())
{
   int next = start + size;
   URI nextUri = builder.clone().build(next, size);
   Link nextLink = Link.fromUri(nextUri)
                     .rel("next").type("application/xml").build();
   links.add(nextLink);
}
// previous link
if (start > 0)
{
   int previous = start - size;
   if (previous < 0) previous = 0;
   URI previousUri = builder.clone().build(previous, size);
    Link previousLink = Link.fromUri(previousUri)
                          .rel("previous")
                          .type("application/xml").build();
   links.add(previousLink);
}
```

If there are more possible customer instances left to be viewed, a next link relationship is calculated using the UriBuilder template defined earlier. A similar calculation is done to see if a previous link relationship needs to be added to the document.

```
}
Customers customers = new Customers();
customers.setCustomers(list);
customers.setLinks(links);
return customers;
}
```

Finally, a `Customers` instance is created and initialized with the `Customer` list and link relationships and returned to the client.

The Client Code

The client initially gets the XML document from the `/customers` URL. It then loops using the next link relationship as the URL to print out all the customers in the database:

```
public class CustomerResourceTest
{
    @Test
    public void testQueryCustomers() throws Exception
    {
        URI uri = new URI("http://localhost:8080/services/customers");
        while (uri != null)
        {
            WebTarget target = client.target(uri);
            String output = target.request().get(String.class);
            System.out.println("** XML from " + uri.toString());
            System.out.println(output);

            Customers customers = target.request().get(Customers.class);
            uri = customers.getNext();
        }
    }
}
```

An interesting thing to note about this is that the server is guiding the client to make state transitions as it browses the customer database. Once the initial URL is invoked, further queries are solely driven by Atom links.

Build and Run the Example Program

Perform the following steps:

1. Open a command prompt or shell terminal and change to the *ex10_1* directory of the workbook example code.

2. Make sure your PATH is set up to include both the JDK and Maven, as described in Chapter 17.

3. Perform the build and run the example by typing mvn `install`.

Example ex10_2: Link Headers

There are two educational goals I want to get across with this example. The first is the use of Link headers within a RESTful application. The second is that if your services provide the appropriate links, you only need one published URL to navigate through your system. When you look at the client code for this example, you'll see that only one URL is hardcoded to start the whole process of the example.

To illustrate these techniques, a few more additional JAX-RS services were built beyond the simple customer database example that has been repeated so many times throughout this book. Chapter 2 discussed the design of an ecommerce application. This chapter starts the process of implementing this application by introducing an order-entry RESTful service.

The Server Code

The Order and LineItem classes are added to the JAXB domain model. They are used to marshal the XML that represents order entries in the system. They are not that interesting, so I'm not going to get into much detail here.

OrderResource

The OrderResource class is used to create, post, and cancel orders in our ecommerce system. The purge operation is also available to destroy any leftover order entries that have been cancelled but not removed from the order entry database. Let's look:

src/main/java/com/restfully/shop/services/OrderResource.java

```java
@Path("/orders")
public class OrderResource
{
    private Map<Integer, Order> orderDB =
                                new Hashtable<Integer, Order>();
    private AtomicInteger idCounter = new AtomicInteger();

    @POST
    @Consumes("application/xml")
    public Response createOrder(Order order, @Context UriInfo uriInfo)
    {
        order.setId(idCounter.incrementAndGet());
        orderDB.put(order.getId(), order);
        System.out.println("Created order " + order.getId());
        UriBuilder builder = uriInfo.getAbsolutePathBuilder();
        builder.path(Integer.toString(order.getId()));
        return Response.created(builder.build()).build();

    }
```

The createOrder() method handles POST /orders requests. It generates new Order IDs and adds the posted Order instance into the order database (the map). The UriInfo.ge tAbsolutePathBuilder() method generates the URL used to initialize the Location header returned by the Response.created() method. You'll see later that the client uses this URL to further manipulate the created order.

```
@GET
@Path("{id}")
@Produces("application/xml")
public Response getOrder(@PathParam("id") int id,
                          @Context UriInfo uriInfo)
{
   Order order = orderDB.get(id);
   if (order == null)
   {
      throw new WebApplicationException(Response.Status.NOT_FOUND);
   }
   Response.ResponseBuilder builder = Response.ok(order);
   if (!order.isCancelled()) addCancelHeader(uriInfo, builder);
   return builder.build();
}
```

The getOrder() method processes GET /orders/{id} requests and retrieves individual orders from the database (the map). If the order has not been cancelled already, a cancel Link header is added to the Response so the client knows if an order can be cancelled and which URL to post a cancel request to:

```
protected void addCancelHeader(UriInfo uriInfo,
                                Response.ResponseBuilder builder)
{
   UriBuilder absolute = uriInfo.getAbsolutePathBuilder();
   URI cancelUrl = absolute.clone().path("cancel").build();
   builder.links(Link.fromUri(cancelUrl).rel("cancel").build());
}
```

The addCancelHeader() method creates a Link object for the cancel relationship using a URL generated from UriInfo.getAbsolutePathBuilder().

```
@HEAD
@Path("{id}")
@Produces("application/xml")
public Response getOrderHeaders(@PathParam("id") int id,
                                @Context UriInfo uriInfo)
{
   Order order = orderDB.get(id);
   if (order == null)
   {
      throw new WebApplicationException(Response.Status.NOT_FOUND);
   }
   Response.ResponseBuilder builder = Response.ok();
   builder.type("application/xml");
   if (!order.isCancelled()) addCancelHeader(uriInfo, builder);
   return builder.build();
}
```

The getOrderHeaders() method processes HTTP HEAD /orders/{id} requests. This is a convenience operation for HTTP clients that want the link relationships published by the resource but don't want to have to parse an XML document to get this information. Here, the getOrderHeaders() method returns the cancel Link header with an empty response body:

```
@POST
@Path("{id}/cancel")
public void cancelOrder(@PathParam("id") int id)
{
    Order order = orderDB.get(id);
    if (order == null)
    {
        throw new WebApplicationException(Response.Status.NOT_FOUND);
    }
    order.setCancelled(true);
}
```

Users can cancel an order by posting an empty message to /orders/{id}/cancel. The cancelOrder() method handles these requests and simply looks up the Order in the database and sets its state to cancelled.

```
@GET
@Produces("application/xml")
@Formatted
public Response getOrders(@QueryParam("start") int start,
                          @QueryParam("size") @DefaultValue("2") int size,
                          @Context UriInfo uriInfo)
{
...
    Orders orders = new Orders();
    orders.setOrders(list);
    orders.setLinks(links);
    Response.ResponseBuilder responseBuilder = Response.ok(orders);
    addPurgeLinkHeader(uriInfo, responseBuilder);
    return responseBuilder.build();
}
```

The getOrders() method is similar to the CustomerResource.getCustomers() method discussed in the ex10_1 example, so I won't go into a lot of details. One thing it does differently, though, is to publish a purge link relationship through a Link header. Posting to this link allows clients to purge the order entry database of any lingering cancelled orders:

```
protected void addPurgeLinkHeader(UriInfo uriInfo,
                                  Response.ResponseBuilder builder)
{
    UriBuilder absolute = uriInfo.getAbsolutePathBuilder();
    URI purgeUri = absolute.clone().path("purge").build();
    builder.links(Link.fromUri(purgeUri).rel("purge").build());
}
```

The addPurgeLinkHeader() method creates a Link object for the purge relationship using a URL generated from UriInfo.getAbsolutePathBuilder().

```
@HEAD
@Produces("application/xml")
public Response getOrdersHeaders(@QueryParam("start") int start,
                    @QueryParam("size") @DefaultValue("2") int size,
                    @Context UriInfo uriInfo)
{
   Response.ResponseBuilder builder = Response.ok();
   builder.type("application/xml");
   addPurgeLinkHeader(uriInfo, builder);
   return builder.build();
}
```

The getOrdersHeaders() method is another convenience method for clients that are interested only in the link relationships provided by the resource:

```
@POST
@Path("purge")
public void purgeOrders()
{
   synchronized (orderDB)
   {
      List<Order> orders = new ArrayList<Order>();
      orders.addAll(orderDB.values());
      for (Order order : orders)
      {
         if (order.isCancelled())
         {
            orderDB.remove(order.getId());
         }
      }
   }
}
```

Finally, the purgeOrders() method implements the purging of cancelled orders.

StoreResource

One of the things I want to illustrate with this example is that a client needs to be aware of only one URL to navigate through the entire system. The StoreResource class is the base URL of the system and publishes Link headers to the relevant services of the application:

src/main/java/com/restfully/shop/services/StoreResource.java

```
@Path("/shop")
public class StoreResource
{
   @HEAD
   public Response head(@Context UriInfo uriInfo)
   {
      UriBuilder absolute = uriInfo.getBaseUriBuilder();
      URI customerUrl = absolute.clone().path(CustomerResource.class).build();
```

```
        URI orderUrl = absolute.clone().path(OrderResource.class).build();

        Response.ResponseBuilder builder = Response.ok();
        Link customers = Link.fromUri(customerUrl)
                             .rel("customers")
                             .type("application/xml").build();
        Link orders = Link.fromUri(orderUrl)
                         .rel("orders")
                         .type("application/xml").build();
        builder.links(customers, orders);
        return builder.build();
    }
}
```

This class accepts HTTP HEAD /shop requests and publishes the customers and or
ders link relationships. These links point to the services represented by the Customer
Resource and OrderResource classes.

The Client Code

The client code creates a new customer and order. It then cancels the order, purges it,
and, finally, relists the order entry database. All URLs are accessed via Link headers or
Atom links:

```
public class OrderResourceTest
{
    @Test
    public void testCreateCancelPurge() throws Exception
    {
        String base = "http://localhost:8080/services/shop";
        Response response = client.target(base).request().head();

        Link customers = response.getLink("customers");
        Link orders = response.getLink("orders");
        response.close();
```

The testCreateCancelPurge() method starts off by doing a HEAD request to /shop
to obtain the service links provided by our application. The Response.getLink()
method allows you to query for a Link header sent back with the HTTP response.

```
        System.out.println("** Create a customer through this URL: "
                          + customers.getHref());

        Customer customer = new Customer();
        customer.setFirstName("Bill");
        customer.setLastName("Burke");
        customer.setStreet("10 Somewhere Street");
        customer.setCity("Westford");
        customer.setState("MA");
        customer.setZip("01711");
        customer.setCountry("USA");
```

```
response = client.target(customers).request().post(Entity.xml(customer));
Assert.assertEquals(201, response.getStatus());
response.close();
```

We create a customer in the customer database by POSTing an XML representation to the URL referenced in the customers link relationship. This relationship is retrieved from our initial HEAD request to /shop.

```
Order order = new Order();
order.setTotal("$199.99");
order.setCustomer(customer);
order.setDate(new Date().toString());
LineItem item = new LineItem();
item.setCost("$199.99");
item.setProduct("iPhone");
order.setLineItems(new ArrayList<LineItem>());
order.getLineItems().add(item);

System.out.println();
System.out.println("** Create an order through this URL: "
                                    + orders.getUri().toString());
response = client.target(orders).request().post(Entity.xml(order));
Assert.assertEquals(201, response.getStatus());
URI createdOrderUrl = response.getLocation();
response.close();
```

Next, we create an order entry by posting to the orders link relationship. The URL of the created order is extracted from the returned Location header. We will need this later when we want to cancel this order:

```
System.out.println();
System.out.println("** New list of orders");
response = client.target(orders).request().get();
String orderList = response.readEntity(String.class);
System.out.println(orderList);
Link purge = response.getLink("purge");
response.close();
```

A GET /orders request is initiated to show all the orders posted to the system. We extract the purge link returned by this invocation so it can be used later when the client wants to purge cancelled orders:

```
response = client.target(createdOrderUrl).request().head();
Link cancel = response.getLink("cancel");
response.close();
```

Next, the client cancels the order that was created earlier. A HEAD request is made to the created order's URL to obtain the cancel link relationship:

```
if (cancel != null)
{
    System.out.println("** Cancelling the order at URL: "
```

```
                            + cancel.getUri().toString());
        response = client.target(cancel).request().post(null);
        Assert.assertEquals(204, response.getStatus());
        response.close();
    }
```

If there is a cancel link relationship, the client posts an empty message to this URL to cancel the order:

```
        System.out.println();
        System.out.println("** New list of orders after cancel: ");
        orderList = client.target(orders).request().get(String.class);
        System.out.println(orderList);
```

The client does another GET /orders to show that the state of our created order was set to cancelled:

```
        System.out.println();
        System.out.println("** Purge cancelled orders at URL: "
                            + purge.getUri().toString());
        response = client.target(purge).request().post(null);
        Assert.assertEquals(204, response.getStatus());
        response.close();

        System.out.println();
        System.out.println("** New list of orders after purge: ");
        orderList = client.target(orders).request().get(String.class);
        System.out.println(orderList);
    }
```

Finally, by posting an empty message to the purge link, the client cleans the order entry database of any cancelled orders.

Build and Run the Example Program

Perform the following steps:

1. Open a command prompt or shell terminal and change to the *ex10_2* directory of the workbook example code.

2. Make sure your PATH is set up to include both the JDK and Maven, as described in Chapter 17.

3. Perform the build and run the example by typing mvn install.

CHAPTER 25

Examples for Chapter 11

In Chapter 11, you learned about HTTP caching techniques. Servers can tell HTTP clients if and how long they can cache retrieved resources. You can revalidate expired caches to avoid resending big messages by issuing conditional GET invocations. Conditional PUT operations can be invoked for safe concurrent updates.

Example ex11_1: Caching and Concurrent Updates

The example in this chapter expands on the `CustomerResource` example repeated throughout this book to support caching, conditional GETs, and conditional PUTs.

The Server Code

The first thing is to add a `hashCode()` method to the `Customer` class:

src/main/java/com/restfully/shop/domain/Customer.java

```
@XmlRootElement(name = "customer")
public class Customer
{
...
   @Override
   public int hashCode()
   {
      int result = id;
      result = 31 * result + (firstName != null
                              ? firstName.hashCode() : 0);
      result = 31 * result + (lastName != null
                              ? lastName.hashCode() : 0);
      result = 31 * result + (street != null
                              ? street.hashCode() : 0);
      result = 31 * result + (city != null ? city.hashCode() : 0);
      result = 31 * result + (state != null ? state.hashCode() : 0);
      result = 31 * result + (zip != null ? zip.hashCode() : 0);
```

```
        result = 31 * result + (country != null
                                    ? country.hashCode() : 0);
        return result;
    }
}
```

This method is used in the `CustomerResource` class to generate semi-unique `ETag` header values. While a hash code calculated in this manner isn't guaranteed to be unique, there is a high probability that it will be. A database application might use an incremented version column to calculate the `ETag` value.

The `CustomerResource` class is expanded to support conditional GETs and PUTs. Let's take a look at the relevant pieces of code:

src/main/java/com/restfully/shop/services/CustomerResource.java

```
@Path("/customers")
public class CustomerResource
{
...

    @GET
    @Path("{id}")
    @Produces("application/xml")
    public Response getCustomer(@PathParam("id") int id,
                                @Context Request request) {
        Customer cust = customerDB.get(id);
        if (cust == null)
        {
            throw new WebApplicationException(Response.Status.NOT_FOUND);
        }

        if (sent == null) System.out.println("No ETag sent by client");

        EntityTag tag = new EntityTag(Integer.toString(cust.hashCode()));

        CacheControl cc = new CacheControl();
        cc.setMaxAge(5);
```

The `getCustomer()` method first starts out by retrieving the current `Customer` object identified by the `id` parameter. A current `ETag` value is created from the hash code of the `Customer` object. A new `Cache-Control` header is instantiated as well.

```
        Response.ResponseBuilder builder =
                    request.evaluatePreconditions(tag);
        if (builder != null) {
            System.out.println(
                    "** revalidation on the server was successful");
            builder.cacheControl(cc);
            return builder.build();
        }
```

Next, `Request.evaluatePreconditions()` is called to perform a conditional GET. If the client has sent an `If-None-Match` header that matches the calculated current `ETag`, the method returns immediately with an empty response body. In this case, a new `Cache-Control` header is sent back to refresh the `max-age` the client will use.

```
         // Preconditions not met!

         cust.setLastViewed(new Date().toString());
         builder = Response.ok(cust, "application/xml");
         builder.cacheControl(cc);
         builder.tag(tag);
         return builder.build();
      }
   }
```

If no `If-None-Match` header was sent or the preconditions were not met, the `Customer` is sent back to the client with an updated `Cache-Control` header.

```
   @Path("{id}")
   @PUT
   @Consumes("application/xml")
   public Response updateCustomer(@PathParam("id") int id,
                                  @Context Request request,
                                  Customer update ) {
      Customer cust = customerDB.get(id);
      if (cust == null)
          throw new WebApplicationException(Response.Status.NOT_FOUND);
      EntityTag tag = new EntityTag(Integer.toString(cust.hashCode()));
```

The `updateCustomer()` method is responsible for updating a customer. It first starts off by finding the current `Customer` with the given `id`. From this queried customer, it generates the up-to-date value of the `ETag` header.

```
      Response.ResponseBuilder builder =
                      request.evaluatePreconditions(tag);

      if (builder != null) {
         // Preconditions not met!
         return builder.build();
      }
```

The current `ETag` header is compared against any `If-Match` header sent by the client. If it does match, the update can be performed:

```
      // Preconditions met, perform update

      cust.setFirstName(update.getFirstName());
      cust.setLastName(update.getLastName());
      cust.setStreet(update.getStreet());
      cust.setState(update.getState());
      cust.setZip(update.getZip());
      cust.setCountry(update.getCountry());
```

```
        builder = Response.noContent();
        return builder.build();
    }
}
```

Finally, the update is performed.

The Client Code

The client code first performs a conditional GET. It then tries to do a conditional PUT using a bad ETag value.

```
public class CustomerResourceTest
{
    @Test
    public void testCustomerResource() throws Exception
    {
        WebTarget customerTarget =
            client.target("http://localhost:8080/services/customers/1");
        Response response = customerTarget.request().get();
        Assert.assertEquals(200, response.getStatus());
        Customer cust = response.readEntity(Customer.class);

        EntityTag etag = response.getEntityTag();
        response.close();
```

The testCustomerResource() method starts off by fetching a preinitialized Customer object. It does this so that it can obtain the current ETag of the Customer representation.

```
        System.out.println("Doing a conditional GET with ETag: "
                                            + etag.toString());
        response = customerTarget.request()
                            .header("If-None-Match", etag).get();
        Assert.assertEquals(304, response.getStatus());
        response.close();
```

This code is performing a conditional GET. We set the If-None-Match header using the previously fetched ETag value. The client is expecting that the server will return a 304, "Not Modified," response.

```
        // Update and send a bad etag with conditional PUT
        cust.setCity("Bedford");
        response = customerTarget.request()
                .header("If-Match", "JUNK")
                .put(Entity.xml(cust));
        Assert.assertEquals(412, response.getStatus());
        response.close();
    }
}
```

Finally, the code does a conditional PUT with a bad `ETag` value sent with the `If-Match` header. The client is expecting this operation to fail with a 412, "Precondition Failed," response.

Build and Run the Example Program

Perform the following steps:

1. Open a command prompt or shell terminal and change to the *ex11_1* directory of the workbook example code.
2. Make sure your PATH is set up to include both the JDK and Maven, as described in Chapter 17.
3. Perform the build and run the example by typing `mvn install`.

Another interesting thing you might want to try is to start up and leave the application running by using `mvn jetty:run`. Open your browser to *http://localhost:8080/customers/1*. Continually refresh this URL. You will be able to see if your browser performs a conditional GET request or not by viewing the `<last-viewed>` element of the returned XML. I found that Firefox 3.5.2 does a conditional GET, while Safari 4.0.1 does not.

CHAPTER 26

Examples for Chapter 12

In Chapter 12, you learned how filters and interceptors can be used to augment your JAX-RS service classes. In this chapter, we through how to build and run some of the examples shown in that chapter. Specifically, we'll go write a `ContainerResponseFil`ter, a `DynamicFeature`, and an implementation of a `WriterInterceptor`. If you want to see examples of a `ClientRequestFilter` and a `ContainerRequestFilter` bound via a `@NameBinding`, check out Chapter 29.

Example ex12_1 : ContainerResponseFilter and DynamicFeature

ex12_1 implements the `@MaxAge` and `CacheControlFilter` example in the section "DynamicFeature" on page 179.

The Server Code

The `@MaxAge`, `CacheControlFilter`, and `MaxAgeFeature` classes were explained pretty well in "DynamicFeature" on page 179, so I'm not going to go into them again here. We applied the `@MaxAge` annotation to the `CustomerResource.getCustomer()` method:

src/main/java/com/restfully/shop/services/CustomerResource

```
@GET
@Path("{id}")
@Produces("application/xml")
@MaxAge(500)
public Customer getCustomer(@PathParam("id") int id)
{
    Customer customer = customerDB.get(id);
    if (customer == null)
    {
        throw new WebApplicationException(Response.Status.NOT_FOUND);
```

```
        }
        return customer;
    }
```

Applying this annotation to this method will cause the `CacheControlFilter` to be bound to this method when it is executed. The filter will cause a `Cache-Control` header to be added to the HTTP response with a max age of 500 seconds. Let's also take a look at how these classes are registered:

src/main/java/com/restfully/shop/services/ShoppingApplication.java

```
@ApplicationPath("/services")
public class ShoppingApplication extends Application
{
    private Set<Object> singletons = new HashSet<Object>();
    private Set<Class<?>> classes = new HashSet<Class<?>>();

    public ShoppingApplication()
    {
        singletons.add(new CustomerResource());
        classes.add(MaxAgeFeature.class);
    }

    @Override
    public Set<Class<?>> getClasses()
    {
        return classes;
    }

    @Override
    public Set<Object> getSingletons()
    {
        return singletons;
    }
}
```

Notice that we only register the `MaxAgeFeature` class. This class handles the registration of the `CacheControlFilter` if the JAX-RS method is annotated with `@MaxAge`.

The Client Code

The client code hasn't changed much from other examples. We first start off by creating a `Customer` on the server. We then do a GET request to get the customer, checking for the `Cache-Control` header generated by the `CacheControlFilter` on the server side:

src/test/java/com/restfully/shop/test/CustomerResourceTest.java

```
    ...

        System.out.println("*** GET Created Customer **");
        response = client.target(location).request().get();
        CacheControl cc = CacheControl.valueOf(
```

```
                    response.getHeaderString(HttpHeaders.CACHE_CONTROL));
        System.out.println("Max age: " + cc.getMaxAge());
```

There is nothing really special about this code other than it shows you how to create a
CacheControl object from a header string.

Build and Run the Example Program

Perform the following steps:

1. Open a command prompt or shell terminal and change to the *ex12_1* directory of
   the workbook example code.

2. Make sure your PATH is set up to include both the JDK and Maven, as described
   in Chapter 17.

3. Perform the build and run the example by typing `mvn` `install`.

Example ex12_2: Implementing a WriterInterceptor

In this example, we implement support for generating the Content-MD5 header. This
header is defined in the HTTP 1.1 specification. Its purpose is to provide an additional
end-to-end message integrity check of the HTTP message body. While not proof against
malicious attacks, it's a good way to detect accidental modification of the message body
in transit just in case it was transformed by a proxy, cache, or some other intermediary.
Well, OK, I admit it's a pretty lame header, but let's show how we can implement support
for it using a WriterInterceptor:

```
public class ContentMD5Writer implements WriterInterceptor
{
    @Override
    public void aroundWriteTo(WriterInterceptorContext context)
                    throws IOException, WebApplicationException
    {
        MessageDigest digest = null;
        try
        {
            digest = MessageDigest.getInstance("MD5");
        }
        catch (NoSuchAlgorithmException e)
        {
            throw new IllegalArgumentException(e);
        }
```

To implement a WriterInterceptor, we must define an aroundWriteTo() method. We
start off in this method by creating a java.security.MessageDigest. We'll use this
class to create an MD5 hash of the entity we're marshalling.

```
ByteArrayOutputStream buffer = new ByteArrayOutputStream();
DigestOutputStream digestStream = new DigestOutputStream(buffer, digest);

OutputStream old = context.getOutputStream();
context.setOutputStream(digestStream);
```

Next we create a java.io.ByteArrayOutputStream and wrap it with a java.securi ty.DigestOutputStream. The MD5 hash is created from the marshalled bytes of the entity. We need to buffer this marshalling in memory, as we need to set the Content-MD5 before the entity is sent across the wire. We override the OutputStream of the ContainerRequestContext so that the MessageBodyWriter that performs the marshalling uses the DigestOutputStream.

```
try
{
   context.proceed();

   byte[] hash = digest.digest();
   String encodedHash = Base64.encodeBytes(hash);
   context.getHeaders().putSingle("Content-MD5", encodedHash);
```

Next, context.proceed() is invoked. This continues with the interceptor chain and until the underlying MessageBodyWriter is invoked. After proceed() finishes, we obtain the hash from the MessageDigest and Base-64–encode it using a RESTEasy utility class. We then set the Content-MD5 header value with this encoded string.

```
   byte[] content = buffer.toByteArray();
   old.write(content);
}
```

After the header is set, we write the buffered content to the real OutputStream.

```
finally
{
   context.setOutputStream(old);
}
     }
   }
}
```

Finally, if you override the context's OutputStream it is always best practice to revert it after you finish intercepting. We do this in the finally block.

We enable this interceptor for all requests that return an entity by registering it within our Application class. I won't go over this code, as you should be familiar with how to do this by now.

The Client Code

The client code is basically the same as *ex12_1* except we are viewing the returned Content-MD5 header:

---

src/test/java/com/restfully/shop/test/CustomerResourceTest.java

```
@Test
public void testCustomerResource() throws Exception
{
...
    System.out.println("*** GET Created Customer **");
    response = client.target(location).request().get();
    String md5 = response.getHeaderString("Content-MD5");
    System.out.println("Content-MD5: " + md5);
}
```

Build and Run the Example Program

Perform the following steps:

1. Open a command prompt or shell terminal and change to the *ex12_2* directory of the workbook example code.

2. Make sure your PATH is set up to include both the JDK and Maven, as described in Chapter 17.

3. Perform the build and run the example by typing **mvn install**.

CHAPTER 27

Examples for Chapter 13

In Chapter 13, you learned how clients can invoke HTTP requests in the background. You also learned how the server side can detach response processing from the original calling thread with an AsyncResponse. In this chapter, we'll use both of these features to implement a customer chat service.

Example ex13_1: Chat REST Interface

Before we dive into code, let me explain the REST interface for our chat service. The service will share a URL to both send and receive chat messages. The service will work much like Twitter in that if one user posts a chat, anybody listening for chats will see it. Posting a chat is a simple HTTP POST request. Here's an example request:

```
POST /chat HTTP/1.1
Host: localhost:8080
Content-Type: text/plain

Hello everybody
```

As you can see, all the user has to do is post a simple text message to the */chat* URL and messages will be sent to all listeners.

To receive chat messages, clients will make a blocking GET request to the chat server:

```
GET /chat HTTP/1.1
Host: localhost:8080
```

When a chat becomes available, this GET request returns with the next chat message. Additionally, a next Link header is sent back with the HTTP response:

```
HTTP/1.1 200 OK
Content-Type: text/plain
Link: </chat?current=1>; rel=next

Hello everybody
```

We do not want the chat client to lose any messages while it is processing a response. The next link is a placeholder into the list of messages that are posted to the server. After displaying the chat message, the client will do a new GET request to the server using the URL contained within the next Link header:

```
GET /chat?current=1 HTTP/1.1
Host: localhost:800
```

The next link's URI contains a query parameter identifying to the server the last message the client read. The server will use this index to obtain the next message so that the client sees all messages in order. This new GET request will either block again, or immediately return a queued chat message. The pattern then repeats itself. The response will contain a new next Link header with a new pointer into the message queue:

```
HTTP/1.1 200 OK
Content-Type: text/plain
Link: </chat?current=2>; rel=next

What's up?
```

The server will buffer the latest 10 chat messages in a linked list so that it can easily find the next message a particular chat client needs. This is an example of a HATEOAS flow, where the client transitions its state using a link passed back from the server.

The Client Code

The client is a console program that takes input from the command line while at the same time printing out the current chat message. To run the client, you must specify the name you want to use to post messages as an initial argument when you start up the program.

src/main/java/ChatClient.java

```
public class ChatClient
{
    public static void main(String[] args) throws Exception
    {
        String name = args[0];
...
}
```

After grabbing the client's name from the argument list, we then initialize a Client that we'll use to invoke on the customer chat service:

```
final Client client = new ResteasyClientBuilder()
                        .connectionPoolSize(3)
                        .build();
WebTarget target = client.target("http://localhost:8080/services/chat");
```

By default, RESTEasy allows only one connection per Client to be open at one time. So we use the proprietary ClientBuilder implementation of RESTEasy to set a connection pool size of 3. We also initialize a WebTarget with the URL of the chat service.

Next, we use the JAX-RS client asynchronous callback API to set up a loop to pull chat messages from the server:

```
target.request().async().get(new InvocationCallback<Response>()
{
   @Override
   public void completed(Response response)
   {
      Link next = response.getLink("next");
      String message = response.readEntity(String.class);
      System.out.println();
      System.out.print(message);// + "\r");
      System.out.println();
      System.out.print("> ");
      client.target(next).request().async().get(this);
   }

   @Override
   public void failed(Throwable throwable)
   {
      System.err.println("FAILURE!");
   }
});
```

The code starts off by making an async request to the base chat URI. This invocation registers an InvocationCallback interface that we've implemented as a Java inner class. When the initial GET request is complete, the InvocationCallback.complete() method is invoked, passing in the Response from the server. We first extract the next Link header and the chat message from the Response. We then print the message to the console. Finally, we make a new asynchronous GET request using the URI contained in the next Link header. We register the current InvocationCallback instance with this new request. This will set up a continuous pull request with the chat service.

After we've set up our receive loop, we set up another loop that allows us to send chat messages:

```
while (true)
{
   System.out.print("> ");
   BufferedReader br = new BufferedReader(
                            new InputStreamReader(System.in));
   String message = br.readLine();
```

```
    target.request().post(Entity.text(name + ": " + message));
}
```

We simply read from stdin until the user hits Enter and then do an HTTP POST request to the chat service with the command-line input.

The Server Code

The server side is doing a lot of different things to implement our chat service. Let's break it down:

src/main/java/com/restfully/shop/services/CustomerChat.java

```
@Path("chat")
public class CustomerChat
{
    class Message
    {
        String id;
        String message;
        Message next;
    }
```

The CustomerChat class is annotated with @Path to specify the root resource path of our JAX-RS service. It then declares a simple inner class called Message that will represent the queued chat messages. A message is represented by a String id and a String message, and also contains a reference to the next queued Message.

```
    protected Message first;
    protected Message last;
```

The service remembers what the current first and last message is. It stores these in the first and last member variables of the class.

```
    protected int maxMessages = 10;
    protected LinkedHashMap<String, Message> messages =
                                    new LinkedHashMap<String, Message>()
    {
        @Override
        protected boolean removeEldestEntry(Map.Entry<String, Message> eldest)
        {
            boolean remove = size() > maxMessages;
            if (remove) first = eldest.getValue().next;
            return remove;
        }
    };
```

Message objects are stored in a java.util.LinkedHashMap so that they can be easily looked up when a chat client makes a GET request. The key of this map is the id of the Message. The service will always queue the last 10 messages posted to the server. We use a LinkedHashMap so that we can easily evict the oldest chat message when the maximum

---

number of buffered messages is reached. The `removeEldestEntry()` method is used to determine when to evict the oldest entry in the map. It simply checks to see if the size of the map is greater than the maximum amount of messages. It then resets what the `first` message is. Returning `true` triggers the removal of the eldest entry.

```
protected AtomicLong counter = new AtomicLong(0);
```

The `AtomicLong counter` variable is used to generate message IDs.

```
LinkedList<AsyncResponse> listeners = new LinkedList<AsyncResponse>();
```

The `listeners` variable stores a list of waiting chat clients. We'll see how this is used later.

```
ExecutorService writer = Executors.newSingleThreadExecutor();
```

We will have one and only one thread that is responsible for writing response messages back to the chat clients. Having one *writer* thread is what makes this whole application scale very well. Without asynchronous JAX-RS, this service would require a thread per blocking chat client. While most modern operating systems can handle one or two thousand threads, system performance starts to degrade quickly with all the context switching the operating system has to do. Asynchronous JAX-RS allows us to scale to a much larger number of concurrent users.

Posting a new message

Let's look at how the service handles a new chat message:

```
@Context
protected UriInfo uriInfo;

@POST
@Consumes("text/plain")
public void post(final String text)
{
    final UriBuilder base = uriInfo.getBaseUriBuilder();
    writer.submit(new Runnable());
```

The `post()` method consumes plain-text data. The first thing we do is store a `UriBuild er` in a local variable of the base URI of our service. We then queue up a task for our writer thread. We cannot use the `UriInfo` member variable in this background task. The `CustomerChat` class is a singleton and can accept requests concurrently. Because of this, the `UriInfo uriInfo` member variable is a proxy that delegates to the request's actual `UriInfo` by using an underlying `ThreadLocal` in most JAX-RS vendor implementations. If the *writer* background thread invokes on this proxy, it would get an error because `ThreadLocal` data is not transferred between different threads.

```
    writer.submit(new Runnable());
    {
        @Override
```

```
public void run()
{
    synchronized (messages)
    {
        Message message = new Message();
        message.id = Long.toString(counter.incrementAndGet());
        message.message = text;
```

Each new message post is queued up for the *writer* thread in an implementation of the Runnable interface. This task starts off by synchronizing on the messages variable. This protects the critical parts of our message service by serializing access to the messages map. The code then creates a Message instance using an id generated from the counter.

```
        if (messages.size() == 0)
        {
            first = message;
        }
        else
        {
            last.next = message;
        }
```

The *writer* thread next checks to see if this is the initial message to the system. If so, it sets the first member variable to point to the first message posted to the service. Otherwise, it points the tail of the Message linked list to this new Message instance.

```
        messages.put(message.id, message);
        last = message;
```

The code then stores the new message in the messages map and sets the last member variable to point to this new message.

```
        for (AsyncResponse async : listeners)
        {
            try
            {
                send(base, async, message);
            }
            catch (Exception e)
            {
                e.printStackTrace();
            }
        }
        listeners.clear();
    }
}
});
}
```

Finally, the *writer* thread loops through all waiting chat clients and sends them the new message.

Handling poll requests

The `CustomerChat.receive()` method handles GET requests from chat clients:

```
@GET
public void receive(@QueryParam("current") String id,
                    @Suspended AsyncResponse async)
{
    final UriBuilder base = uriInfo.getBaseUriBuilder();
    Message message = null;
    synchronized (messages)
    {
        Message current = messages.get(id);
        if (current == null) message = first;
        else message = current.next;

        if (message == null) {
            queue(async);
        }
    }
    // do this outside of synchronized block to reduce lock hold time
    if (message != null) send(base, async, message);
}
```

The `receive()` method takes a query parameter, `current`. This parameter is the `id` of the last message the chat client read. This parameter is allowed to be `null` if this is the chat client's first pull request. Injecting the `async` parameter via the `@Suspended` annotation detaches HTTP response processing from this request thread.

The method then begins by defining a `synchronized` block on the `messages` variable. This block allows the `receive()` method to perform atomic actions that do not conflict with the *writer* thread. Within the block, the code looks up the `current` query parameter in the `messages` map. If the message is `null`, then the code sets this variable to the `first` member variable of the class. Otherwise, it sets the message to the found message's `next` field. If the message is still `null`, then there is no message available and the `AsyncResponse` is queued for the *writer* thread to pick up when a message is available.

Finally, after the `synchronized` block, if the message is not `null`, it is sent immediately back to the chat client.

```
protected void queue(AsyncResponse async)
{
    listeners.add(async);
}
```

The `queue()` method just adds the `AsyncResponse` to the `listeners` list so the *writer* thread can pick it up.

```
protected void send(UriBuilder base, AsyncResponse async, Message message)
{
```

```
            URI nextUri = base.clone().path(CustomerChat.class)
                    .queryParam("current", message.id).build();
            Link next = Link.fromUri(nextUri).rel("next").build();
            Response response = Response.ok(message.message, MediaType.TEXT_PLAIN_TYPE)
                                       .links(next).build();
            async.resume(response);
    }
```

The send() method can be called by the *writer* thread or the receive() method. It
creates a Response populated with the message that will be sent back to the chat client.
It also calculates and adds a next Link header to send back with the response. At the
end of the method, the AsyncResponse.resume() method is invoked with the built
Response.

Build and Run the Example Program

You'll need multiple console windows to run this example. In the first console window,
perform the following steps:

1. Change to the *ex13_1* directory of the workbook example code.

2. Make sure your PATH is set up to include both the JDK and Maven, as described
   in Chapter 17.

3. Perform the build and run the example by typing **mvn jetty:run**.

This will start the JAX-RS services for the example.

Open another console window and do the following.

1. Change to the *ex13_1* directory of the workbook example code.

2. Run the chat client by typing **mvn exec:java -Dexec.mainClass=ChatClient -
   Dexec.args="*your-name*"**.

Replace *your-name* with your first name. Repeat this process in yet another console
window to run a second chat client. Finally, start typing chat messages.

CHAPTER 28

Examples for Chapter 14

In Chapter 14, you learned a bit about how JAX-RS fits in the grander scheme of things like Java EE and Spring. In this chapter, there are two similar examples that define the services illustrated in Chapter 2. The first marries JAX-RS with EJB. The second uses Spring to write our JAX-RS services. Instead of using in-memory maps like the earlier examples in the workbook, both examples use the Java Persistence API (JPA) to map Java objects to a relational database.

Example ex14_1: EJB and JAX-RS

This example shows how you can use JAX-RS with EJB and JPA. It makes use of some of the integration code discussed in Chapter 14.

Project Structure

To implement *ex14_1*, the Wildfly 8.0 Application Server is used to deploy the example. Wildfly is the community version of the JBoss application server. It is Java EE 7–compliant, so JAX-RS 2.0 is already built in. As a result, our Maven *pom.xml* file needs to change a little to support this example. First, let's look at the dependency changes in this build file:

pom.xml

```
<dependencies>
    <dependency>
        <groupId>org.jboss.resteasy</groupId>
        <artifactId>resteasy-jaxrs</artifactId>
        <version>3.0.5.Final</version>
        <scope>provided</scope>
    </dependency>
</dependencies>
```

Because JAX-RS 2.0 is built in, we do not have to add all the RESTEasy third-party dependencies to our WAR file. The provided scope is used to tell Maven that the JAR dependencies are needed only for compilation and to not include them within the WAR.

Next, we need to include a Wildfly Maven plug-in:

```
<plugins>
    <plugin>
        <groupId>org.jboss.as.plugins</groupId>
        <artifactId>jboss-as-maven-plugin</artifactId>
        <version>7.1.1.Final</version>
        <executions>
            <execution>
                <id>jboss-deploy</id>
                <phase>pre-integration-test</phase>
                <goals>
                    <goal>deploy</goal>
                </goals>
            </execution>
            <execution>
                <id>jboss-undeploy</id>
                <phase>post-integration-test</phase>
                <goals>
                    <goal>undeploy</goal>
                </goals>
            </execution>
        </executions>
    </plugin>
```

The jboss-as-maven-plugin is configured to run after the WAR is built, but before the unit tests are run. It uses the Wildfly remote deployment interface to automatically deploy our WAR to the Wildfly application server. We'll see later how to start the example.

The EJBs

The EJB code is very similar to *ex10_2* from Chapter 24, except the code has been expanded to save created order entries into a relational database instead of an in-memory map. Like all of our previous examples, the JAXB classes that define our XML data format live in the com.restfully.shop.domain package. A separate parallel Java package, com.restfully.shop.persistence, was created for the example's JPA classes. These JPA classes are almost a carbon copy of the JAXB ones, except they are using JPA annotations to map to a relational database.

You could use JAXB and JPA annotations together within one class hierarchy, but this isn't the best idea, as there are a few problems you might encounter. The first has to do with how JPA works. Objects like the OrderEntity have relationships to other classes like LineItemEntity, ProductEntity, and CustomerEntity. In JPA, it is common to lazy-load these objects as their object graphs are traversed. This can save on database access time. The problem where JAX-RS is concerned is that the JAX-RS runtime will usually turn the Java object into an XML document outside the scope of an EJB request. This might cause lazy-load exceptions when JAXB tries to traverse the entire object graph.

You can write your code so that it is careful not to introduce lazy-load exceptions, but there is one other major problem you may encounter. You will often want to support older clients that use older versions of the XML format. This can cause a divergence between your XML schema and your database schema. The best way to avoid this problem is to create two separate class hierarchies. That way, your XML and database mappings can evolve separately from one another. Yes, it's a little more code for you to write, but it will save you headaches in the long run.

I'm going to skip a lot of the details of this example. You've already seen how JAXB classes work and this book isn't an exercise on learning JPA, so I'll focus on how JAX-RS interacts with EJB. Let's take a look at one of the EJBs:

ejb/src/main/java/com/restfully/shop/services/CustomerResource.java

```java
@Path("/customers")
public interface CustomerResource
{
    @POST
    @Consumes("application/xml")
    Response createCustomer(Customer customer,
                                        @Context UriInfo uriInfo);

    @GET
    @Produces("application/xml")
    @Formatted
    Customers getCustomers(@QueryParam("start") int start,
                    @QueryParam("size") @DefaultValue("2") int size,
                    @QueryParam("firstName") String firstName,
                    @QueryParam("lastName") String lastName,
                    @Context UriInfo uriInfo);

    @GET
    @Path("{id}")
    @Produces("application/xml)
    Customer getCustomer(@PathParam("id") int id);
}
```

For a non-JAX-RS-aware EJB container to work with JAX-RS, you need to define your JAX-RS annotations on the EJB's business interface. The `CustomerResource` interface does just this.

Our EJB business logic is defined within the `CustomerResourceBean` class:

ejb/src/main/java/com/restfully/shop/services/CustomerResourceBean.java

```
@Stateless
public class CustomerResourceBean implements CustomerResource
{
    @PersistenceContext
    private EntityManager em;
```

Our EJB class is annotated with the @javax.ejb.Stateless annotation to mark it as a stateless session EJB. The CustomerResourceBean class implements the CustomerRe source interface.

There is a javax.persistence.EntityManager field named em. The annotation @jav ax.persistence.PersistenceContext injects an instance of the EntityManager into that field. The EntityManager persists Java objects into a relational database. These are all facilities of EJB and JPA.

```
public Response createCustomer(Customer customer, UriInfo uriInfo)
{
    CustomerEntity entity = new CustomerEntity();
    domain2entity(entity, customer);
    em.persist(entity);
    em.flush();

    System.out.println("Created customer " + entity.getId());
    UriBuilder builder = uriInfo.getAbsolutePathBuilder();
    builder.path(Integer.toString(entity.getId()));
    return Response.created(builder.build()).build();

}
```

The createCustomer() method implements the RESTful creation of a Customer in the database. The Customer object is the unmarshalled representation of the XML document posted through HTTP. The code allocates an instance of com.restful ly.shop.persistence.CustomerEntity and copies the data from Customer to this instance. The EntityManager then persists the CustomerEntity instance into the database. Finally, the method uses UriInfo.getAbsolutePathBuilder() to create a URL that will populate the value of the Location header that is sent back with the HTTP response.

```
public Customer getCustomer(int id)
{
    CustomerEntity customer = em.getReference(CustomerEntity.class,
                                              id);
    return entity2domain(customer);
}
```

The getCustomer() method services GET /customers/<id> requests and retrieves Cus tomerEntity objects from the database using the EntityManager. The entity2do main() method call converts the CustomerEntity instance found in the database into an instance of the JAXB class `Customer`. This `Customer` instance is what is returned to the JAX-RS runtime.

```
public static void domain2entity(CustomerEntity entity,
                                 Customer customer)
{
   entity.setId(customer.getId());
   entity.setFirstName(customer.getFirstName());
   entity.setLastName(customer.getLastName());
   entity.setStreet(customer.getStreet());
   entity.setCity(customer.getCity());
   entity.setState(customer.getState());
   entity.setZip(customer.getZip());
   entity.setCountry(customer.getCountry());
}

public static Customer entity2domain(CustomerEntity entity)
{
   Customer cust = new Customer();
   cust.setId(entity.getId());
   cust.setFirstName(entity.getFirstName());
   cust.setLastName(entity.getLastName());
   cust.setStreet(entity.getStreet());
   cust.setCity(entity.getCity());
   cust.setState(entity.getState());
   cust.setZip(entity.getZip());
   cust.setCountry(entity.getCountry());
   return cust;
}
```

The `domain2entity()` and `entity2domain()` methods simply convert to and from the JAXB and JPA class hierarchies.

```
public Customers getCustomers(int start,
                              int size,
                              String firstName,
                              String lastName,
                              UriInfo uriInfo)
{
   UriBuilder builder = uriInfo.getAbsolutePathBuilder();
   builder.queryParam("start", "{start}");
   builder.queryParam("size", "{size}");

   ArrayList<Customer> list = new ArrayList<Customer>();
   ArrayList<Link> links = new ArrayList<Link>();
```

The `getCustomers()` method is expanded as compared to previous examples in this book. The `firstName` and `lastName` query parameters are added. This allows clients to search for customers in the database with a specific first and last name.

```
   Query query = null;
   if (firstName != null && lastName != null)
```

```
{
    query = em.createQuery(
            "select c from Customer c where c.firstName=:first
                and c.lastName=:last");
    query.setParameter("first", firstName);
    query.setParameter("last", lastName);

}
else if (lastName != null)
{
    query = em.createQuery(
            "select c from Customer c where c.lastName=:last");
    query.setParameter("last", lastName);
}
else
{
    query = em.createQuery("select c from Customer c");
}
```

The getCustomers() method builds a JPA query based on the values of firstName and lastName. If these are both set, it searches in the database for all customers with that first and last name. If only lastName is set, it searches only for customers with that last name. Otherwise, it just queries for all customers in the database.

```
List customerEntities = query.setFirstResult(start)
        .setMaxResults(size)
        .getResultList();
```

Next, the code executes the query. You can see that doing paging is a little bit easier with JPA than the in-memory database we used in Chapter 24. The setMaxResults() and query.setFirstResult() methods set the index and size of the dataset you want returned.

```
for (Object obj : customerEntities)
{
    CustomerEntity entity = (CustomerEntity) obj;
    list.add(entity2domain(entity));
}
```

Next, the code iterates through all the CustomerEntity objects returned by the executed query and creates Customer JAXB object instances.

```
// next link
// If the size returned is equal then assume there is a next
if (customerEntities.size() == size)
{
    int next = start + size;
    URI nextUri = builder.clone().build(next, size);
    Link nextLink = Link.fromUri(nextUri)
                        .rel("next")
                        .type("application/xml").build();
    links.add(nextLink);
```

```
        }
        // previous link
        if (start > 0)
        {
            int previous = start - size;
            if (previous < 0) previous = 0;
            URI previousUri = builder.clone().build(previous, size);
            Link previousLink = Link.fromUri(previousUri)
                                    .rel("previous")
                                    .type("application/xml").build();
            links.add(previousLink);
        }
        Customers customers = new Customers();
        customers.setCustomers(list);
        customers.setLinks(links);
        return customers;
    }

}
```

Finally, the method calculates whether the next and previous Atom links should be added to the Customers JAXB object returned. This code is very similar to the examples described in Chapter 24.

The other EJB classes defined in the example are pretty much extrapolated from the *ex10_2* example and modified to work with JPA. I don't want to rehash old code, so I won't get into detail on how these work.

The Remaining Server Code

There's a few more server-side classes we need to go over.

The ExceptionMappers

The EntityManager.getReference() method is used by various EJBs in this example to locate objects within the database. When this method cannot find an object within the database, it throws a javax.persistence.EntityNotFoundException. If we deployed this code as is, JAX-RS would end up eating this exception and returning a 500, "Internal Server Error," to our clients if they tried to access an unknown object in the database. The 404, "Not Found," error response code makes a lot more sense to return in this scenario. To facilitate this, a JAX-RS ExceptionMapper is used. Let's take a look:

ejb/src/main/java/com/restfully/shop/services/EntityNotFoundExceptionMapper.java

```
@Provider
public class EntityNotFoundExceptionMapper
            implements ExceptionMapper<EntityNotFoundException>
{
    public Response toResponse(EntityNotFoundException exception)
    {
```

```
        return Response.status(Response.Status.NOT_FOUND).build();
    }
}
```

This class catches EntityNotFoundExceptions and generates a 404 response.

Changes to Application class

The ShoppingApplication class has been simplified a bit. Because all of our code is implemented as EJBs, there's no special registration we need to do in our Applica tion class. Here's what it looks like now:

war/src/main/java/com/restfully/shop/services/ShoppingApplication.java

```
@ApplicationPath("/services")
public class ShoppingApplication extends Application
{
}
```

The Wildfly application server will scan the WAR for any annotated JAX-RS classes and automatically deploy them. In this deployment, all of our JAX-RS services are EJBs and contained in the *WEB-INF/classes* folder of our WAR.

The Client Code

Let's take a look at the client code:

ear/src/test/java/com/restfully/shop/test/ShoppingTest.java

```
protected void populateDB() throws Exception
{
    Response response =
            client.target("http://localhost:8080/ex14_1/services/shop")
                    .request().head();
    Link products = response.getLink("products");
    response.close();

    System.out.println("** Populate Products");

    Product product = new Product();
    product.setName("iPhone");
    product.setCost(199.99);
    response = client.target(products).request().post(Entity.xml(product));
    Assert.assertEquals(201, response.getStatus());
    response.close();

    product = new Product();
    product.setName("MacBook Pro");
    product.setCost(3299.99);
    response = client.target(products).request().post(Entity.xml(product));
    Assert.assertEquals(201, response.getStatus());
    response.close();
```

```
        product = new Product();
        product.setName("iPod");
        product.setCost(49.99);
        response = client.target(products).request().post(Entity.xml(product));
        Assert.assertEquals(201, response.getStatus());
        response.close();
    }
```

The populateDB() method makes HTTP calls on the ProductResource JAX-RS service to create a few products in the database.

```
    @Test
    public void testCreateOrder() throws Exception
    {
        populateDB();

        Response response = client.target
          ("http://localhost:8080/ex14_1/services/shop").request().head();
        Link customers = response.getLink("customers");
        Link products = response.getLink("products");
        Link orders = response.getLink("orders");
        response.close();
```

The test starts off by initializing the server's database by calling populateDB(). Like *ex10_2*, the client interacts with the StoreResource JAX-RS service to obtain links to all the services in the system.

```
        System.out.println("** Buy an iPhone for Bill Burke");
        System.out.println();
        System.out.println("** First see if Bill Burke exists as a customer");
        Customers custs = client.target(customers)
                                    .queryParam("firstName", "Bill")
                                    .queryParam("lastName", "Burke")
                                    .request().get(Customers.class);
        Customer customer = null;
        if (custs.getCustomers().size() > 0)
        {
            System.out.println("- Found a Bill Burke in the database, using that");
            customer = custs.getCustomers().iterator().next();
        }
        else
        {
            System.out.println("- Cound not find a Bill Burke in the database,
                            creating one.");
            customer = new Customer();
            customer.setFirstName("Bill");
            customer.setLastName("Burke");
            customer.setStreet("222 Dartmouth Street");
            customer.setCity("Boston");
            customer.setState("MA");
            customer.setZip("02115");
            customer.setCountry("USA");
```

```
        response = client.target(customers)
                        .request()
                        .post(Entity.xml(customer));
        Assert.assertEquals(201, response.getStatus());
        URI uri = response.getLocation();
        response.close();

        customer = client.target(uri).request().get(Customer.class);
    }
```

The client code checks to see if the customer "Bill Burke" already exists. If that customer doesn't exist, it is created within the customer database.

```
        System.out.println();
        System.out.println("Search for iPhone in the Product database");
        Products prods = client.target(products)
                            .queryParam("name", "iPhone")
                            .request()
                            .get(Products.class);
        Product product = null;
        if (prods.getProducts().size() > 0)
        {
            System.out.println("- Found iPhone in the database.");
            product = prods.getProducts().iterator().next();
        }
        else
        {
            throw new RuntimeException("Failed to find an iPhone in the database!");
        }
```

The customer wants to buy a product called iPhone, so the client searches the product database for it.

```
        System.out.println();
        System.out.println("** Create Order for iPhone");
        LineItem item = new LineItem();
        item.setProduct(product);
        item.setQuantity(1);
        Order order = new Order();
        order.setTotal(product.getCost());
        order.setCustomer(customer);
        order.setDate(new Date().toString());
        order.getLineItems().add(item);
        response = client.target(orders).request().post(Entity.xml(order));
        Assert.assertEquals(201, response.getStatus());
        response.close();

        System.out.println();
        System.out.println("** Show all orders.");
        String xml = client.target(orders).request().get(String.class);
        System.out.println(xml);
    }
}
```

Finally, an order is created within the database.

Build and Run the Example Program

Perform the following steps:

1. Download the latest Wildfly 8.0 Application Server from *http://www.wildfly.org/download/*.

2. Unzip Wildfly 8.0 into any directory you want.

3. Open a command prompt or shell terminal, and then change to the *wildfly-8.0.0.Final/bin* directory.

4. You must start Wildfly manually before you can run the example. To do this, execute *standalone.sh* or *standalone.bat*, depending on whether you are using a Unix- or Windows-based system.

5. Open another command prompt or shell terminal and change to the *ex14_1* directory of the workbook example code.

6. Make sure your PATH is set up to include both the JDK and Maven, as described in Chapter 17.

7. Perform the build and run the example by typing `mvn install`.

As described before, the *pom.xml* file within the project is configured to use a special JBoss plug-in so that it can deploy the WAR file from the example to the application server. After the WAR is deployed, the client test code will be executed. Following the execution of the test, the WAR will be undeployed from JBoss by Maven.

Example ex14_2: Spring and JAX-RS

There isn't much difference between the code of *ex14_1* and *ex14_2*. The Java classes are basically the same, except all the EJB `@Stateless` annotations were removed from the JAX-RS resource classes because the example is using Spring instead of EJB for its component model.

Besides the removal of EJB metadata, the differences between the two projects are mainly packaging and configuration. If you look through the *ex14_2* directory, you'll see that we're back to using embedded Jetty. The *web.xml* file is a tiny bit different than the EJB example, so let's take a look at that first:

src/main/webapp/WEB-INF/web.xml

```
<web-app>
    <context-param>
        <param-name>spring-beans-file</param-name>
        <param-value>META-INF/applicationContext.xml</param-value>
```

```
        </context-param>
    </web-app>
```

This example follows the Spring integration conventions discussed in Chapter 14. The *web.xml* file adds a `<context-param>` to point to the Spring XML file that holds all of the example's Spring configuration. Let's look at this Spring XML file:

src/main/resources/applicationContext.xml

```
<beans xmlns="http://www.springframework.org/schema/beans"
       xmlns:xsi="http://www.w3.org/2001/XMLSchema-instance"
       xmlns:tx="http://www.springframework.org/schema/tx"
       xsi:schemaLocation="
        http://www.springframework.org/schema/beans
        http://www.springframework.org/schema/beans/spring-beans.xsd
        http://www.springframework.org/schema/tx
        http://www.springframework.org/schema/tx/spring-tx.xsd"
       default-autowire="byName">

    <bean id="entityManagerFactory"
        class="org.springframework.orm.jpa.
                        LocalContainerEntityManagerFactoryBean">
        <property name="jpaVendorAdapter">
            <bean class="org.springframework.orm.jpa.vendor
                                    .HibernateJpaVendorAdapter">
                <property name="showSql" value="false"/>
                <property name="generateDdl" value="true"/>
                <property name="databasePlatform"
                        value="org.hibernate.dialect.HSQLDialect"/>
            </bean>
        </property>
    </bean>

    <bean id="dataSource"
        class="org.apache.commons.dbcp.BasicDataSource"
        destroy-method="close">
        <property name="driverClassName"
                    value="org.hsqldb.jdbcDriver"/>
        <property name="url" value="jdbc:hsqldb:test/db/myDB"/>
        <property name="username" value="sa"/>
        <property name="password" value=""/>
    </bean>

    <bean id="transactionManager"
        class="org.springframework.orm.jpa.JpaTransactionManager"/>

    <tx:annotation-driven/>
```

The first part of the Spring configuration file is the configuration required to get JPA and Spring to work together. While the package structure for the Spring example is simpler than the EJB one, you can see that the configuration is a bit more complex.

```
<bean class="org.springframework.orm
        .jpa.support.PersistenceAnnotationBeanPostProcessor"/>

<bean id="customer" class="com.restfully.shop.services
                                   .CustomerResourceBean"/>
<bean id="product" class="com.restfully.shop.services
                                   .ProductResourceBean"/>
<bean id="order" class="com.restfully.shop.services
                                   .OrderResourceBean"/>
<bean id="store" class="com.restfully.shop.services
                                   .StoreResourceBean"/>
</beans>
```

The rest of the Spring XML file defines all of the JAX-RS resource beans.

The Spring XML file is loaded and registered with the JAX-RS runtime by the ShoppingApplication class:

src/main/java/com/restfully/shop/services/ShoppingApplication.java

```
@ApplicationPath("/services")
public class ShoppingApplication extends Application
{
    private Set<Class<?>> classes = new HashSet<Class<?>>();

    public ShoppingApplication()
    {
        classes.add(EntityNotFoundExceptionMapper.class);
    }

    public Set<Class<?>> getClasses()
    {
        return classes;
    }

    protected ApplicationContext springContext;

    @Context
    protected ServletContext servletContext;

    public Set<Object> getSingletons()
    {
        try
        {
            InitialContext ctx = new InitialContext();
            String xmlFile =
                (String)servletContext.getInitParameter("spring-beans-file");
            springContext = new ClassPathXmlApplicationContext(xmlFile);
        }
        catch (Exception ex)
        {
            ex.printStackTrace();
            throw new RuntimeException(ex);
```

```
        }
        HashSet<Object> set = new HashSet();
        set.add(springContext.getBean("customer"));
        set.add(springContext.getBean("order"));
        set.add(springContext.getBean("product"));
        set.add(springContext.getBean("store"));
        return set;
    }

}
```

The `getSingletons()` method is responsible for initializing Spring and registering any JAX-RS resource beans created by Spring with the JAX-RS runtime. It first looks up the name of the Spring XML configuration file. The filename is stored in a servlet context's init parameter named `spring-beans-file`. The `getSingletons()` method looks up this init parameter via the injected `ServletContext`.

After `getSingletons()` gets the name of the config file, it then initializes a Spring `ApplicationContext` from it. Finally, it looks up each JAX-RS bean within the project and registers it with the JAX-RS runtime.

Build and Run the Example Program

Perform the following steps:

1. Open a command prompt or shell terminal and change to the *ex14_2* directory of the workbook example code.

2. Make sure your PATH is set up to include both the JDK and Maven, as described in Chapter 17.

3. Perform the build and run the example by typing `mvn install`.

CHAPTER 29

Examples for Chapter 15

The chapter goes over some example code that illustrates a few of the concepts and APIs you were introduced to in Chapter 15. In the first example, you'll write two custom security plug-ins. In the second example, you'll use JSON Web Encryption to add more security to a chat application.

Example ex15_1: Custom Security

In the first example, we will write two custom security features using JAX-RS filters. The first feature is a custom authentication protocol. The second will be a custom access policy. The example applies these security features to the code we wrote in *ex06_1*.

One-Time Password Authentication

The first custom security feature we'll write is one-time password (OTP) authentication. The client will use a credential that changes once per minute. This credential will be a hash that we generate by combining a static password with the current time in minutes. The client will send this generated one-time password in the Authorization header. For example:

```
GET /customers HTTP/1.1
Authorization: <username> <generated_password>
```

The header will contain the username of the user followed by the one-time password.

The server code

We will enforce OTP authentication only on JAX-RS methods annotated with the @OTPAuthenticated annotation:

src/main/java/com/restfully/shop/features/OTPAuthenticated.java

```
@Target({ElementType.METHOD, ElementType.TYPE})
@Retention(RetentionPolicy.RUNTIME)
@NameBinding
public @interface OTPAuthenticated
{
}
```

When declared on a JAX-RS method, this annotation will trigger the binding of a `ContainerRequestFilter` that implements the OTP algorithm using the `@NameBind ing` technique discussed in "Name Bindings" on page 181. To apply a name binding, the `OTPAuthenticated` annotation interface is annotated with `@NameBinding`.

With our custom annotation defined, let's take a look at the filter that implements the OTP algorithm:

src/main/java/com/restfuly/shop/features/OneTimePasswordAuthenticator.java

```
@OTPAuthenticated
@Priority(Priorities.AUTHENTICATION)
public class OneTimePasswordAuthenticator implements ContainerRequestFilter
{
```

The `OneTimePasswordAuthenticator` class is annotated with `@OTPAuthenticated`. This completes the `@NameBinding` we started when we implemented the `@OTPAuthentica ted` annotation interface. The class is also annotated with `@Priority`. This annotation affects the ordering of filters as they are applied to a JAX-RS method. We'll discuss specifically why we need this later in the chapter, but you usually want authentication filters to run before any other filter.

```
protected Map<String, String> userSecretMap;

public OneTimePasswordAuthenticator(Map<String, String> userSecretMap)
{
   this.userSecretMap = userSecretMap;
}
```

Our filter will be a singleton object and will be initialized with a map. The key of the map will be a username, while the value will be the secret password used by the user to create a one-time password.

```
@Override
public void filter(ContainerRequestContext requestContext) throws IOException
{
   String authorization = requestContext.getHeaderString(
                                      HttpHeaders.AUTHORIZATION);
   if (authorization == null) throw new NotAuthorizedException("OTP");

   String[] split = authorization.split(" ");
   final String user = split[0];
   String otp = split[1];
```

In the first part of our `filter()` method, we parse the `Authorization` header that was sent by the client. The username and encoded password are extracted from the header into the `user` and `otp` variables.

```
String secret = userSecretMap.get(user);
if (secret == null) throw new NotAuthorizedException("OTP");

String regen = OTP.generateToken(secret);
if (!regen.equals(otp)) throw new NotAuthorizedException("OTP");
```

Next, our `filter()` method looks up the secret of the user in its map and generates its own one-time password. This token is compared to the value sent in the `Authoriza tion` header. If they match, then the user is authenticated. If the user does not exist or the one-time password is not validated, then a 401, "Not Authorized," response is sent back to the client.

```
final SecurityContext securityContext =
                            requestContext.getSecurityContext();
requestContext.setSecurityContext(new SecurityContext()
{
    @Override
    public Principal getUserPrincipal()
    {
        return new Principal()
        {
            @Override
            public String getName()
            {
                return user;
            }
        };
    }

    @Override
    public boolean isUserInRole(String role)
    {
        return false;
    }

    @Override
    public boolean isSecure()
    {
        return securityContext.isSecure();
    }

    @Override
    public String getAuthenticationScheme()
    {
        return "OTP";
    }
});
```

After the user is authenticated, the `filter()` method creates a custom `SecurityCon text` implementation within an inner anonymous class. It then overrides the existing `SecurityContext` by calling `ContainerRequestContext.setSecurityContext()`. The `SecurityContext.getUserPrincipal()` is implemented to return a `Principal` initialized with the username sent in the `Authorization` header. Other JAX-RS code can now inject this custom `SecurityContext` to find out who the user principal is.

The algorithm for generating a one-time password is pretty simple. Let's take a look:

src/main/java/com/restfully/shop/features/OTP.java

```java
public class OTP
{
   public static String generateToken(String secret)
   {
      long minutes = System.currentTimeMillis() / 1000 / 60;
      String concat = secret + minutes;
      MessageDigest digest = null;
      try
      {
         digest = MessageDigest.getInstance("MD5");
      }
      catch (NoSuchAlgorithmException e)
      {
         throw new IllegalArgumentException(e);
      }
      byte[] hash = digest.digest(concat.getBytes(Charset.forName("UTF-8")));
      return Base64.encodeBytes(hash);
   }
}
```

OTP is a simple class. It takes any arbitrary password and combines it with the current time in minutes to generate a new `String` object. An MD5 hash is done on this `String` object. The hash bytes are then Base 64–encoded using a RESTEasy-specific library and returned as a `String`.

The `@OTPAuthenticated` annotation is then applied to two methods in the `Customer Resource` class to secure access to them:

src/main/java/com/restfully/shop/services/CustomerResource.java

```java
@GET
@Path("{id}")
@Produces("application/xml")
@OTPAuthenticated
public Customer getCustomer(@PathParam("id") int id)
{
   ...
}

@PUT
```

```
@Path("{id}")
@Consumes("application/xml")
@OTPAuthenticated
@AllowedPerDay(1)
public void updateCustomer(@PathParam("id") int id, Customer update)
{
   ...
}
```

The `getCustomer()` and `updateCustomer()` methods are now required to be OTP authenticated.

Allowed-per-Day Access Policy

The next custom security feature we'll implement is an allowed-per-day access policy. The idea is that for a certain JAX-RS method, we'll specify how many times each user is allowed to execute that method per day. We will do this by applying the @Allowed PerDay annotation to a JAX-RS method:

src/main/java/com/restfuly/shop/features/AllowedPerDay.java

```
@Target({ElementType.METHOD, ElementType.TYPE})
@Retention(RetentionPolicy.RUNTIME)
@NameBinding
public @interface AllowedPerDay
{
    int value();
}
```

As with @OTPAuthenticated, we'll use a @NameBinding to bind the annotation to a specific `ContainerRequestFilter`. Let's take a look at that filter:

src/main/java/com/restfuly/shop/features/PerDayAuthorizer.java

```
@AllowedPerDay(0)
@Priority(Priorities.AUTHORIZATION)
public class PerDayAuthorizer implements ContainerRequestFilter
{
```

The `PerDayAuthorizer` class is annotated with @AllowedPerDay. This completes the @NameBinding we started when we implemented the @AllowedPerDay annotation interface. The class is also annotated with @Priority. This annotation affects the ordering of filters as they are applied to a JAX-RS method. We want this filter to run after any authentication code, but before any application code, as we are figuring out whether or not a user is allowed to invoke the request. If we did not annotate the `OneTimePasswordAuthenticator` and `PerDayAuthorizer` classes with the @Priority annotation, it is possible that the `PerDayAuthorizer` would be invoked before the `One TimePasswordAuthenticator` filter. The `PerDayAuthorizer` needs to know the authenticated user created in the `OneTimePasswordAuthenticator` filter; otherwise, it won't work.

```
@Context
ResourceInfo info;
```

We inject a `ResourceInfo` instance into the filter instance using the `@Context` annotation. We'll need this variable to know the current JAX-RS method that is being invoked.

```
public void filter(ContainerRequestContext requestContext) throws IOException
{
    SecurityContext sc = requestContext.getSecurityContext();
    if (sc == null) throw new ForbiddenException();
    Principal principal = sc.getUserPrincipal();
    if (principal == null) throw new ForbiddenException();
    String user = principal.getName();
```

The `filter()` method first obtains the `SecurityContext` from the `ContainerRequest Context.getSecurityContext()` method. If the context is null or the user principal is null, it returns a 403, "Forbidden," response to the client by throwing a `ForbiddenEx ception`.

```
    if (!authorized(user))
    {
        throw new ForbiddenException();
    }
}
```

The username value is passed to the `authorized()` method to check the permission. If the method returns false, a 401, "Forbidden," response is sent back to the client via a `ForbiddenException`.

```
protected static class UserMethodKey
{
    String username;
    Method method;

    public UserMethodKey(String username, Method method)
    {
        this.username = username;
        this.method = method;
    }

    @Override
    public boolean equals(Object o)
    {
        if (this == o) return true;
        if (o == null || getClass() != o.getClass()) return false;

        UserMethodKey that = (UserMethodKey) o;

        if (!method.equals(that.method)) return false;
```

```
        if (!username.equals(that.username)) return false;

        return true;
    }

    @Override
    public int hashCode()
    {
        int result = username.hashCode();
        result = 31 * result + method.hashCode();
        return result;
    }
}

    protected Map<UserMethodKey, Integer> count =
                         new HashMap<UserMethodKey, Integer>();
```

The filter instance remembers how many times in a day a particular user invoked a particular JAX-RS method. It stores this information in the count variable map. This map is keyed by a custom UserMethodKey class, which contains the username and JAX-RS method that is being tracked.

```
    protected long today = System.currentTimeMillis();

    protected synchronized boolean authorized(String user, AllowedPerDay allowed)
    {
        if (System.currentTimeMillis() > today + (24 * 60 * 60 * 1000))
        {
            today = System.currentTimeMillis();
            count.clear();
        }
```

The authorized() method is synchronized, as this filter may be concurrently accessed and we need to do this policy check atomically. It first checks to see if a day has elapsed. If so, it resets the today variable and clears the count map.

```
        UserMethodKey key = new UserMethodKey(user, info.getResourceMethod());
        Integer counter = count.get(user);
        if (counter == null)
        {
            counter = 0;
        }
```

The authorized() method then checks to see if the current user and method are already being tracked and counted.

```
        AllowedPerDay allowed =
        info.getResourceMethod().getAnnotation(AllowedPerDay.class);
        if (allowed.value() > counter)
        {
            count.put(user, counter + 1);
            return true;
```

```
    }
    return false;
  }
}
```

The method then extracts the `AllowedPerDay` annotation from the current JAX-RS method that is being invoked. This annotation will contain the number of times per day that a user is allowed to invoke the current JAX-RS method. If this value is greater than the current count for that user for that method, then we update the counter and return true. Otherwise, the policy check has failed and we return false.

We then apply this functionality to a JAX-RS resource method by using the `@Allowed PerDay` annotation:

src/main/java/com/restfully/shop/services/CustomerResource.java

```
@PUT
@Path("{id}")
@Consumes("application/xml")
@OTPAuthenticated
@AllowedPerDay(1)
public void updateCustomer(@PathParam("id") int id, Customer update)
{
  ...
}
```

A user will now only be able to invoke the `updateCustomer()` method once per day.

The last thing we have to do is initialize our deployment. Our `Application` class needs to change a little bit to enable this:

src/main/java/com/restfully/shop/services/ShoppingApplication/java

```
@ApplicationPath("/services")
public class ShoppingApplication extends Application
{
  private Set<Object> singletons = new HashSet<Object>();

  public ShoppingApplication()
  {
    singletons.add(new CustomerResource());
    HashMap<String, String> userSecretMap = new HashMap<String, String>();
    userSecretMap.put("bburke", "geheim");
    singletons.add(new OneTimePasswordAuthenticator(userSecretMap));
    singletons.add(new PerDayAuthorizer());
  }

  @Override
  public Set<Object> getSingletons()
  {
    return singletons;
```

```
    }
}
```

The `ShoppingApplication` class populates the user-secret map that must be used to construct the singleton `OneTimePasswordAuthenticator` instance. The `PerDayAuthor izer` class is also a singleton and instantiated by this constructor.

The client code

The first thing we do on the client side is to implement a `ClientRequestFilter` that sets up the `Authorization` header that will be sent to the server:

src/main/java/com/restfully/shop/features/OneTimePasswordGenerator.java

```java
public class OneTimePasswordGenerator implements ClientRequestFilter
{
    protected String user;
    protected String secret;

    public OneTimePasswordGenerator(String user, String secret)
    {
        this.user = user;
        this.secret = secret;
    }

    @Override
    public void filter(ClientRequestContext requestContext) throws IOException
    {
        String otp = OTP.generateToken(secret);
        requestContext.getHeaders().putSingle
        (HttpHeaders.AUTHORIZATION, user + " " + otp);
    }
}
```

This filter is very simple. It is constructed with the username and password we will use to generate the one-time password. The `filter()` method generates the one-time password by calling the `OTP.generateToken()` method we described earlier in this chapter. The `filter()` method then generates and sets the `Authorization` header for the HTTP request.

The client test code is the same as *ex06_1* except that we set it up to use OTP authentication. Let's take a look:

src/test/java/com/restfully/shop/test/CustomerResourceTest.java

```java
@Test
public void testCustomerResource() throws Exception
{
    System.out.println("*** Create a new Customer ***");
    Customer newCustomer = new Customer();
    newCustomer.setFirstName("Bill");
    newCustomer.setLastName("Burke");
```

```
newCustomer.setStreet("256 Clarendon Street");
newCustomer.setCity("Boston");
newCustomer.setState("MA");
newCustomer.setZip("02115");
newCustomer.setCountry("USA");

Response response = client.target(
        "http://localhost:8080/services/customers")
        .request().post(Entity.xml(newCustomer));
if (response.getStatus() != 201) throw new RuntimeException
    ("Failed to create");
String location = response.getLocation().toString();
System.out.println("Location: " + location);
response.close();
```

The testCustomerResource() method starts off the same way as in *ex06_1*. It creates a customer and obtains its URI from the response. Creating a customer is not authenticated so we do not need to worry about setting up authorization here.

```
System.out.println("*** GET Created Customer **");
Customer customer = null;
WebTarget target = client.target(location);
try
{
    customer = target.request().get(Customer.class);
    Assert.fail(); // should have thrown an exception
}
catch (NotAuthorizedException e)
{
}
```

This particular code shows what happens when an unauthenticated request is made. It makes a GET request on the new customer's URI that fails with a NotAuthorizedEx ception because we have not set up our OTP filter yet.

```
target.register(new OneTimePasswordGenerator("bburke", "geheim"));
```

We register an instance of our OneTimePasswordGenerator filter initialized with our username and static password. We can now make an authenticated GET request without error.

```
customer = target.request().get(Customer.class);
System.out.println(customer);
```

To show our allowed-per-day policy in action, the code executes a customer update twice.

```
customer.setFirstName("William");
response = target.request().put(Entity.xml(customer));
if (response.getStatus() != 204)
    throw new RuntimeException("Failed to update");
```
++++
<?hard-pagebreak?>

```
++++
        // Show the update
        System.out.println("**** After Update ***");
        customer = target.request().get(Customer.class);
        System.out.println(customer);

        // only allowed to update once per day
        customer.setFirstName("Bill");
        response = target.request().put(Entity.xml(customer));
        Assert.assertEquals(Response.Status.FORBIDDEN, response.getStatusInfo());

    }
```

The first invocation succeeds, but the second fails because we are allowed to invoke this method only once per day.

Build and Run the Example Program

Perform the following steps:

1. Open a command prompt or shell terminal and change to the *ex15_1* directory of the workbook example code.

2. Make sure your PATH is set up to include both the JDK and Maven, as described in Chapter 17.

3. Perform the build and run the example by typing **mvn install**.

Example ex15_1: JSON Web Encryption

In Chapter 15, you learned a little bit about JSON Web Encryption (JWE) and how it can be used to encrypt HTTP message body or header values. This example augments the customer chat client implemented in Chapter 27. Chat clients will use a shared secret to encrypt and decrypt the messages they send to and receive from the chat server. Chat clients that know the shared secret see the decrypted message, while clients that don't know it see only the JWE encoding. Let's take a look at the code:

src/main/java/ChatClient.java

```
public class ChatClient
{
    public static void main(String[] args) throws Exception
    {
        String name = args[0];
        final String secret = args[1];
```

The ChatClient first starts out by storing the name and secret password that the client will use. It obtains these values from the command line.

```
final Client client = new ResteasyClientBuilder()
                        .connectionPoolSize(3)
                        .build();
WebTarget target = client.target("http://localhost:8080/services/chat");

target.request().async().get(new InvocationCallback<Response>()
{
   @Override
   public void completed(Response response)
   {
      Link next = response.getLink("next");
      String message = response.readEntity(String.class);
      try
      {
         JWEInput encrypted = new JWEInput(message);
         message = encrypted.decrypt(secret).readContent(String.class);
      }
      catch (Exception ignore)
      {
         //e.printStackTrace();
      }
      System.out.println();
      System.out.print(message);
      System.out.println();
      System.out.print("> ");
      client.target(next).request().async().get(this);
   }

   @Override
   public void failed(Throwable throwable)
   {
      System.err.println("FAILURE!");
   }
});
```

The code then implements the receive loop we discussed in Chapter 27. The difference is that it uses the RESTEasy `org.jboss.resteasy.jose.jwe.JWEInput` class to decrypt the received message. A `JWEInput` instance is initialized with the received text message. The `JWEInput.decrypt()` method decrypts the JWE with the shared secret. The `read Context()` method extracts the decrypted bytes into a `String` object that we can output to the console. If the message is not a JWE or if the wrong secret is used, then the original received text message is outputted to the console.

Let's now take a look at how sending a message has changed:

```
while (true)
{
   System.out.print("> ");
   BufferedReader br = new BufferedReader
                        (new InputStreamReader(System.in));
   String message = name + ": " + br.readLine();
```

```
        String encrypted = new JWEBuilder()
                              .contentType(MediaType.TEXT_PLAIN_TYPE)
                              .content(message)
                              .dir(secret);
        target.request().post(Entity.text(encrypted));
}
```

This `while` loop is similar to the code discussed in Chapter 27. The difference is that it uses the RESTEasy `org.jboss.resteasy.jose.jwe.JWEBuilder` class to encrypt the text message we want to post to the server. The `JWEBuilder.contentType()` method sets the `cty` header of the JWE. The `content()` method sets the entity we want to encrypt. The `dir()` method first takes the entity and marshals it using a `MessageBodyReader` picked from the content type and the entity's class. The `dir()` method then generates the JWE based on this marshalled content and shared secret algorithm. Once we have our JWE-encoded string, we then post it to the chat server.

One thing to notice is that we have not changed the server at all. The server is a dumb intermediary that just forwards messages from one client to others. It doesn't care about what is being sent across the wire.

Build and Run the Example Program

You'll need multiple console windows to run this example. In the first console window, perform the following steps:

1. Change to the *ex15_2* directory of the workbook example code.
2. Make sure your PATH is set up to include both the JDK and Maven, as described in Chapter 17.
3. Perform the build and run the example by typing **mvn jetty:run**.

This will start the JAX-RS services for the example.

Open another console window and do the following.

1. Change to the *ex15_2* directory of the workbook example code.
2. Run the chat client by typing **mvn exec:java -Dexec.mainClass=ChatClient -Dexec.args="*your-name your-secret*"**.

Replace *your-name* with your first name and *your-secret* with your shared password. Repeat this process in yet another console window to run a second chat client. You may also want to start different chat clients that use different passwords to see what happens.

Index

Symbols

200 and 204 response codes, 100
404-406 response codes, 100
@ApplicationPath annotation, 39, 206
@BeanParam annotation, 67
@Consumes annotation, 30, 97
@Context annotation, 58, 98
  injecting instances of UriInfo, 63, 149
  injecting reference to HttpHeaders, 130
  obtaining instance of UriInfo interface, 61
  ServletContext and ServletConfig interfaces, 208
  using to get instance of HttpHeaders, 65–66
@CookieParam annotation, 57, 65, 275
@DefaultValue annotation, 72, 274
@DenyAll annotation, 222
@Encoded annotation, 72
@FormParam annotation, 57, 63, 275
@GET annotation, 31, 44
@HeaderParam annotation, 57, 64, 275
@HttpMethod annotation, 44, 263
@MatrixParam annotation, 57, 61, 272
@MaxAge annotation, 181
@NameBinding annotation, 181
  DynamicFeature versus, 182
@Path annotation, 29, 43, 45
  binding URIs, 45
  creating URI from, 147
  expressions, 46
    character encoding, 49
    full dynamic dispatching, 52
    gotchas in request matching, 53
    matrix parameters, 50
    precedence rules for matching, 48
    regular expressions, 47
    subresource locators, 50
    template parameters, 46
    workbook examples, 266–268
@PathParam annotation, 33, 57, 58–61
  content information in, 134
  more than one path parameter, 58
  PathSegment and matrix parameters, 59
    matching with multiple PathSegments, 60
  programmatic URI information, 61
  scope of path parameters, 59
  workbook example, 271
@PermitAll annotation, 222
@POST annotation, 30
@Pretty annotation, 94
@Priority annotation, 177
  advantages of using, 179
@Produces annotation, 31
  matching to Accept headers, 128
  MessageBodyWriter implementation, 92
  setting media for Content-Type header, 79
@Provider annotation
  ExceptionMapper implementations, 108

We'd like to hear your suggestions for improving our indexes. Send email to index@oreilly.com.

DynamicFeature interface, 179, 181
    versus @NameBinding, 182

E

EJB (Enterprise Java Beans)
    Executors or @Asynchronous, use in container, 186
    integration with JAX-RS, 211
        workbook example, 327–340
    JDNI and, 141
    Spring and, 212
encodings
    @Encoded annotation, 72
    adding compression to input/output streams, 173
    character encoding in @Path URI expressions, 49
    dealing with multiple types, 130
    encoding negotiation, 127
encryption, 215
    enforcing, 221
    JSON Web Encryption (JWE), 351–353
    message bodies, 232
    of message bodies, 228
Enterprise Java Beans (see EJB)
Entity class, 119
EntityNotFoundMapper class, 108
EntityTag class, 163
enum, using with injection annotation, 69
error responses, 100
    numeric range for codes, 105
ETag headers, 162, 165
    strong and weak, 162
Exception class, 106
exception handling, 106–111
    AsyncResponse API, 194
    client requests, 122
    exception hierarchy for HTTP error conditions, 109
    exception mapping, 108
    futures in AsyncInvoker client API, 187
    mapping default exceptions, 111
    WebApplicationException, 107
ExceptionMapper object, 108, 183
    EJB and JAX-RS (workbook example), 333
    writing, workbook example, 287–290
exceptions, processing for filters or interceptors, 183
ExecutionException, 187

Executors class, 199
Expires headers, 158

F

Fielding, Roy, 3
File class, 78
file suffixes, mapping to media types and languages, 135
FileInputStream class, 77
filters, 169
    client-side, 174–176
    deploying, 177
    exception processing for, 183
    implementing SecurityContext interface, 225
    ordering, 177
    per JAX-RS method bindings, 179
        name bindings, 181
    reader and writer interceptors, 172–174
        workbook example, 315–317
    server-side, 169
        server request filters, 170
        server response filters, 171
    workbook examples, 313–315
ForbiddenException, 110
forms
    Form class, 120
    injecting form data, 275
    java.net package and, 240
    key feature of the Internet, 139
    MultivaluedMap<String, String> containing form input, 80
full dynamic dispatching, 52
Future interface, 186
futures
    exception handling, 187
    using in AsyncInvoker client API, 185–187
        callbacks versus, 191
        exception handling, 187

G

GenericEntity class, 106
GenericType class, 118
GET method (HTTP), 8
    conditional GETs, 308
    getting list of Orders, Products, or Customers, 20
    invoking with Invocation.Builder, 117
    JAX-RS annotation for, 43

About the Author

Bill Burke is a Fellow at the JBoss division of Red Hat, Inc. A longtime JBoss contributor and architect, his current project is RESTEasy, RESTful Web Services for Java.

Colophon

The animal on the cover of *RESTful Java with JAX-RS 2.0*, Second Edition is an Australian bee-eater (*Merops ornatus*). It is commonly referred to as a rainbow bee-eater because of the vibrant colored feathers that adorn its body. Its bronze crown and nape, blue rump, and green and bronze wings make it easily distinguishable. Its red eye sits inside of a black stripe, outlined in blue, that extends from its bill to its ears. Females and males look alike and are only differentiated by the female's shorter and thicker tail streamers.

Distributed throughout Australia, Papua New Guinea, and eastern Indonesia, the Australian bee-eater usually lives in cleared areas and often uses quarries or mines to build its nesting tunnels. Of course, tunnels in such places are subject to destruction as a result of human activity. Other threats to the bee-eater's survival include foxes and wild dogs that dig up its nesting tunnels.

It is believed that Australian bee-eaters are monogamous. The female builds the nesting tunnels, while her male partner catches food for both of them. To dig the tunnel, the female balances on her wings and feet, using her bill to dig and her feet to move loose soil backward. On average, she can dig about three inches per day.

Although the nesting tunnels are very narrow, bee-eaters have been known to share tunnels with other bee-eaters and sometimes even other bird species. The female can lay as many as seven eggs at a time. Both parents are responsible for incubating them (for about 24 days) and feeding them once they hatch. Often older birds that never found a mate or whose mate has died will help feed others' young as well.

Not surprisingly, the Australian bee-eater preys on bees, and though it is unaffected by the bee's sting, it is very careful to rub the bee on its perch to remove its stinger before consuming it. The bird always takes care to close its eye to prevent any poison from the bee's broken poison sac getting in it. The Australian bee-eater can consume several bees in the course of a single day and thus beekeepers generally aren't fans of the bird. Its diet consists of other insects as well, including dragonflies, beetles, butterflies, and moths.

The cover image is from *Cassell's Natural History*, Vol. III. The cover fonts are URW Typewriter and Guardian Sans. The text font is Adobe Minion Pro; the heading font is Adobe Myriad Condensed; and the code font is Dalton Maag's Ubuntu Mono.

Get even more for your money.

Join the O'Reilly Community, and register the O'Reilly books you own. It's free, and you'll get:

- $4.99 ebook upgrade offer
- 40% upgrade offer on O'Reilly print books
- Membership discounts on books and events
- Free lifetime updates to ebooks and videos
- Multiple ebook formats, DRM FREE
- Participation in the O'Reilly community
- Newsletters
- Account management
- 100% Satisfaction Guarantee

Signing up is easy:

1. Go to: oreilly.com/go/register
2. Create an O'Reilly login.
3. Provide your address.
4. Register your books.

Note: English-language books only

To order books online:
oreilly.com/store

For questions about products or an order:
orders@oreilly.com

To sign up to get topic-specific email announcements and/or news about upcoming books, conferences, special offers, and new technologies:
elists@oreilly.com

For technical questions about book content:
booktech@oreilly.com

To submit new book proposals to our editors:
proposals@oreilly.com

O'Reilly books are available in multiple DRM-free ebook formats. For more information:
oreilly.com/ebooks

O'REILLY®

Lightning Source UK Ltd.
Milton Keynes UK
UKOW05f1158290716

279437UK00003B/4/P